IMAGES
of America

POST ROCK COUNTRY

I0806213

On the Cover: Pictured is the Paul Dinges farm, located north of Schoenchen near the Smoky Hill River in southern Ellis County. The house, barn, and nearly all of the outbuildings were constructed of native stone known as Post Rock limestone. Fences constructed of Post Rock limestone and barbed wire are also visible around the farmstead. The stone was undoubtedly quarried nearby, as there were once a number of quarries in the area. Schoenchen's native-stone St. Anthony's Catholic Church is visible in the background. (Courtesy Rush County Historical Society.)

IMAGES
of America

POST ROCK COUNTRY

Bradley R. Penka and the
Rush County Historical Society

ARCADIA
PUBLISHING

ISBN 978-1-4671-1248-2

Published by Arcadia Publishing
Charleston, South Carolina

Printed in the United States of America

Library of Congress Control Number: 2014941639

For all general information, please contact Arcadia Publishing:
Telephone 843-853-2070
Fax 843-853-0044
E-mail sales@arcadiapublishing.com
For customer service and orders:
Toll-Free 1-888-313-2665

Visit us on the Internet at www.arcadiapublishing.com

This book is dedicated to those individuals who had the foresight to preserve this important part of our history through the Rush County Historical Society.

Contents

Acknowledgments

I would like to thank all of the individuals who have contributed to this book. First, I want to extend a special thanks to the Rush County Historical Society, especially president Lawrence Erbes and vice president/curator Judith Reynolds, for providing access to the society's image archives and assisting with historical information. Second, I want to acknowledge the Kansas Barbed Wire Museum for providing research facilities and image-scanning equipment.

I extend my gratitude to the Fort Hays State University Department of Geosciences and Sternberg Museum of Natural History in Hays, Kansas, for assistance with research about the geology of Post Rock. I also extend appreciation to Fort Hays State University's Forsyth Library and the Barnard Library in La Crosse, Kansas, for providing and verifying historical information about the early settlers of Rush and Ellis Counties.

A special thank-you goes out to the most important person in my life, Tricia, for providing moral support and for helping whenever possible.

I would also like to thank Liz Gurley, Maggie Bullwinkel, and Sara Miller, from Arcadia Publishing, for providing technical assistance and bearing with me through the process.

Finally, I want to remember all of the pioneering individuals who have lived and worked in the area of Kansas known as Post Rock Country. Without their foresight and perseverance, this work would not have been possible.

Unless otherwise noted, all images appear courtesy of the Rush County Historical Society. Images in the society's archives were donated by various individuals, the Barnard Library, the Ivan Krug family, and the Harry Grass family. Images courtesy of the Kansas Barbed Wire Museum are labeled "KBWM," and images from the author's collection are labeled "AC." Original photography by the author is indicated as such.

INTRODUCTION

The story of the Post Rock Museum begins in 1963, when a group of businessmen in La Crosse, Kansas, had an idea that could satisfy the curiosity of people who traveled through the area. Local barber Bill Appel, like many others in the community, was often asked about the peculiar monuments that dotted the highways and back roads of Rush County. A woman reportedly once commented, "Every place has a peculiar way of doing things, but this is the first place I have ever been that has its cemeteries beside the highways."

Appel gathered a group of community leaders, including banker Harry Grass and Southwestern Bell Telephone Company manager Roy Ehly, for a meeting. After a bit of barbershop talk and $100 of seed money from Appel, the group came to a consensus: there needed to be a formal way to tell the story of Post Rock, and what better way than with a museum?

To establish a governing structure for the museum, the group reactivated the Rush County Historical Society, an organization that had initially been founded to celebrate the Kansas Centennial in 1961. The group reactivated the society, began raising funds, and secured a parcel of land. After raising $7,500, the group began to prepare the land, located on the south edge of La Crosse, which had been donated to the city by Grass's family in 1954. Thus began the museum—which opened on Sunday, May 17, 1964—that would preserve a curious element of the history of central Kansas.

So, why La Crosse? La Crosse is situated at the south end of a region in Kansas known as Post Rock Country, which stretches diagonally from north of Dodge City across the state to the Nebraska border. Post Rock Country takes its name from a rock formation consisting of Fencepost limestone, commonly known as Post Rock, that serves as a dividing line between the Greenhorn limestone formation and the Carlile Shale. In Post Rock Country, the rock lies at or within a few feet of the surface, making it abundant and relatively easy to quarry. Area pioneers, who lacked both money and the trees needed to construct homes and buildings, realized Post Rock was the answer to their needs.

The story of the Post Rock region has been documented many times in various ways. The history of the majestic cathedrals constructed by the Volga Germans when they settled in Ellis County has been told through the personal interviews, letters, and diaries of those early settlers. The unusual Garden of Eden—a collection of sculptures and buildings in Lucas, Kansas, built of Post Rock and cement—has been featured in television and print. The town of Lincoln, Kansas, is known as the "Post Rock Capital of Kansas" and lies at the end of a stretch of highway known as the Post Rock Scenic Byway. One piece of the history of Post Rock Country that remains to be told is that of the area in and around Rush County, the home of the Post Rock Museum and the place where the history of Post Rock is preserved.

To completely tell the story of Post Rock, it is necessary to go back a century to the time when the first pioneers arrived in Rush County. Kansas was a vast, dry prairie, and because of frequent droughts and a high occurrence of prairie fires, trees were scarce. Since the pioneers could not afford to ship lumber from back east to build their homes, they searched for an alternative to wood; they found it in the ground itself. By digging into hillsides and scraping out sod (soil that was tightly bound by prairie grass), they were able to fashion crude homes called dugouts. Some settlers fashioned bricks from the sod and built simple homes. Although the sod structures offered some protection from the elements, they were far from sanitary and had dirt floors and ill-fitting windows and doors. Additionally, dugouts and sod houses required constant maintenance and were subject to destruction due to heavy rains and fires. Consequently, settlers searched for a better and more permanent method for building homes.

The pioneers eventually discovered Post Rock. It was readily available, and the formation was the perfect thickness (8 to 12 inches) to use in building. When limestone is first uncovered, it is soft and chalky, making it easy to drill and form. Once the stone is exposed to air, it hardens, making it an exceptionally strong building material. At first, settlers used limestone blocks instead of sod bricks for the walls of dugouts. Once they discovered the limestone's potential as well as its innate beauty, they began to use it for more permanent buildings. In addition to homes, limestone was used to build schools, churches, and bridges. People soon discovered that it also could be quarried for other uses, including as sidewalks, steps, hitching posts, feed and water troughs, and tombstones.

Pioneers faced another problem on the treeless prairie—a need to protect crops from cattle and wildlife. The range laws, at the time, allowed livestock to graze freely and required landowners to protect their own crops. A type of tree known as Osage orange grew quickly, required little water, and, when fully grown, created a dense hedge that impeded cattle and wildlife from feeding on crops. Some farmers fashioned fence posts from the Osage orange wood, but it was difficult to maintain and required time to grow to a usable size. Then, settlers found another use for Post Rock—fence posts. In fact, this unique limestone gained its name from its extensive use in the construction of fence posts. At first, settlers built fences with smooth wire stretched between the stone posts. When barbed wire was invented in the 1870s, they strung it between limestone posts to create very strong fences that withstood the elements and the test of time.

Post Rocks were quarried from slightly thinner beds (usually eight inches) than building stones. Holes were drilled 24 to 36 inches apart in the stone, eight inches from the outer edge of the limestone bed. Tools known as "feather and wedges" were used to split the stone along a drilled line, and posts were then split into lengths of about six feet. Typically, only about 25 posts could be quarried in a day. Each post weighed between 250 and 450 pounds, and a team of horses could only transport about six to eight at a time, though they were often transported one at a time. Transporting posts involved driving a wagon over a post while still in the quarry, attaching the post to the underside of the wagon with a sling, and then driving the post to the fence line. The end of the post was suspended over the post hole and released from the wagon, and after the wagon was moved, one end was slipped into the hole, and the post was lifted upright. The soil was then compacted before builders repeated the process about 10 steps (30 feet) away.

Post Rock proved to be an excellent building material. Many buildings constructed of stone quarried by hand well over a century ago are still standing, and many of the Post Rock fences also continue to guard crops or protect animals in the same manner as they did 100 years ago.

One

Geology of the Post Rock

It may be hard to imagine that the drought-stricken Kansas regions of the 1930s were once at the bottom of a vast inland sea. The differing layers that appear in outcroppings along roadways provide a chronological history of the sea that covered Kansas over 60 million years ago. The unusual geological formations and layers visible in rocks in Kansas are the results of erosion and sedimentary deposits left behind as the sea receded. One of these layers, the Greenhorn limestone, is composed of chalky limestone and gray shale. At the top of this layer is the thin bed of limestone—known as Fencepost limestone—that is only found in a small region of central Kansas. This layer, which is about 12 inches thick, tells a small part of a much bigger geologic story spanning millions of years. The geology of the Post Rock is only the beginning.

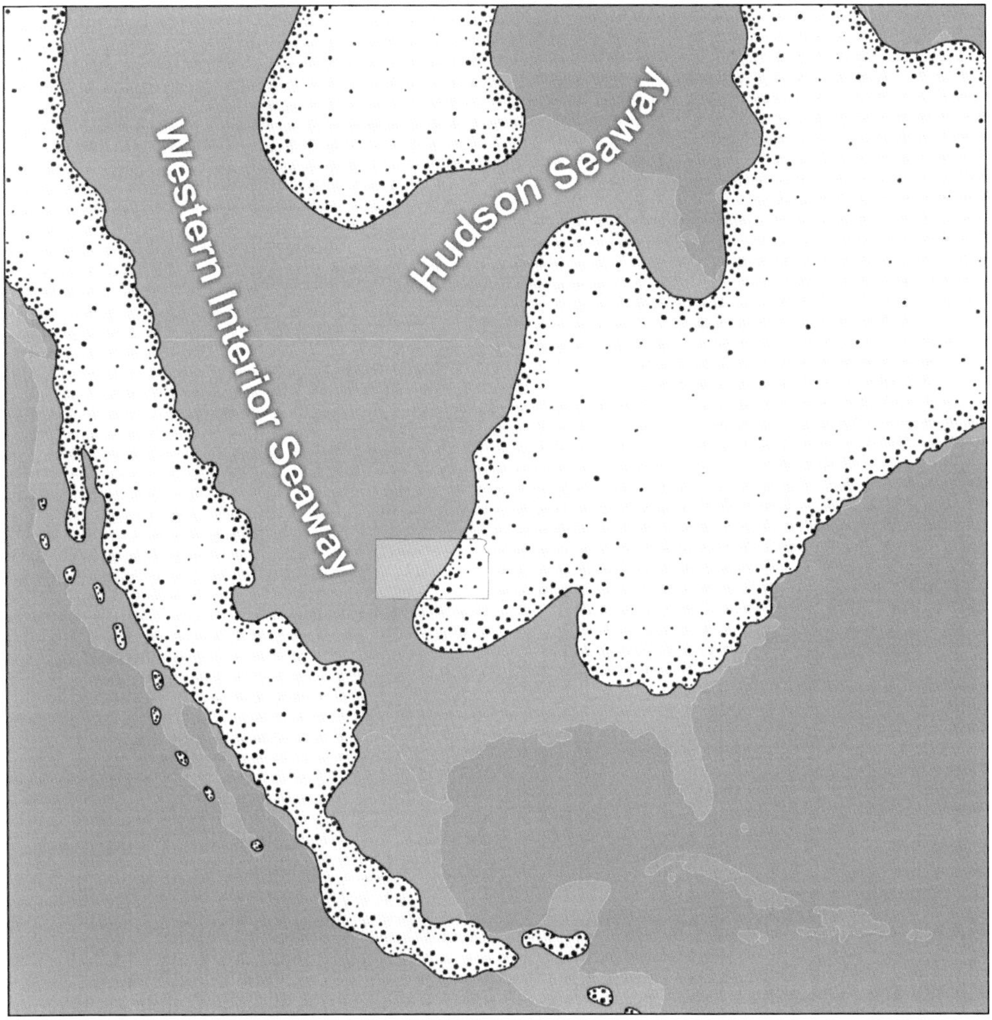

The Western Interior Seaway can be traced back millions of years to a time when Kansas was covered by a large inland sea that stretched from the Gulf of Mexico to Alaska and was nearly 1,000 miles wide from east to west. The area that would become Kansas was somewhat near the middle of this ancient sea. This geological period of time is known as the Cretaceous Period, which means "chalk-bearing." The Cretaceous Period lasted about 70 million years before ending approximately 60 million years ago. Animal life was abundant in this sea, especially very small and microscopic forms covered in shells made of calcium carbonate (lime). Frequently, large numbers of these microscopic animals succumbed to the inhospitable environment, dying and slowly settling like tiny snowflakes on the muddy floor of the sea. After many years, the accumulations of these organisms formed multiple layers of fine-grained limestone. The Fencepost limestone bed—the origin of Post Rock—lies at the top of those rock layers. (Courtesy Sternberg Museum of Natural History.)

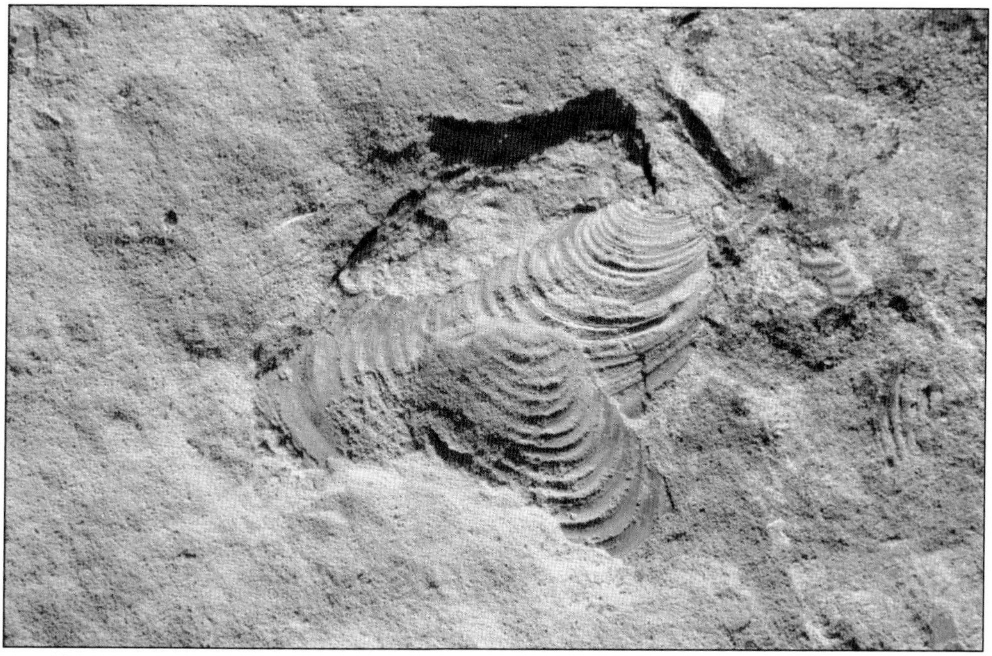

In addition to the microscopic shells that existed in the ancient sea, it contained several larger, shellfish-like oysters, clams, and ammonites – forms similar to those that exist in seas today. Many impressions of these ancient shells can be seen in the Fencepost limestone bed. The ancient sea also contained sharks, fishes, swimming reptiles, and strange birds with teeth. The fossilized remains of these creatures have been discovered within the Cretaceous formation known as Greenhorn limestone. Fossilized clams (above) and ammonites (below) are commonly found in Post Rock limestone. (Both photographs by the author.)

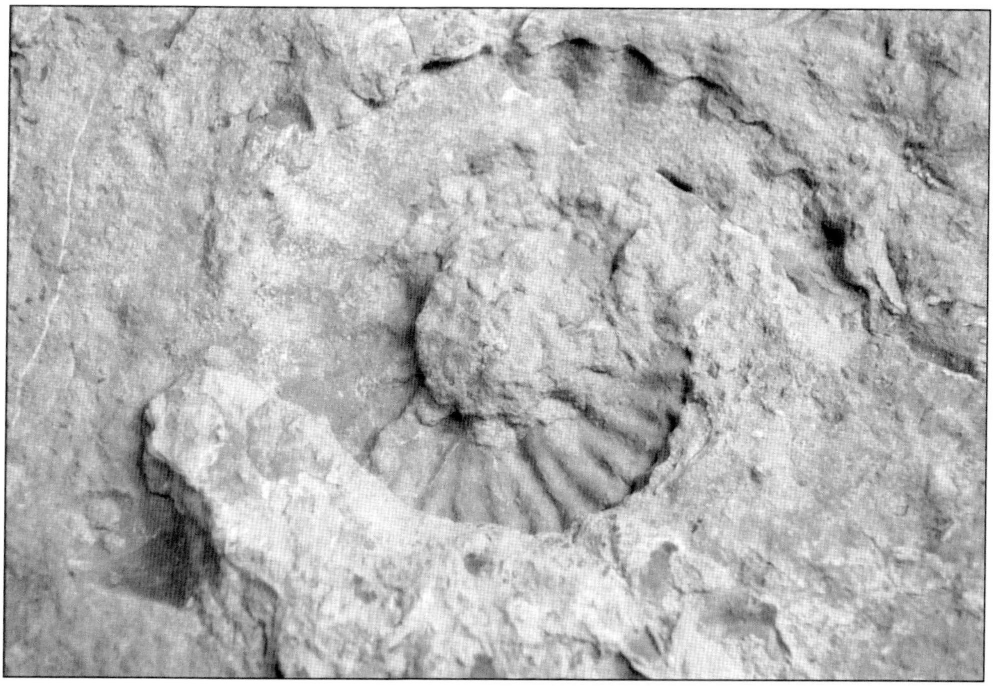

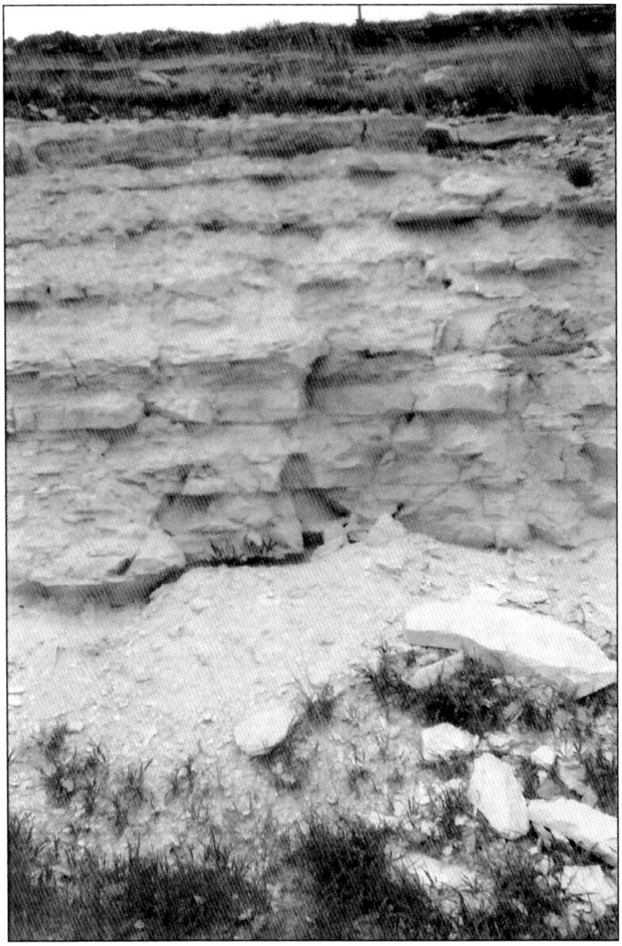

The multiple layers of the Greenhorn limestone bed are easily visible alongside road cuts in central Kansas. The stratified layers are the result of millions of years of sediment being deposited by the ebb and flow of the inland sea that once covered Kansas. Geologists study the variations in these layers and, through comparison, can gain insight about weather conditions, water temperature, and other environmental conditions of the time.

Natural rock outcrops are often visible in uncultivated fields in Kansas. This view is probably similar to what pioneers may have found upon first arriving in the area. Although this outcropping exhibits multiple layers, only the uppermost layer is Post Rock. A Post Rock fence is barely visible on the horizon.

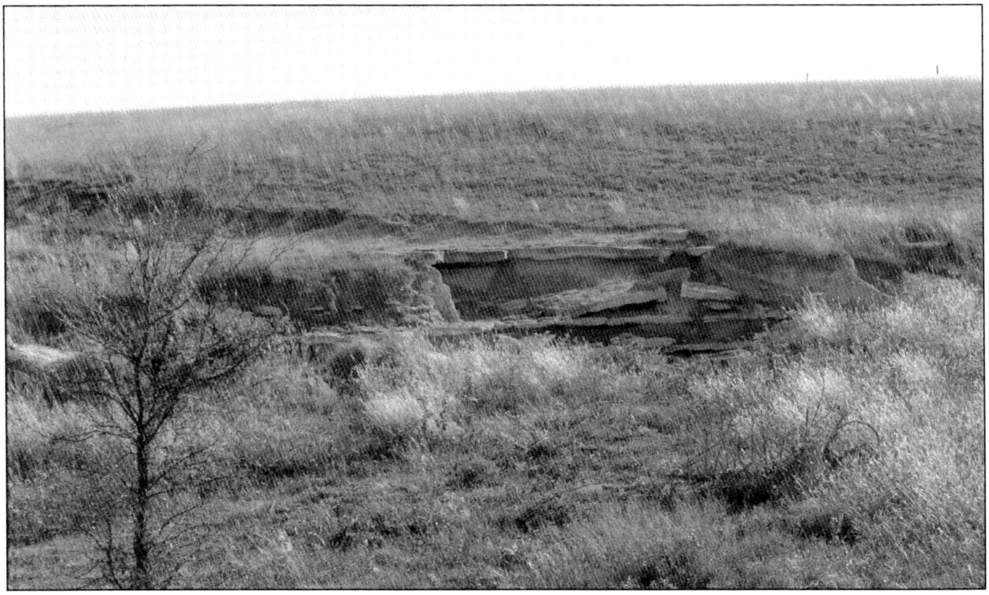

The Fencepost limestone layer (Post Rock) is prominent in outcroppings. Its consistency and relative strength often allow it to remain intact and create a sort of shelf after other layers are worn away by erosion. Although there are other similar layers within the Greenhorn formation, only the top layer is actually Post Rock. This image shows Harry Grass, one of the founders of the Post Rock Museum, pointing out the Post Rock layer.

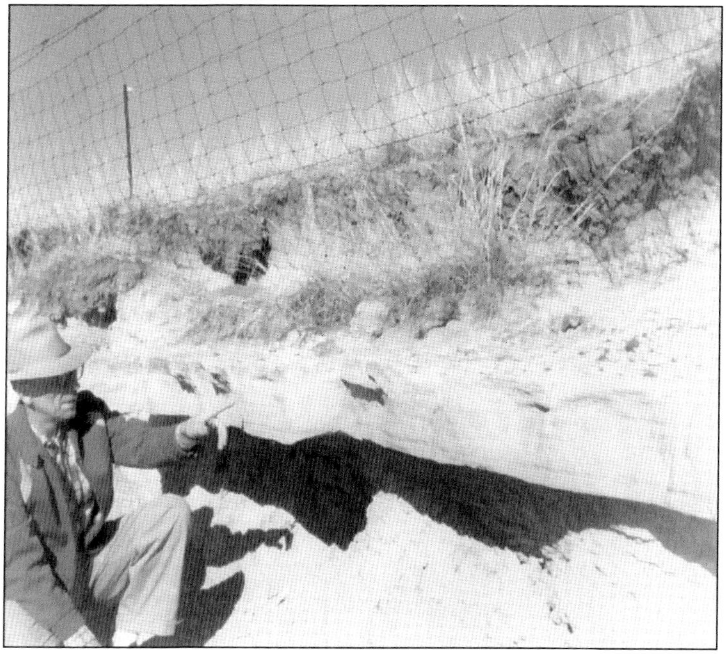

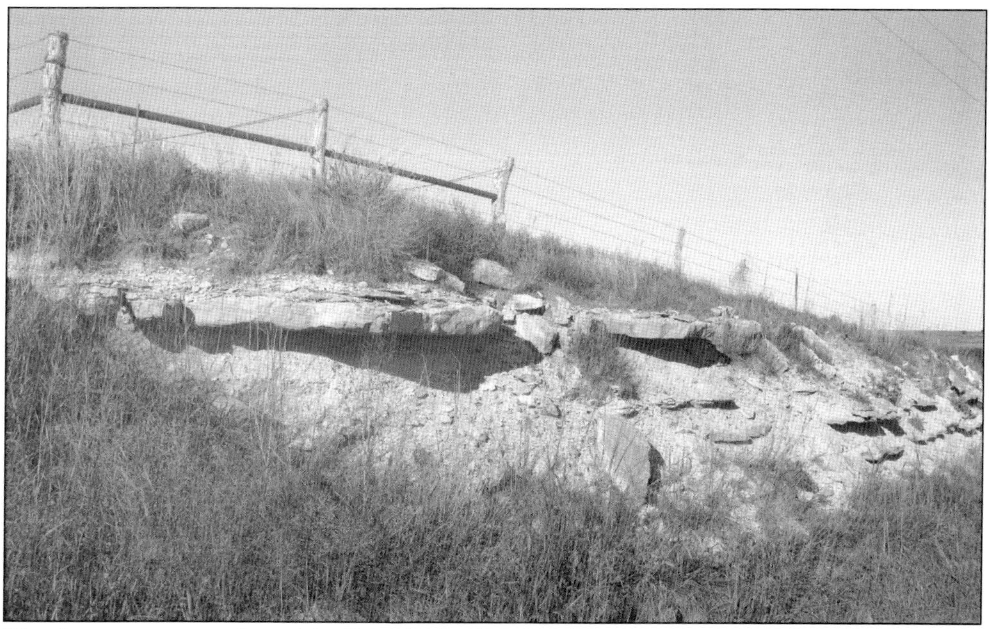

This formation was made visible when the land was graded for construction of a road. The image shows how close the Post Rock bed is to the surface. Note the wooden posts that, by the 1930s, had begun to replace Post Rock in fence construction.

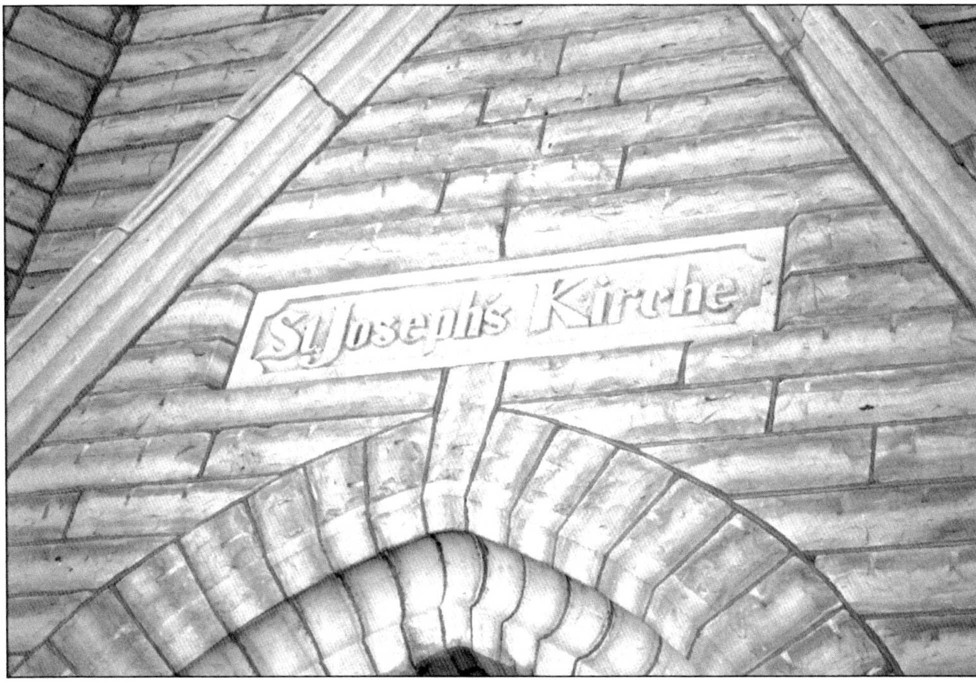

Depending upon placement of stones, fossils may or may not be visible in posts and buildings. When viewed from the side, cut stones exhibit a pattern of layers. The fossils are found parallel to the plane of these layers. Posts were often randomly placed during fence construction. Since all faces of the posts are exposed, it is generally easy to find fossils within them. Depending on how the stones are placed in buildings, fossils may or may not be visible. If stones are placed horizontally in their natural state, a multicolor pattern of grain will be visible on the surface of the wall (as shown in the above photograph of St. Joseph's Kirche). Drill marks from quarrying are also visible, creating an interesting pattern to finished buildings. However, since fossils lie on the plane, they are hidden. If stones are placed perpendicularly to their grain, fossils may be visible, but the stones exhibit a more consistent beige color (as shown in the below photograph of Memorial Union at Fort Hays State University).

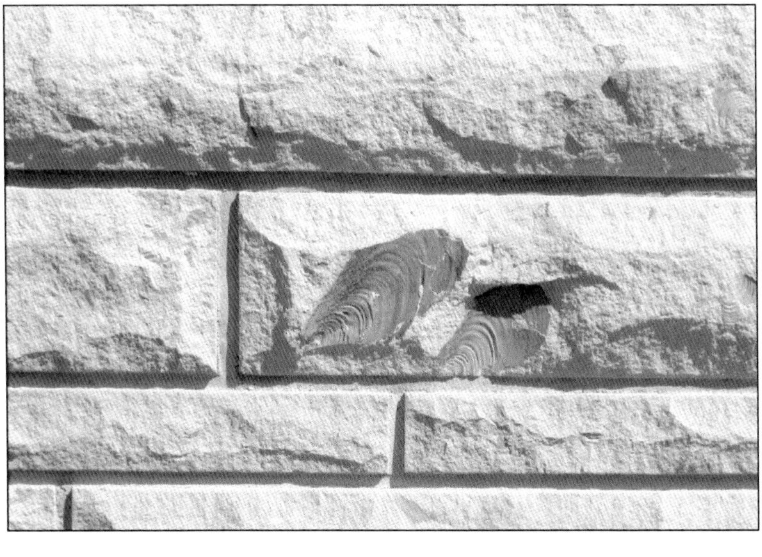

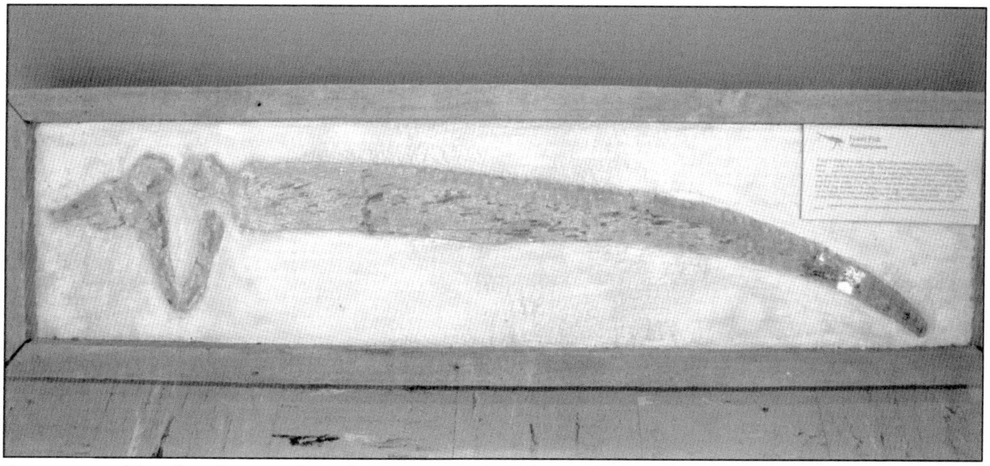

A variety of fossilized examples of marine animals from the Cretaceous period can be found in formations containing Post Rock limestone. *Protosphyraena* resembles a modern swordfish with its long, toothed beak with a sharp, projecting spear. Its long, sickle-like fins were each four feet long and had sharp, serrated edges. This specimen of a *Protosphyraena* pectoral fin is on exhibit at the Post Rock Museum.

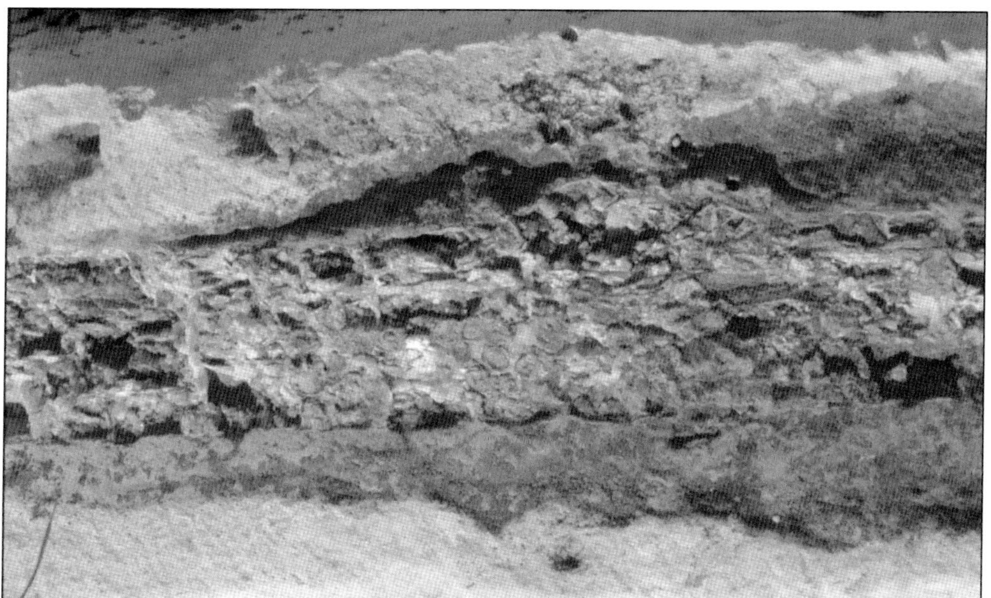

Fossilized (or petrified) wood specimens are commonly found in formations along with Post Rock limestone. Fossilization of the wood occurs after the specimen is buried in sediment. Empty spaces within an organism's cells fill with mineral-rich water. Under extreme pressure, the minerals harden and leave behind deposits of a variety of minerals.

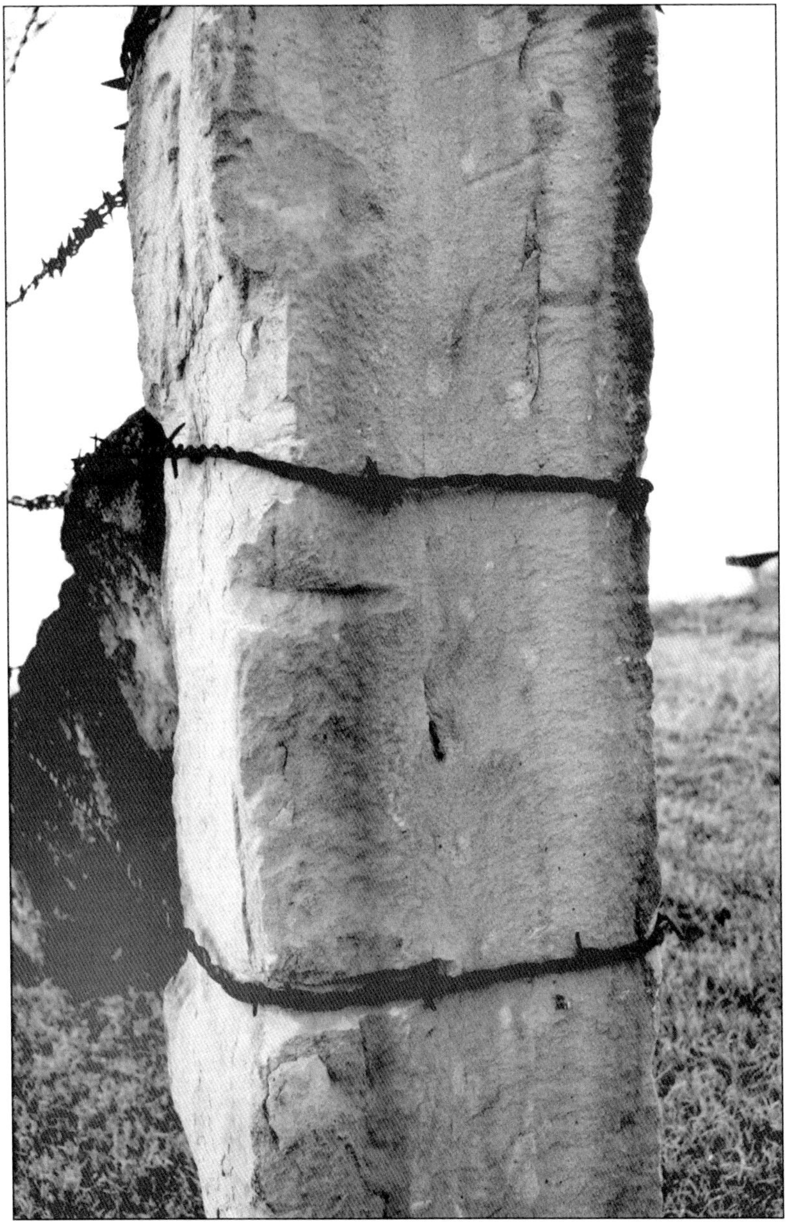

One feature that distinguishes Fencepost limestone from similar layers is its characteristic brown streak. This streak—a form of iron ore known as limonite or, more commonly, rust—is thought to have been derived from the crystallization and oxidation of iron-rich water, wood, and other debris that washed up along the shoreline as the Western Interior Seaway receded. It is characteristically much harder than the rest of the Post Rock layer. The brown streak also helps to determine the location where the limestone was quarried. In the upper northeast portion of Post Rock Country, the brown streak is narrow and well defined and appears more centralized. Farther to the southwest, the brown streak begins to lose definition and sometimes separates into two or more streaks. At the southwestern extreme of Post Rock Country, the streaks may be wider and appear faded and poorly developed. The post pictured shows the brown streak off-center to the left side of the post, characteristic of Post Rocks quarried in the Rush County area.

Two

QUARRYING POST ROCK

When the pioneers first arrived in western and central Kansas, they were faced with a dilemma: the vast, open prairie was lacking in trees and other traditional building materials. However, they found a solution at their feet: Post Rock, which occurs naturally in a uniform bed about 12 inches thick and lies at or near the surface. Although Post Rock appeared to be the perfect answer for buildings and fence posts, it was not simple to harvest and prepare. Quarrying was slow and labor-intensive. After the layer was exposed, it had to be drilled and split by hand and transported a few pieces at a time by horse and wagon. Once on site, it needed to be prepared with crude tools and laid by hand with only a rudimentary block-and-tackle system to assist. However, the pioneers were no strangers to hard work, and they managed to quarry thousands of building stones and fenceposts during the late 19th and early 20th centuries.

Post Rock Country

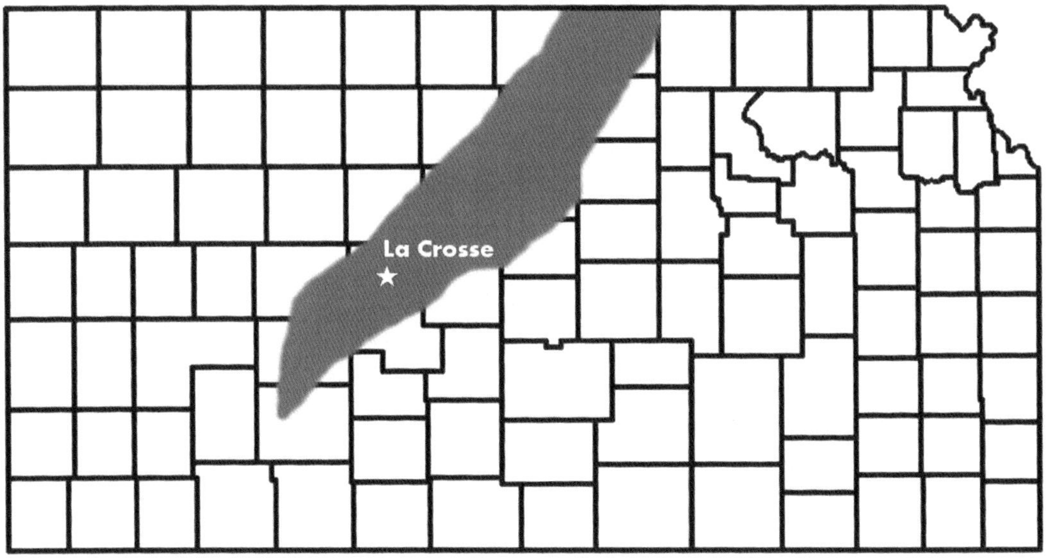

The Kansas Geological Survey has divided the state into 11 physiographic regions. The largest regions include the High Plains in the west, the Smoky Hills region in central Kansas, Flint Hills in the east central area, the Glaciated Region in the northeast, and the Osage Cuestas in the southeast. Post Rock Country is situated in the middle of the Smoky Hills region. It stretches 200 miles diagonally from north of Dodge City to the Nebraska border. A number of native-stone buildings can be found in this region, but among the most unique aspects are the miles of fences constructed with large and colorful posts made of stone. The unique heritage of the region is exhibited in several areas. The city of Lincoln is known as the "Post Rock Capital of Kansas" and features a number of beautiful buildings constructed of the stone. The Post Rock Scenic Byway is an 18-mile stretch of highway that travels from Lucas to Wilson through Russell, Lincoln, and Ellsworth Counties. The Post Rock Museum in La Crosse tells the story and preserves the heritage of Post Rock.

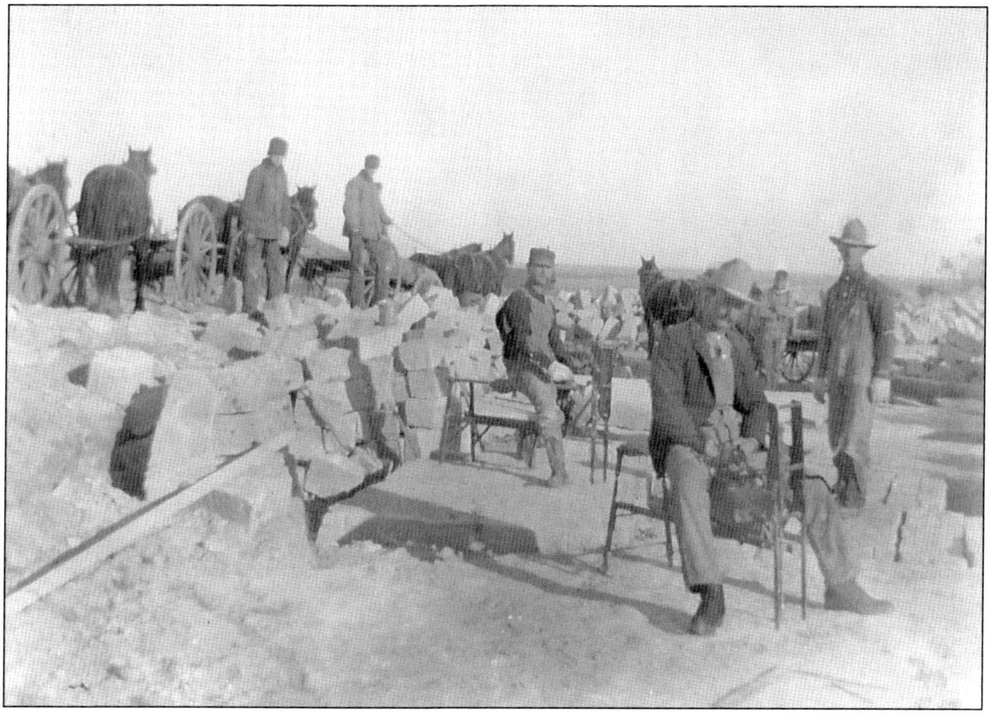

Initially, the quarrying of Post Rock was done primarily with homemade tools. Holes were drilled into the rock with hand-operated drills, which used the weight of the operator to drive the bit into the stone. Some drills had large stone wheels attached above the bit to add weight. The stones were split by driving a beveled wedge point-side down between two other wedges inserted with the wide end down into the holes. Just before the rock was ready to split, the wedge made a distinctive pinging sound when struck. When the entire row was "tuned" to this sound, an additional strike with a hammer caused the stone to split along the line. Pictured above and below is a stone quarry located south of Alexander in southwestern Rush County.

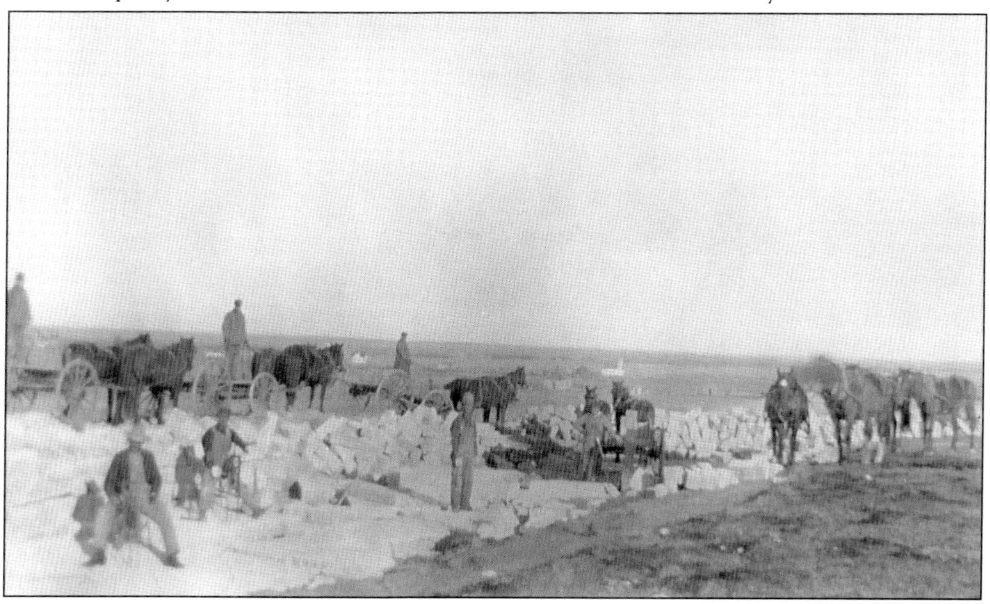

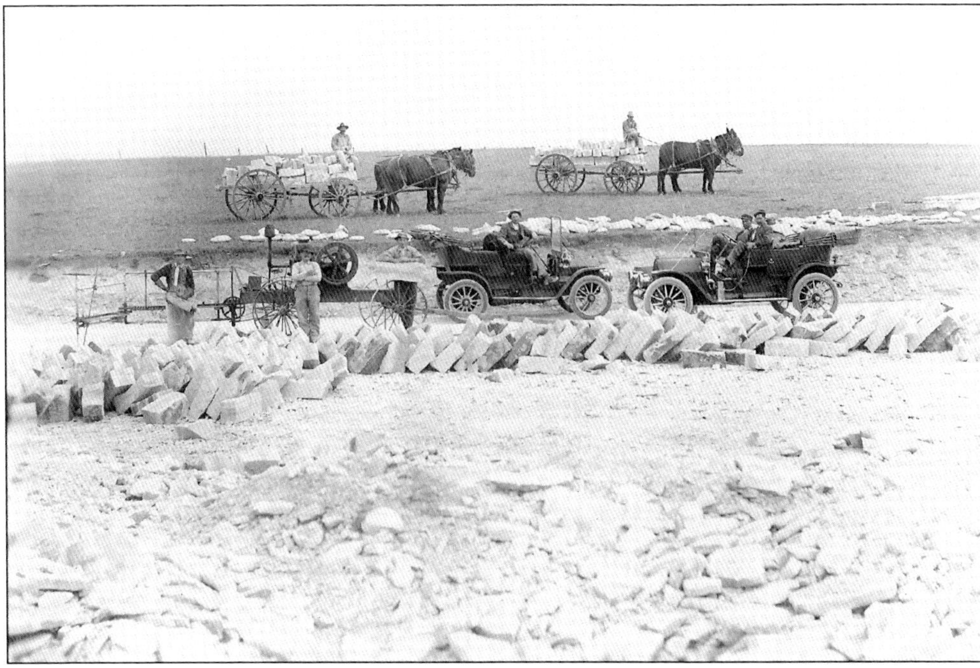

The methods of rock quarrying remained virtually unchanged into the 20th century. However, power-driven machinery started to take the place of manual equipment and horse-drawn transportation. Since money was scarce, settlers resorted to inventive means of recycling unused objects into useful equipment. Rock drills were powered by motors salvaged from washing machines. The motor was connected to the drill by a pulley, and the mechanism had small metal wheels that allowed it to be moved along the face of the rock. Once the row of holes was drilled, the stone was split in the conventional manner. Although automobiles were beginning to gain popularity, stones were still transported by horse and wagon. These two photographs, dated December 14, 1911, show a quarry in Russell County; the quarry's exact location is unknown.

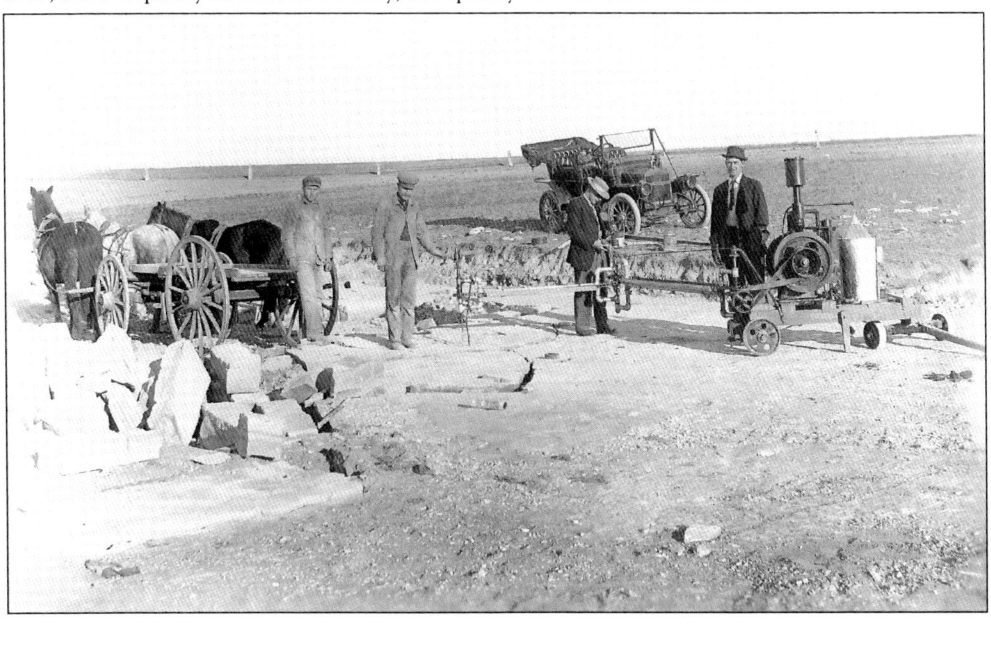

This drill was salvaged from an early quarry. Masons modified a typical brace-and-bit drill by attaching a stone weight to increase the pressure of the drill bit against the rock. Although the weight helped, the continuous hand-cranking was still highly labor-intensive. The weight also served as a depth gauge.

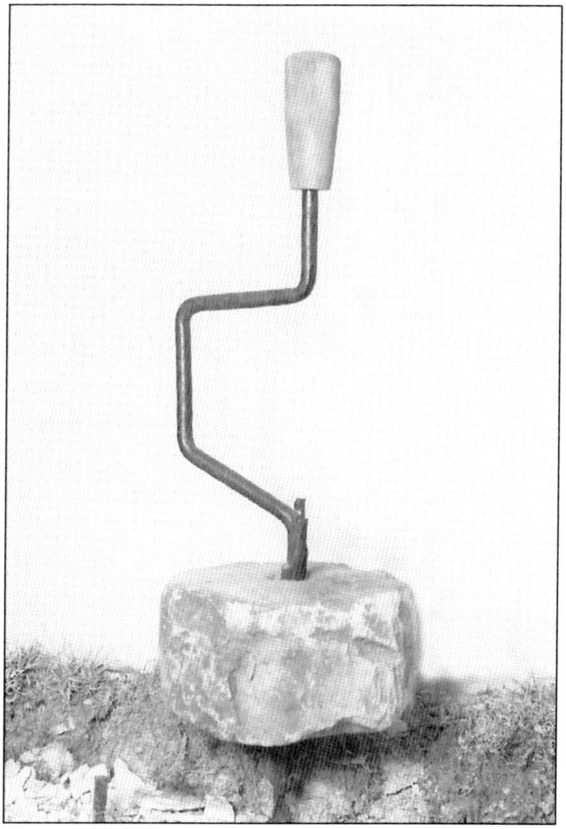

The design of this gasoline-powered drill features a motor salvaged from a 1920s washing machine and mounted to an iron-frame drilling buck. The motor is connected by a pulley to the gear box above the drill, which rotates the drill mechanism while the operator presses a lever, pushing the bit into the rock. The drill has two small metal wheels that allow it to be moved along the face of the rock.

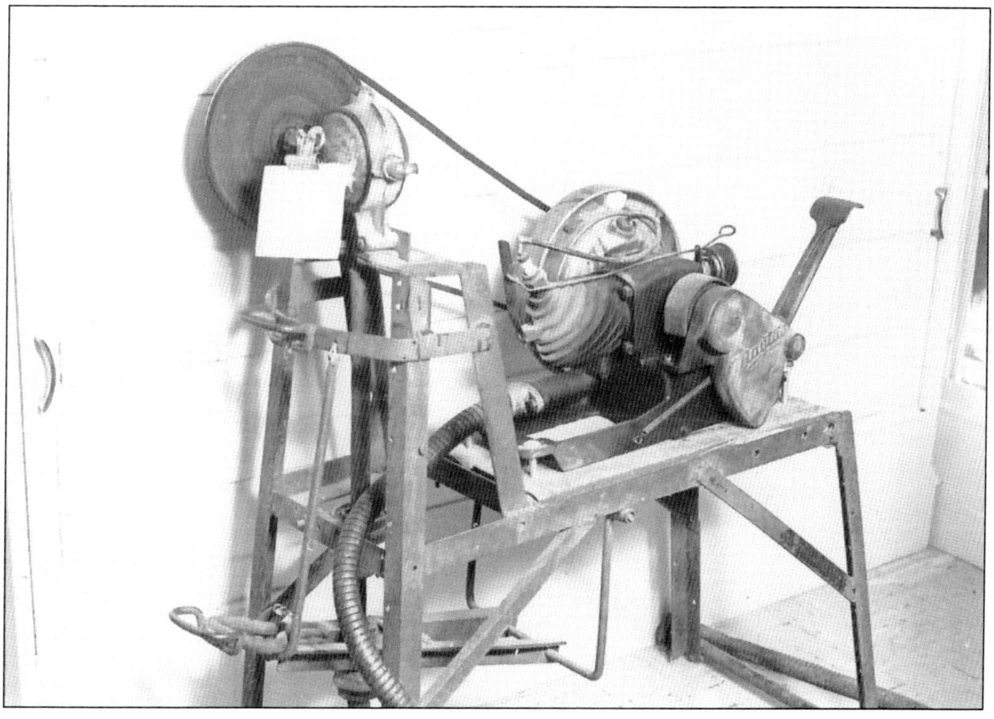

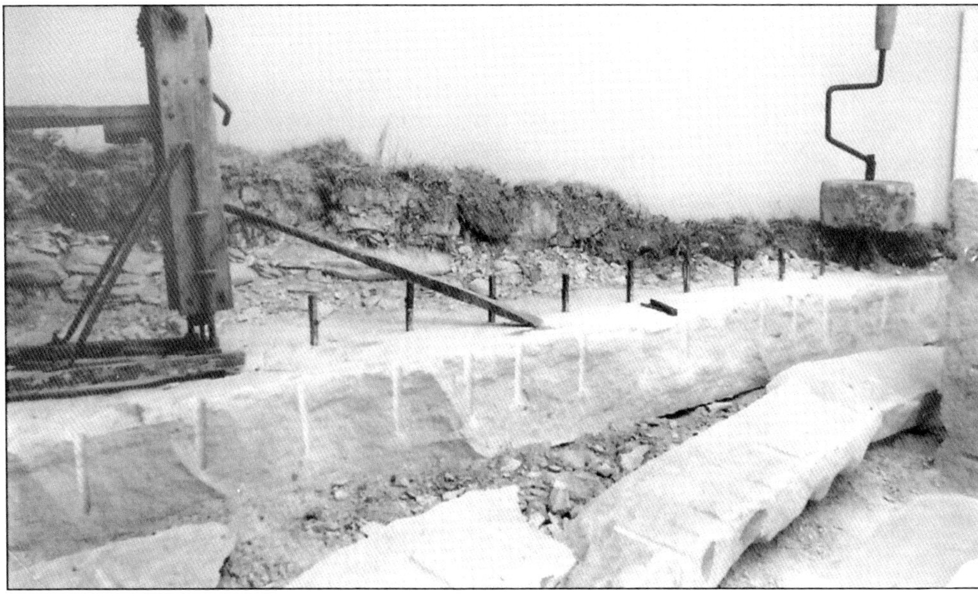

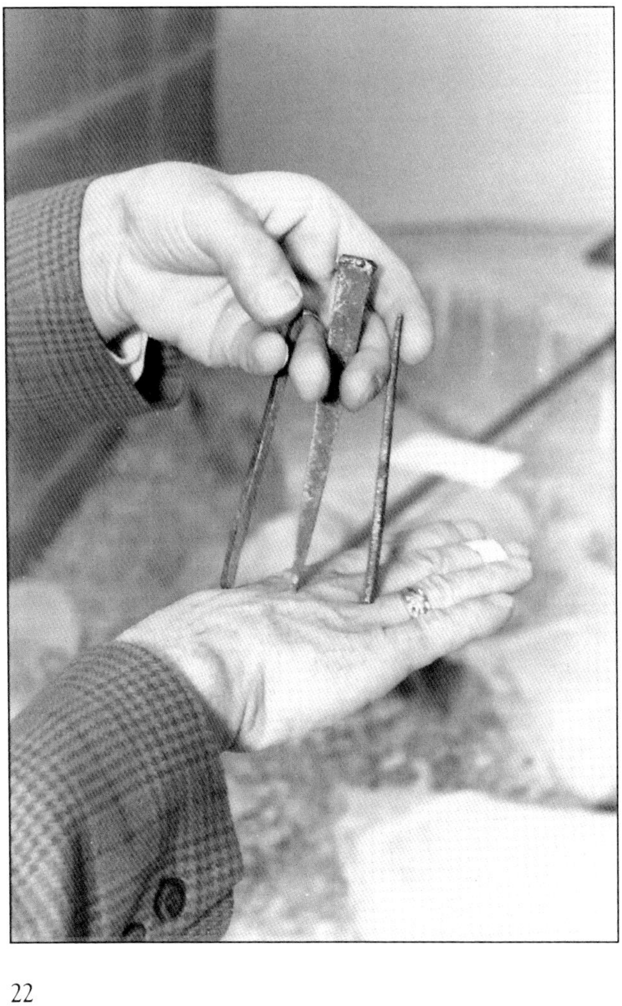

The 1964 image above shows several sets of feather and wedges positioned in a line of holes along a limestone bed in a model quarry in the Post Rock Museum. To split the stone, a stonemason would go up and down the row and strike each of the wedges. Experienced stonemasons would listen for a distinctive pinging sound. At that point, the next hammer strike would systematically split the stone along the line.

These items are collectively known as "feather and wedges." Feathers consisted of two pieces of metal, each flat on one side and slightly rounded on the other, that work as shims. The wedge, which resembled a chisel, was driven between the two feathers, putting pressure against the stone and eventually forcing it to split.

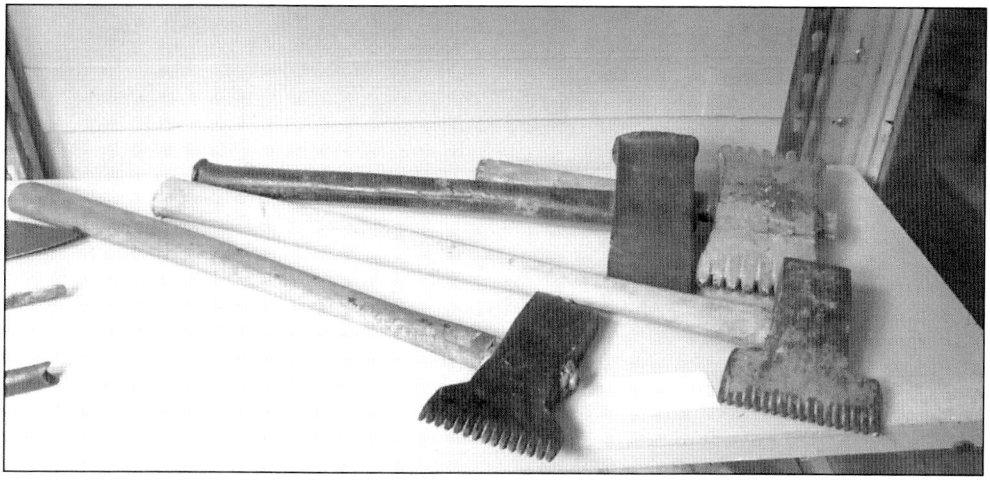

These stonemasons' hammers were combination tools designed for both splitting and dressing stones. Dressing was primarily reserved for stones used in building and involved striking the face with a serrated hammer, which removed imperfections and squared the stones or created various patterns in the stone's face.

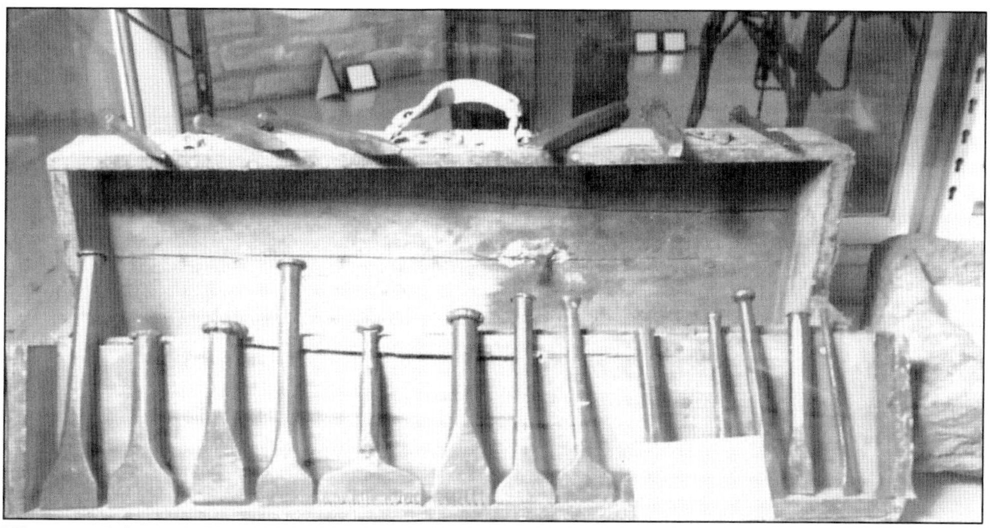

This is a 19th-century stonemason's toolbox. Stonemasons used a variety of chisels with different patterns to create a variety of designs on the exposed face of the stone. Depending on the type of building, dressing stones could involve smoothing jagged edges or carving intricate patterns.

Dressing Post Rock Limestone

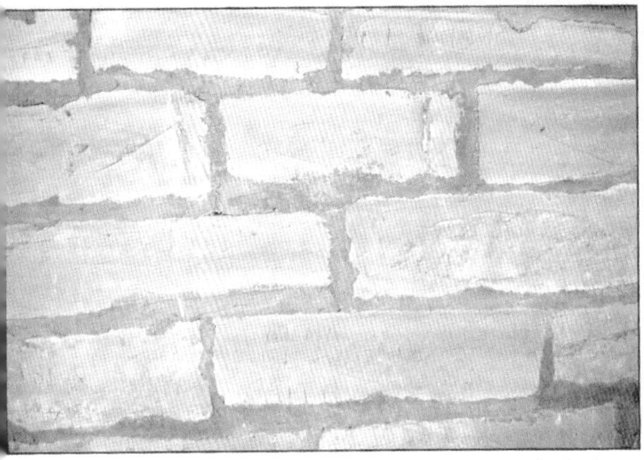

Rough Hewn

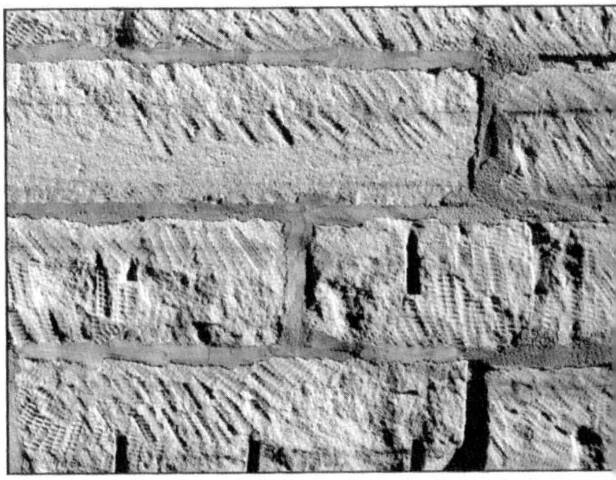

Quarry Face

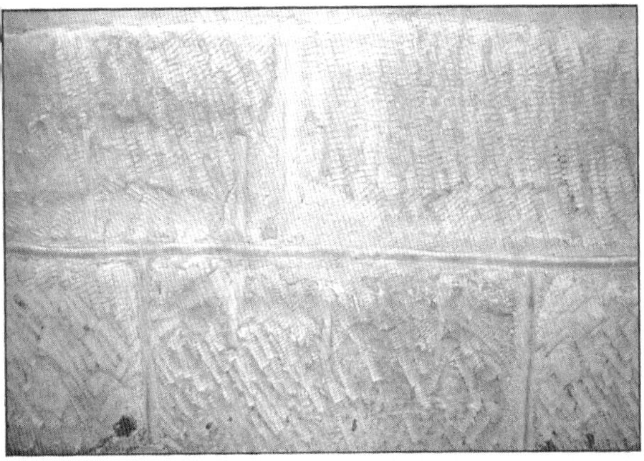

Hammered Face

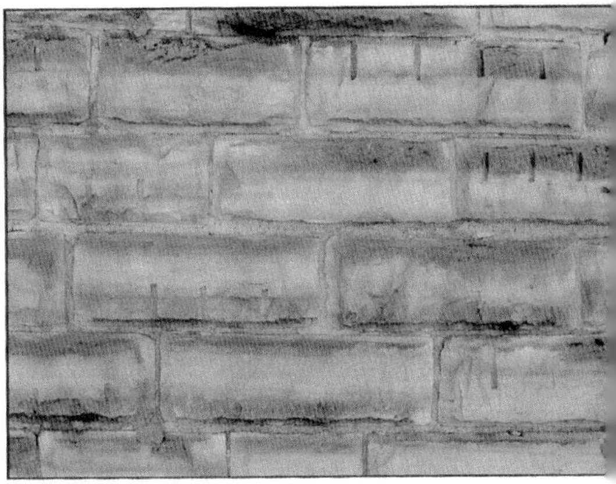

Pitch Face

There are five commonly used methods of dressing stones for buildings. Rough-hewn stones were left in the condition they were in when removed from the ground; this resulted in mortar joints that were often crude and irregular. Quarry-faced stones had four sides joined, sawed, and squared off, but left the face untouched to retain a natural appearance. Pitch-face stones resembled quarry-faced stones, with the edges to be joined neatly squared off, but on the exposed side, edges were chiseled back to produce a protruding face—this allowed for straight mortar lines and gave the stones a three-dimensional look. Hammered-face stones were dressed the same as pitch-faced stones, with smooth-cut edges and a cut-back, protruding face, but designs (ranging from simple to complex patterns) were then chiseled into the surface. A fifth, less-popular method of finishing known as sawed face was similar to quarry face, except the face was trimmed smooth. (Photograph by the author.)

Post Rock Construction Styles

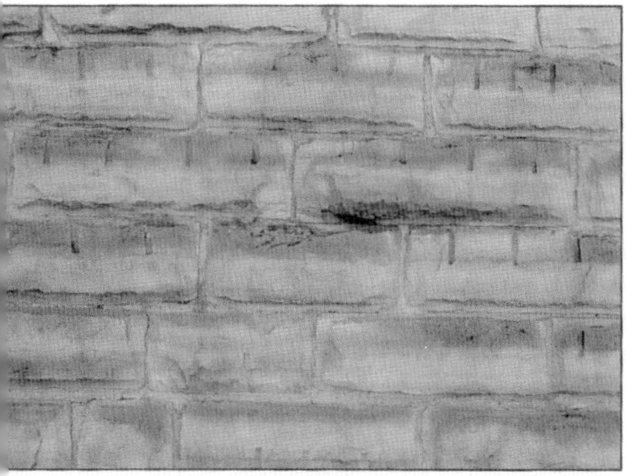

Traditional

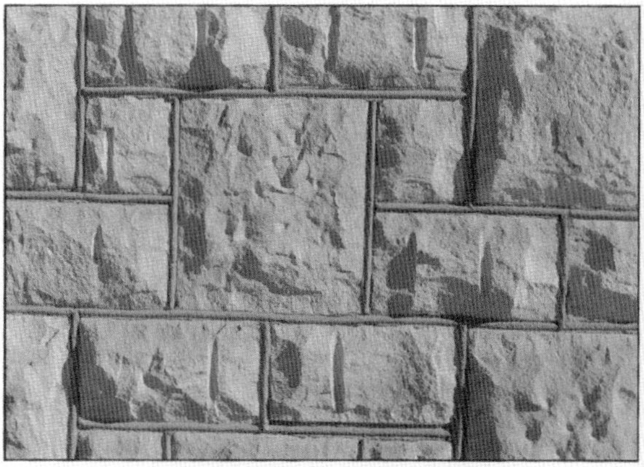

Random Ashler

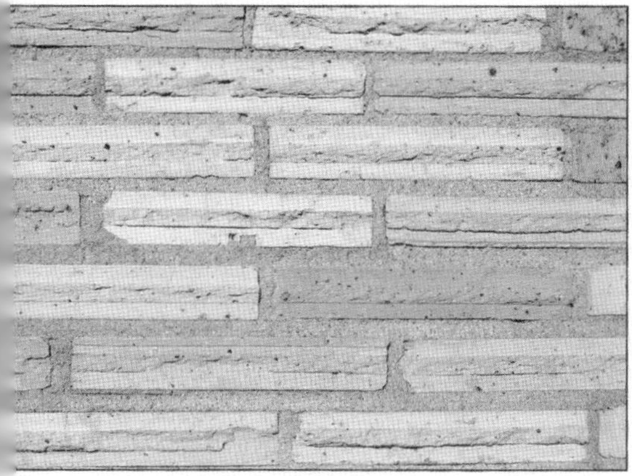

Flagging

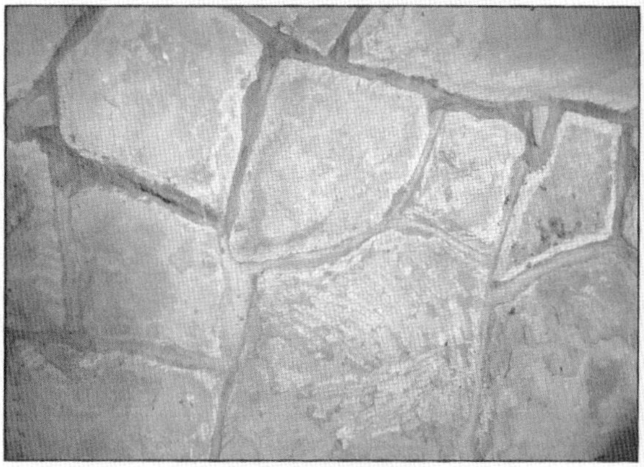

Rubble

Stones were traditionally placed using the same method as that used for brick, in even courses with the joints alternated to increase strength. To add to the attractiveness of the wall, other methods can be employed. Random ashlars are laid on a level plane, but using stones of two or more heights in various widths and arranging them in a pattern, resulting in a strong, yet attractive, design. Flagstones are half-height stones created by splitting stones along the grain or at natural fractures; they are generally used for sidewalks and flooring. However, stonemasons discovered that natural fractures in the Fencepost limestone bed created a lot of scrap and found that by dressing these small, broken pieces, they could use them as attractive building stones. Another method of utilizing scrap in construction is called rubble; stone fragments of irregular shapes and sizes—but with at least one straight surface—could be placed in a random pattern that required very little preparation or dressing. (Photograph by the author.)

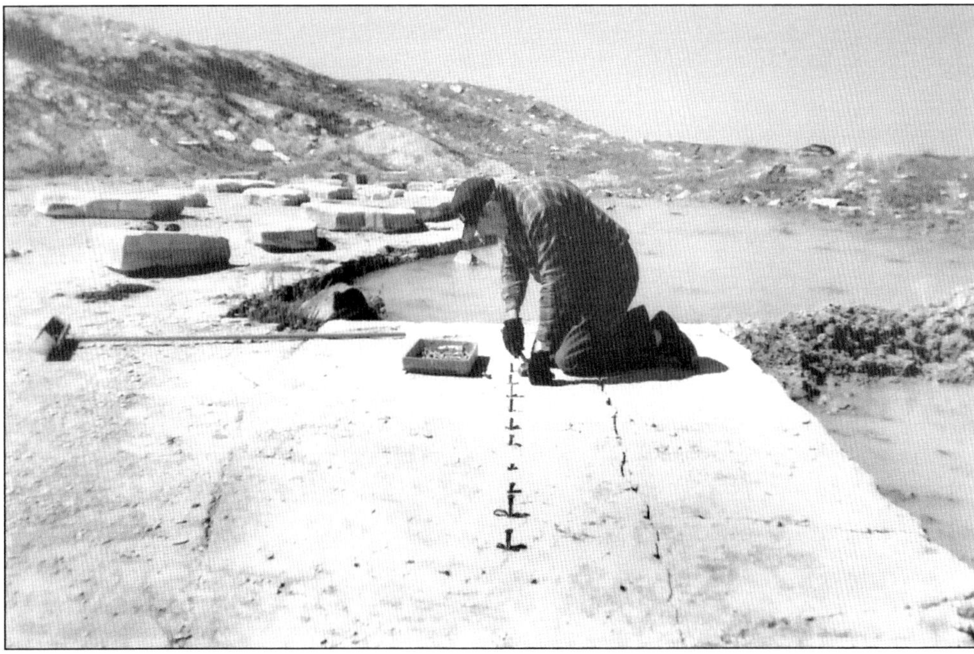

Glen Schneipp, of Bazine, Kansas, prepares to split a slab of stone intended to be used for a step. As each of the wedges is struck with the hammer, the stone will split along the line and separate from the bed. Note how smooth the surface of the Post Rock layer is once the overburden has been removed. (Courtesy Lawrence Erbes.)

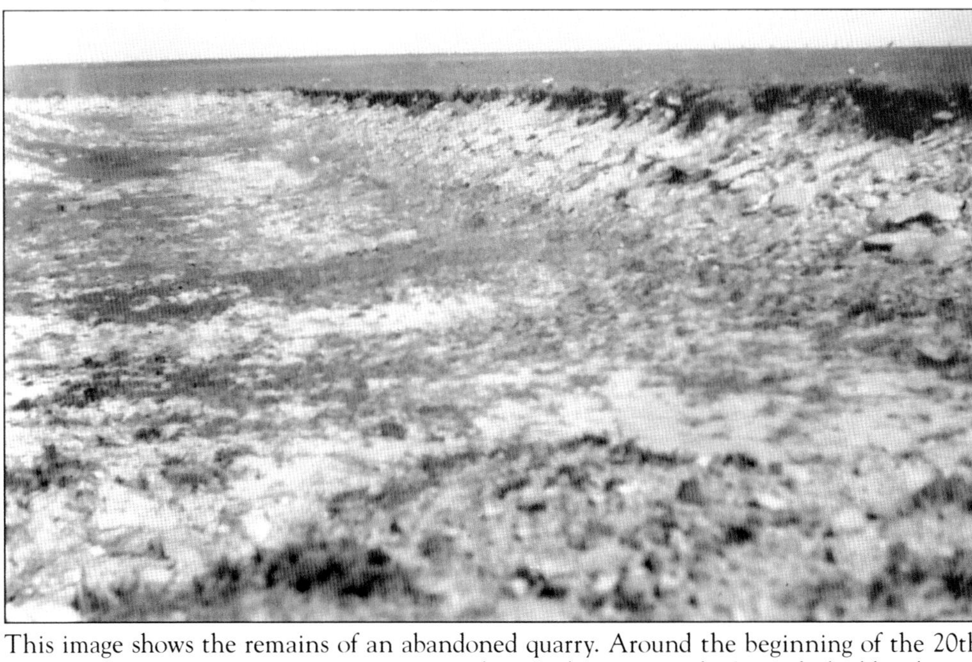

This image shows the remains of an abandoned quarry. Around the beginning of the 20th century, numerous stone quarries were scattered across the countryside. Stone for building homes or churches was usually quarried near the location where it was to be used, then quarries were abandoned when the building was completed. In this image, the Post Rock layer has been removed, and vegetation has started to grow within the remaining rock layer.

Three

Post Rock on the Farm

Rural settlers were forced to use as many natural resources as possible to survive. At first, their buildings were made of sod. However, sod was susceptible to the elements, hard to maintain, and hardly sanitary. Once people discovered that Post Rock was an extremely sturdy and permanent—and readily available—building material, they began to use it for homes, barns, outbuildings, and fences, as well as for other creative structures. Since wood was scarce, stone was used for clothesline supports, well covers, and even telephone poles. The use of Post Rock for fence posts was further enhanced by the 1874 invention known as barbed wire. Because it was inexpensive, available, and very strong, barbed wire proved to be an excellent companion for Post Rock in fence construction. The combination of barbed wire and stone posts made for strong and durable fences that survived the harsh environment and abuse from large animals for many years. Several miles of fences constructed in the early 1900s are still in use today—a testament to the durability of this unique stone.

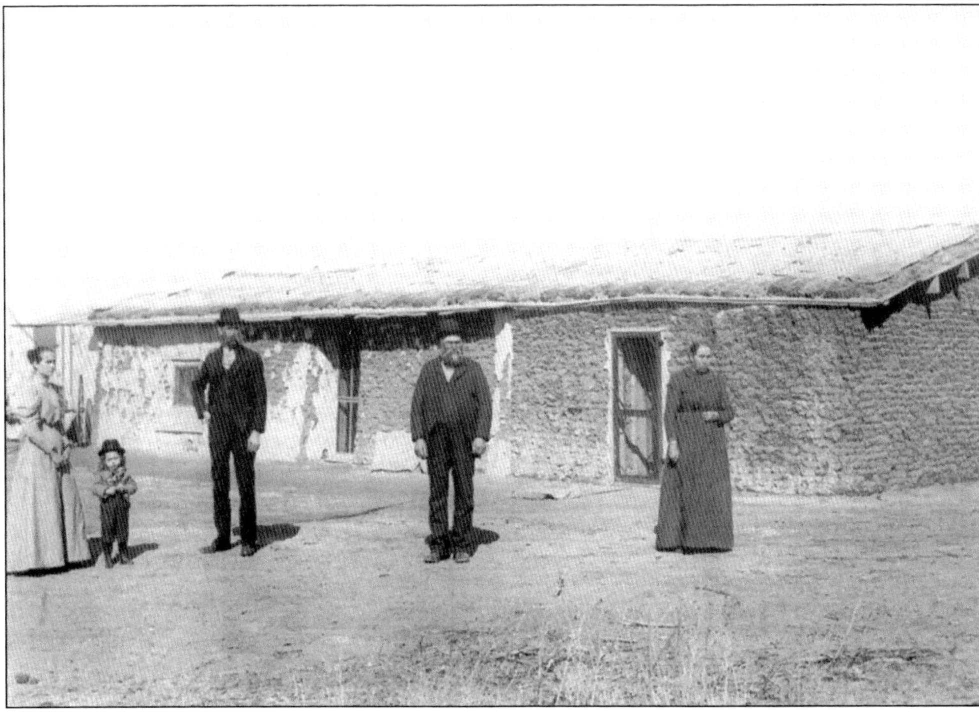

Sod homes were built from "bricks" cut from the prairie earth. These could be constructed quickly and at almost no cost. This rural home outside of La Crosse was one of the first in the area. Pictured here are, from left to right, Edna Robbins Olson, Lloyd Robbins Olson, Nelson Pederson Olson, Nils Olson, and Isle Olson.

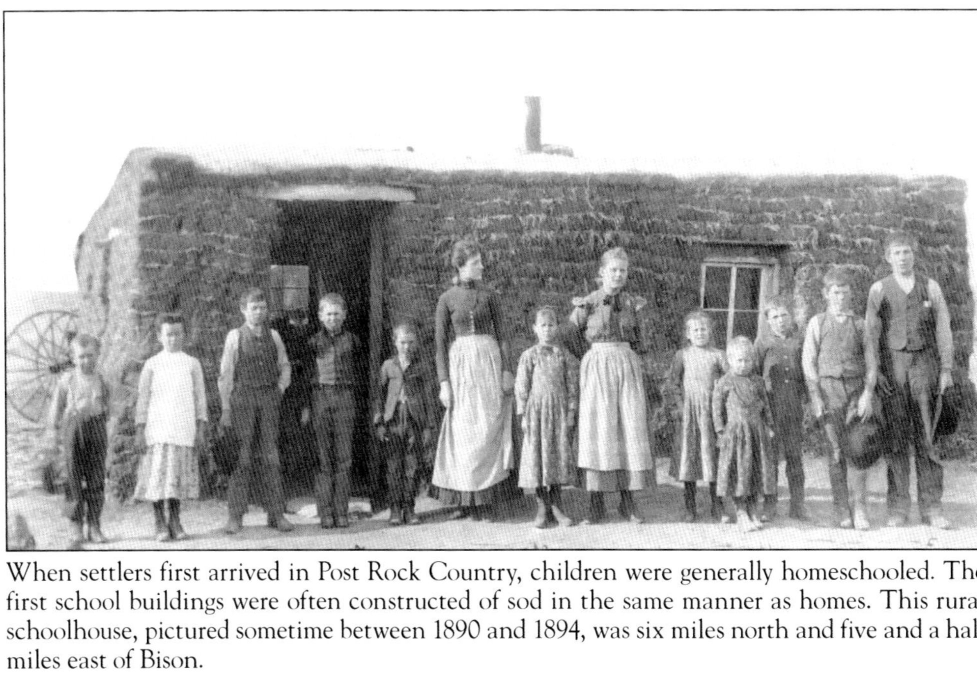

When settlers first arrived in Post Rock Country, children were generally homeschooled. The first school buildings were often constructed of sod in the same manner as homes. This rural schoolhouse, pictured sometime between 1890 and 1894, was six miles north and five and a half miles east of Bison.

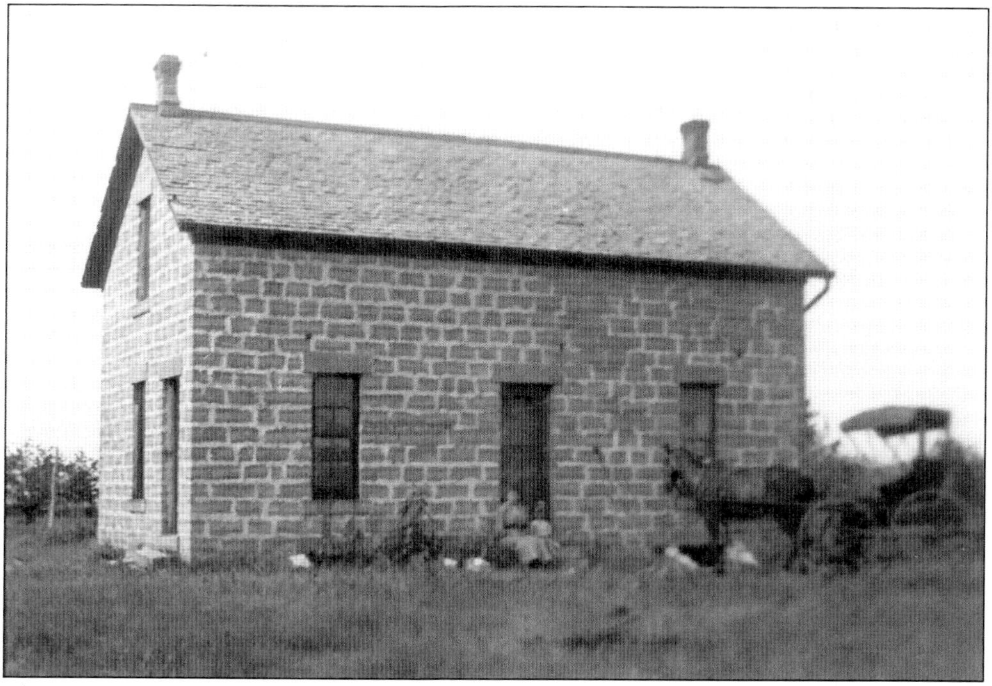

This two-story Post Rock farm home was located near Timken. Bohemian settlers first arrived in the Timken area in 1878. The town is named for Henry Timken, inventor of the Timken buggy spring and Timken roller bearing. Timken, who never lived in the area, attempted to purchase land there, but when he was unable to secure adequate property, he chose to construct his factory back east.

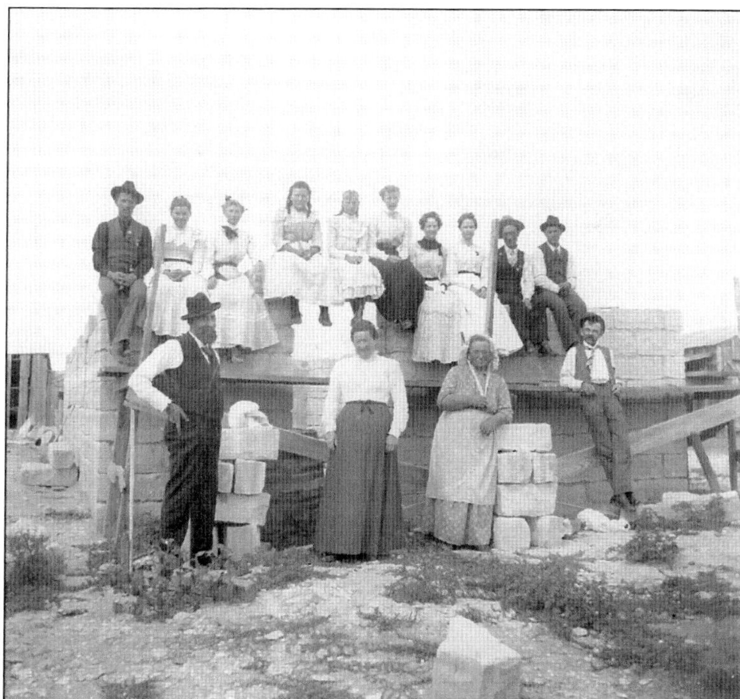

This group posed for a picture on the uncompleted barn at the Adam Kirch farm located northwest of Rush Center. Most of the people are well dressed, indicating that they were probably not in the process of construction at the time. In the late 1800s, stones were often mortared with mud or a mixture of limestone dust and water.

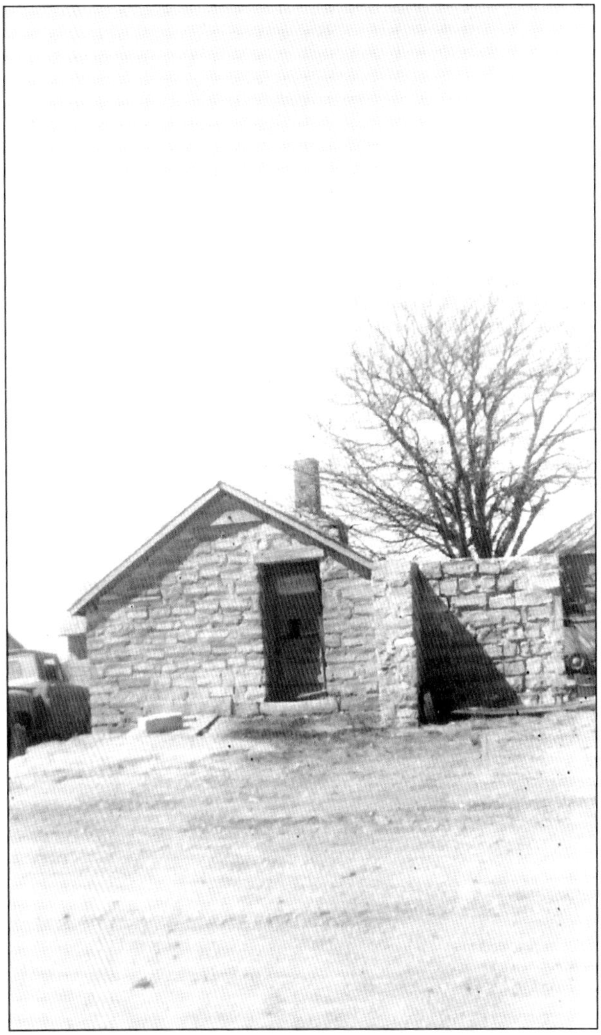

Alexander Harvey built this simple homestead between 1874 and 1876. Harvey, one of the first settlers in Rush County, served in Custer's 6th Cavalry in 1869. After he was mustered out of the Army in 1872, he took over a former military trading post on the Fort Hays–Fort Dodge Trail. His trading post, known as "Harvey's Ranche," was situated northwest of Walnut Creek near what is now the town of Alexander, which was named in Harvey's honor.

This is another view of Harvey's modest home. Before white settlers arrived, the area around Alexander was a hunting ground for southern Native American tribes. As the town was being settled, frequent reports of impending Indian attacks spurred residents to take up arms; however, there are no existing records of any conflicts. Explorers have found hide scrapers and flint arrows in creek banks near the area.

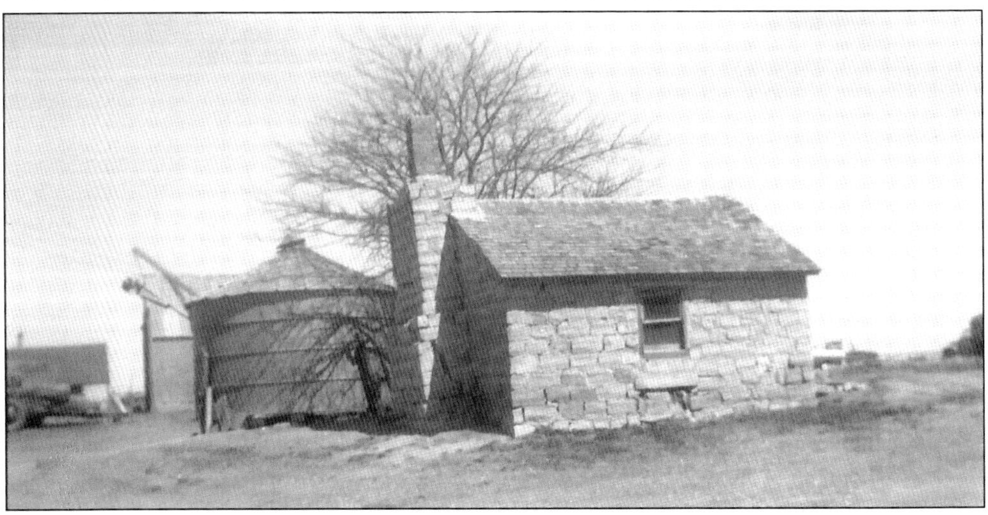

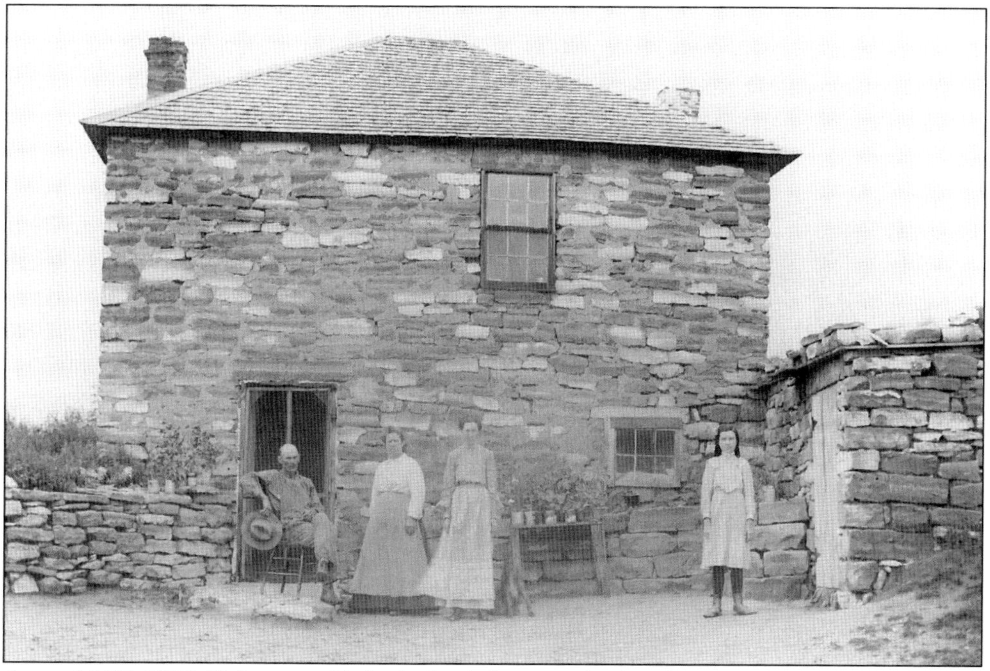

Around 1870, W.C. Holmes established a land claim south of Rush Center. After first living in a dugout, he built this rock house from stone quarried on his land. A portion of the house is built into an adjacent hillside. Pictured here are, from left to right, W.C.; his wife, Hettie; and their daughters Cecelia and Mollie.

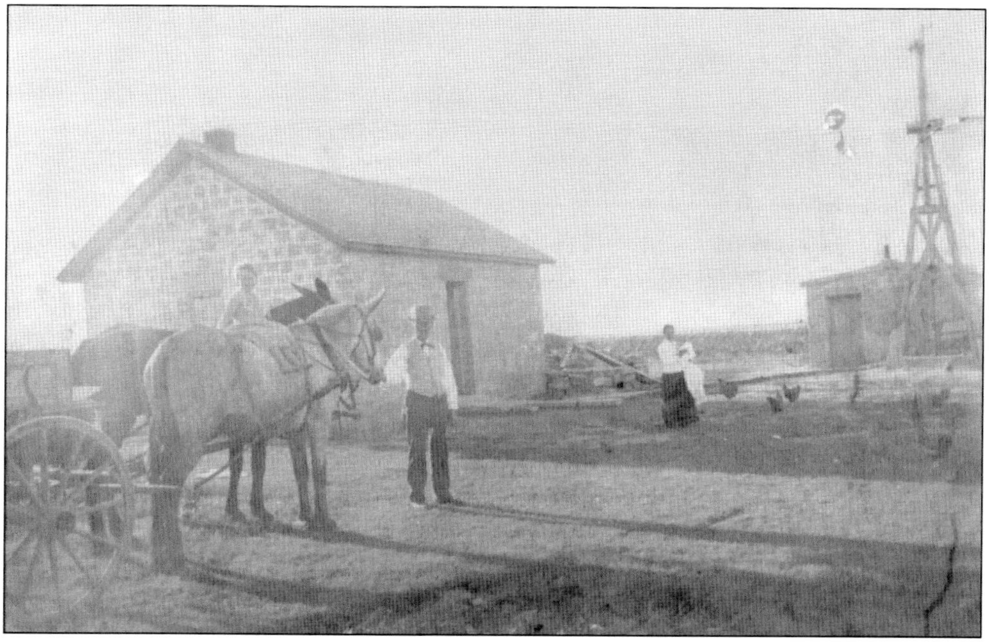

This image of a pioneer homestead illustrates a purely functional design that utilized native limestone construction. These early homes typically contained one room and had minimal windows and doors. Inhabitants of the homes would hang blankets from the ceiling to serve as makeshift walls that separated sleeping quarters from the rest of the house.

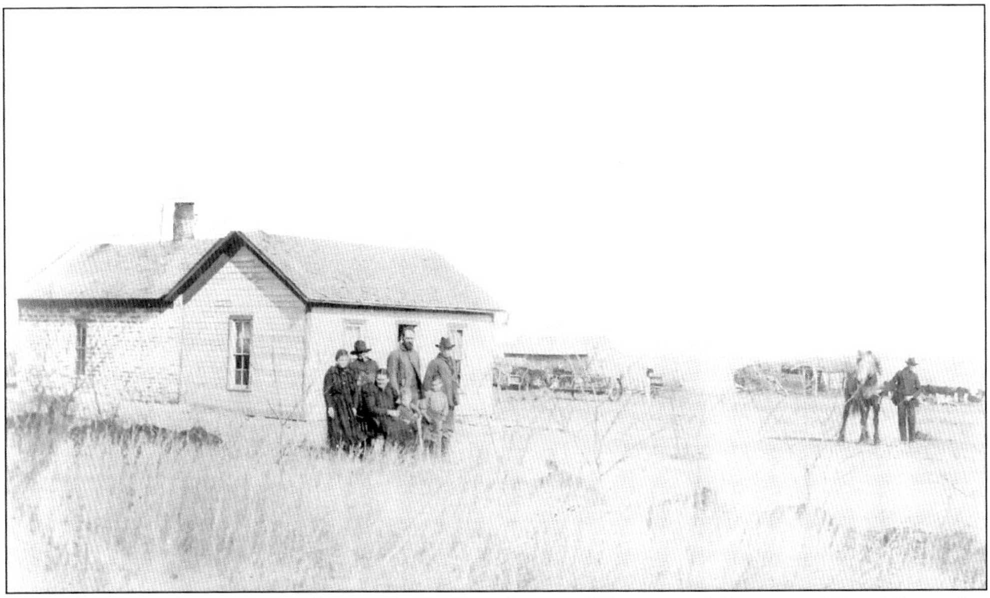

According to the Homestead Act of 1862, settlers could receive 160 acres of land from the government at little or no cost if they promised to establish residency on the parcel. This c. 1890 photograph shows the homestead, located northeast of Hargrave, of W.M. Greenway. Note the native limestone addition to the wood-frame home.

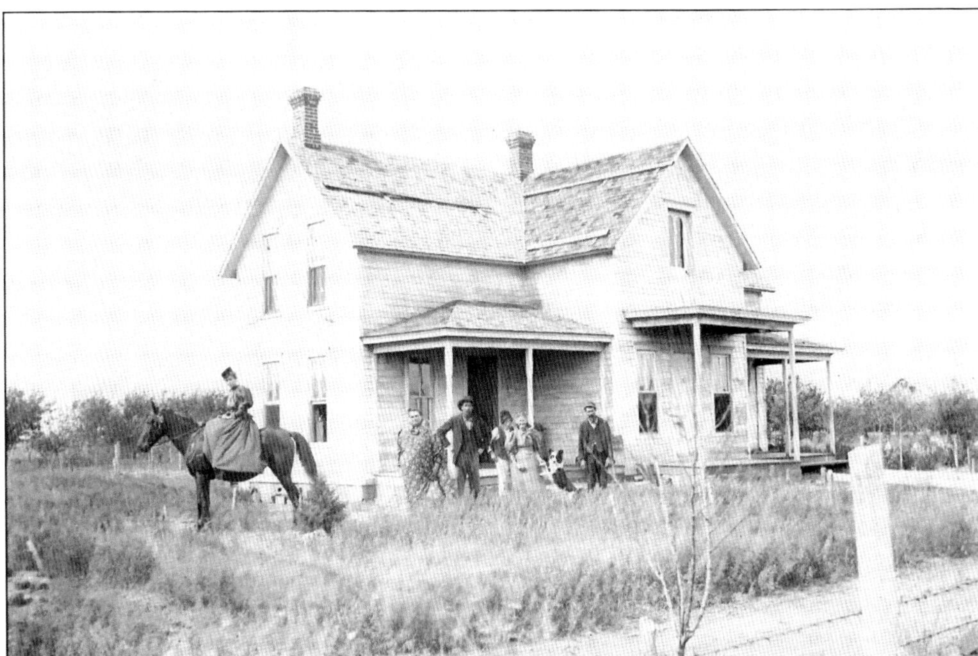

Limestone was used for home construction in a variety of ways and by a variety of social classes. This traditional two-story, wood-frame farmhouse, situated on a stone foundation, is an example of a rural home that shows evidence of having been enlarged, probably to accommodate a growing family.

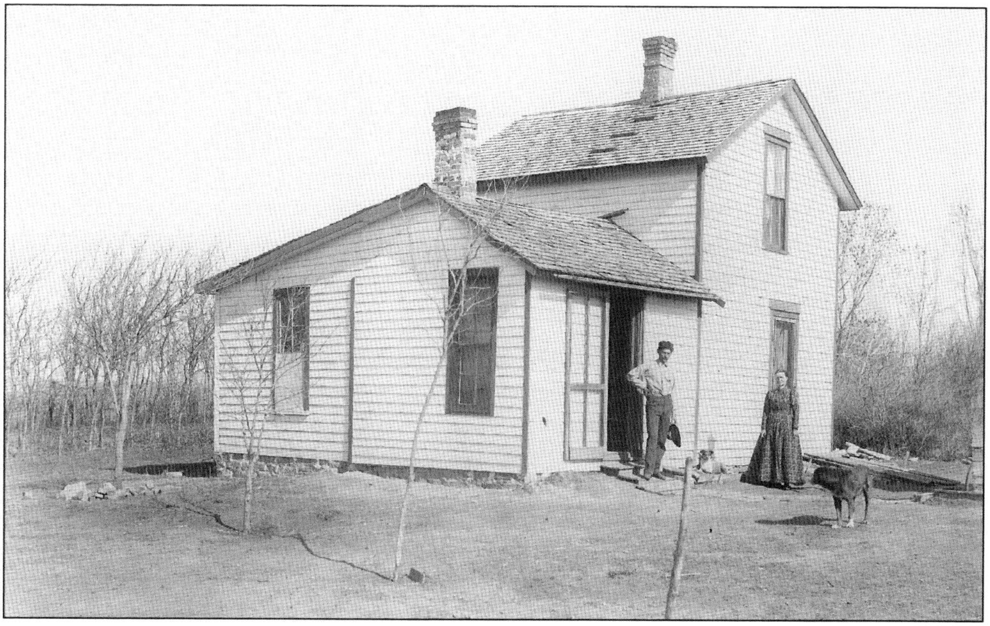

Many rural homes were situated on limestone foundations with small stone cellars. The cellar served a dual purpose: it provided a cool place to store canned goods and could also be used as a tornado shelter if necessary. This image shows the home of Tabitha Isideen Perkins Forney, located near Russell, Kansas, in the 1880s. Forney noted on the back of the photograph that she was married in this house in 1881.

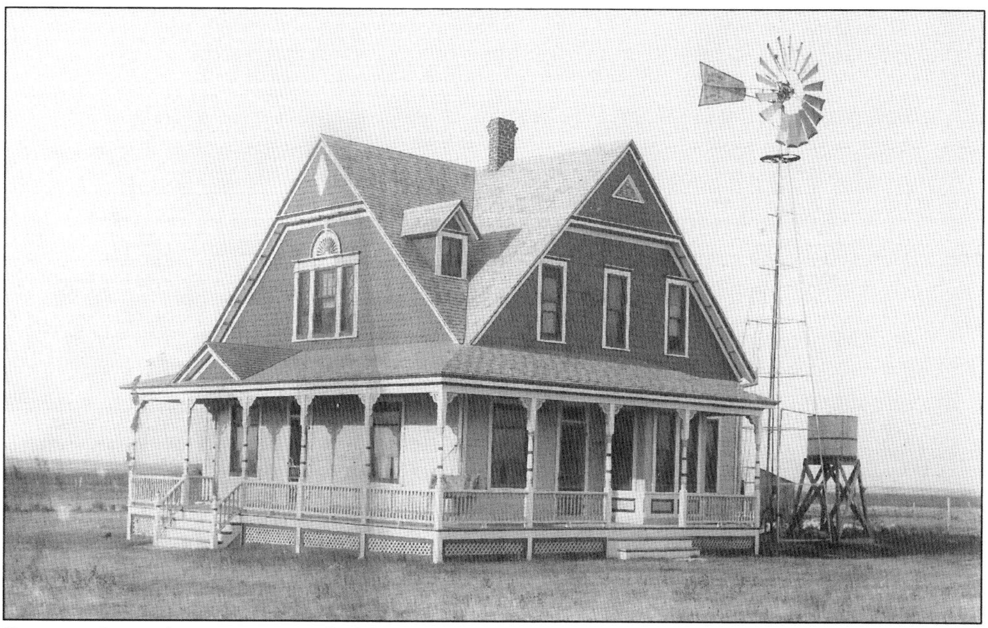

Some early settlers constructed elaborate homes on their farms. In 1900, W.M. Russell built this house a half-mile south of La Crosse. Limestone was used in the foundation of the house. In 1921, Jacob Erbes purchased this home, and it remains in his family today. The home was later occupied by Jacob's son Loris Erbes and then by Loris's son Lawrence. This photograph was taken in 1903.

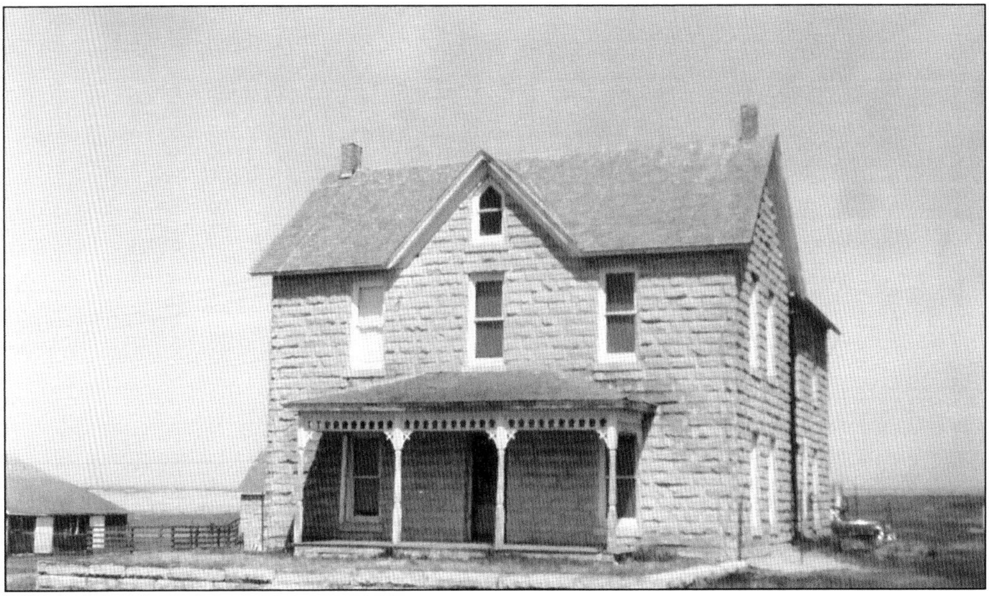

This magnificent house is located southwest of Liebenthal. Known as the Jefferis home, it is perhaps one of the most elaborate and well-preserved rural residences in Rush County. The property also contains a native-stone barn. This home is known for its appearance in a scene in the 1973 movie *Paper Moon*.

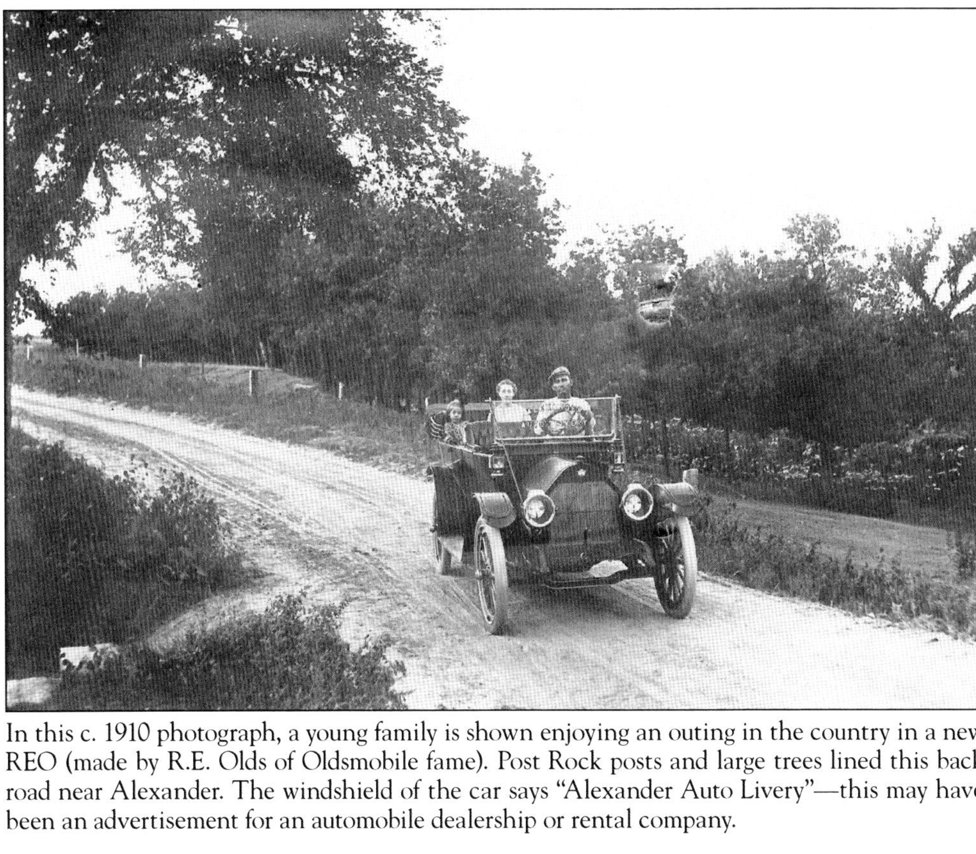

In this c. 1910 photograph, a young family is shown enjoying an outing in the country in a new REO (made by R.E. Olds of Oldsmobile fame). Post Rock posts and large trees lined this back road near Alexander. The windshield of the car says "Alexander Auto Livery"—this may have been an advertisement for an automobile dealership or rental company.

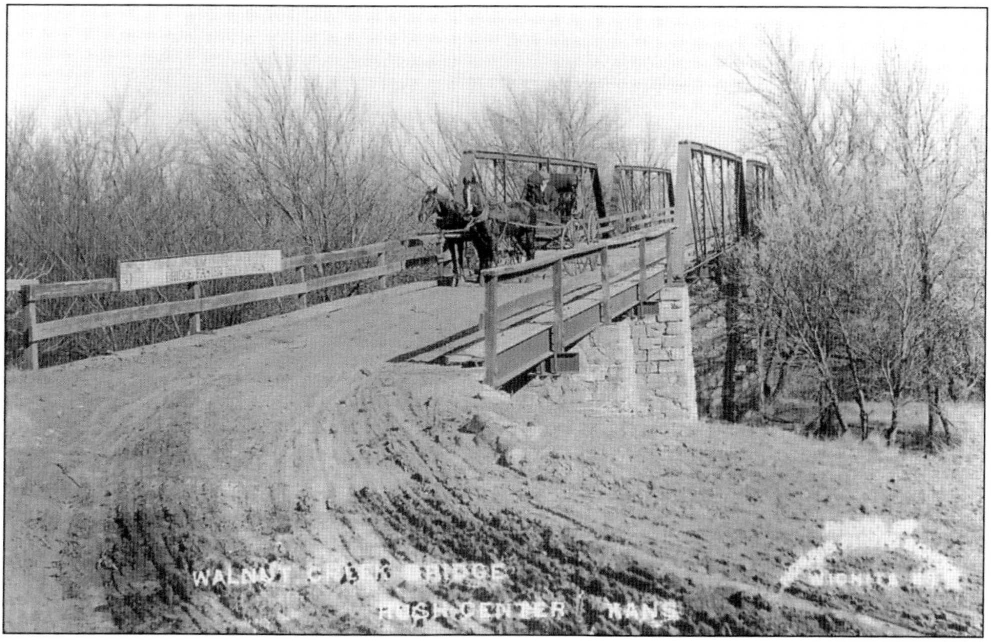

This one-lane pin-truss bridge, shown in 1915, spanned Walnut Creek south of Rush Center and was the main crossing over the creek for many years. It was supported by native-stone abutments and piers. The sign on the railing instructed travelers not to drive over the bridge "faster than a walk."

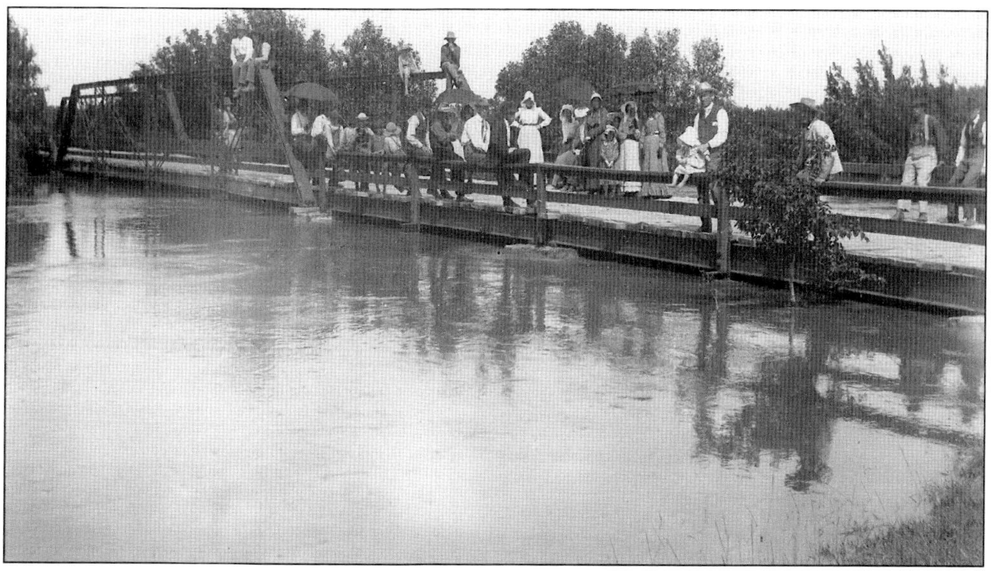

The town of Rush Center is situated in Walnut Valley adjacent to Walnut Creek. In the early 20th century, the creek was subject to frequent flooding. This 1901 image shows Walnut Creek at flood stage with water reaching the underside of the bridge.

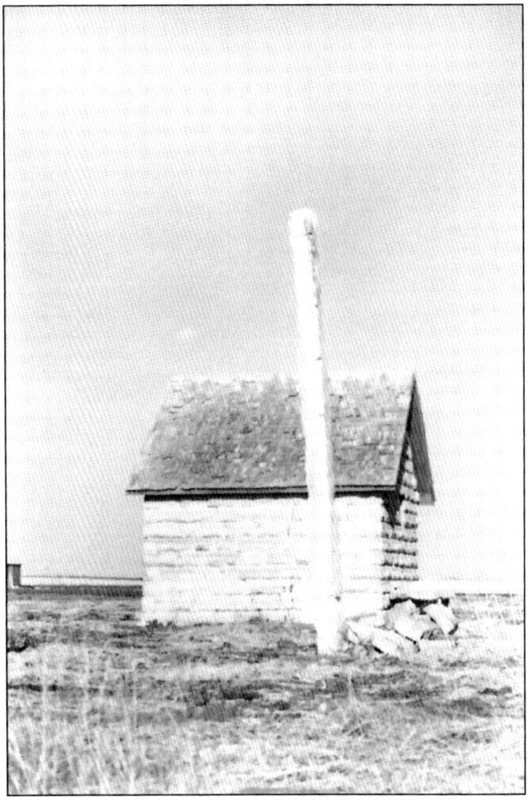

With wood scarce, settlers resorted to ingenious means to create otherwise common items. This telephone pole cut from Post Rock limestone is estimated to weigh in excess of 1,000 pounds. The building behind the pole was probably used as a washhouse.

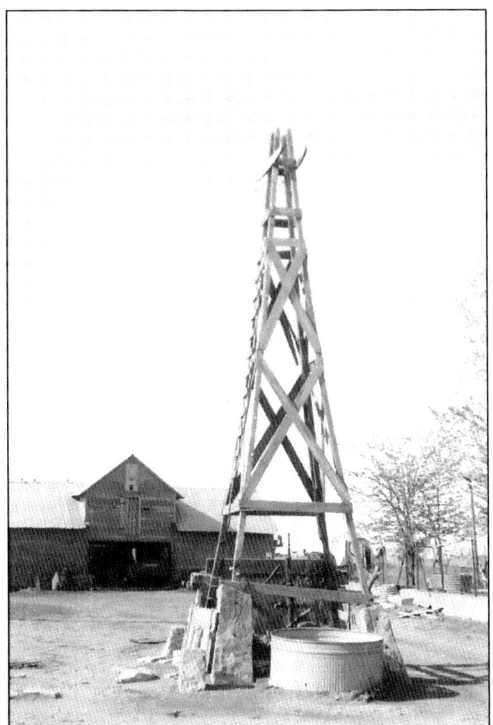

Because of the high winds on the open prairie, fence posts were often used as supports for windmills. Wooden windmills were top-heavy, and posts were set in the ground with one at each corner to match the angles of the windmill legs. The builder then drilled holes through the posts and attached them to the legs with iron bolts. The wooden posts of the windmill were attached a few inches above ground to help prevent the wood from rotting.

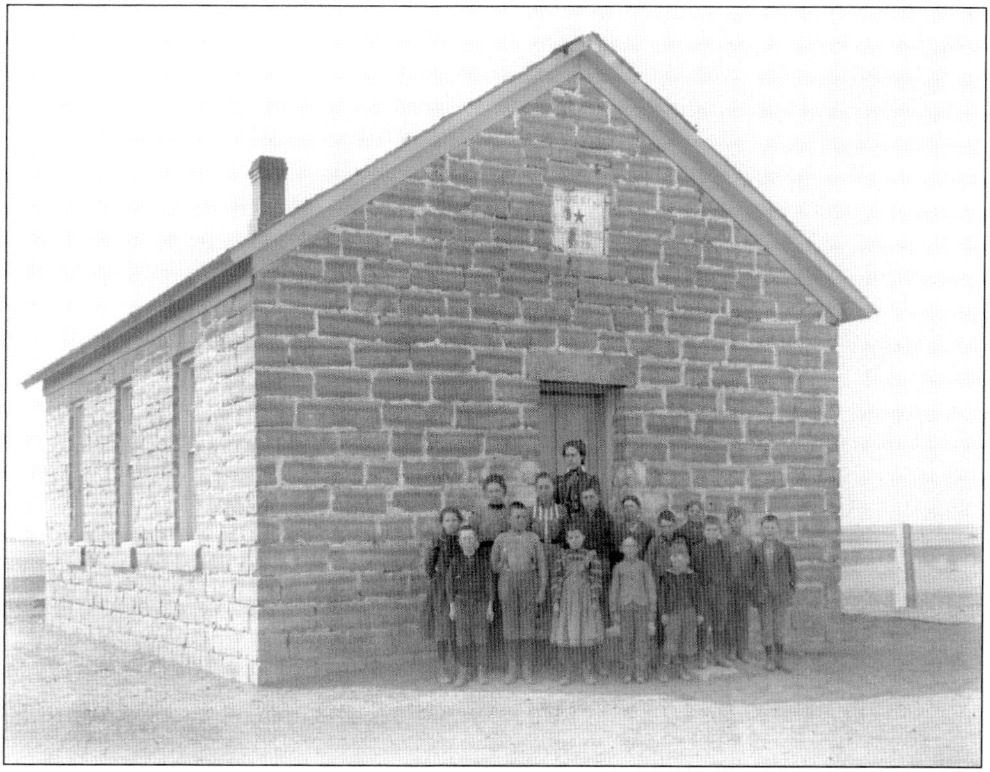

Located 1.5 miles west of Bison, the Lone Star School building was constructed in 1878 for use as a German-speaking Methodist church and school. Rev. C.G. Fritsche, the church's first pastor, carved a lone star on the east gable end "in reverence to the Holy Land and its Lone Star, Our Lord, Jesus Christ." Around 1890, the church relocated and then sold this building to School District 34, which held classes there until 1947. A vestibule later constructed on the east end of the building hides the lone star emblem. The photograph above shows the emblem and the words "Lone Star Schoolhouse—1879." The c. 1940 picture below shows the vestibule. The restored building is now listed in the National Register of Historic Places.

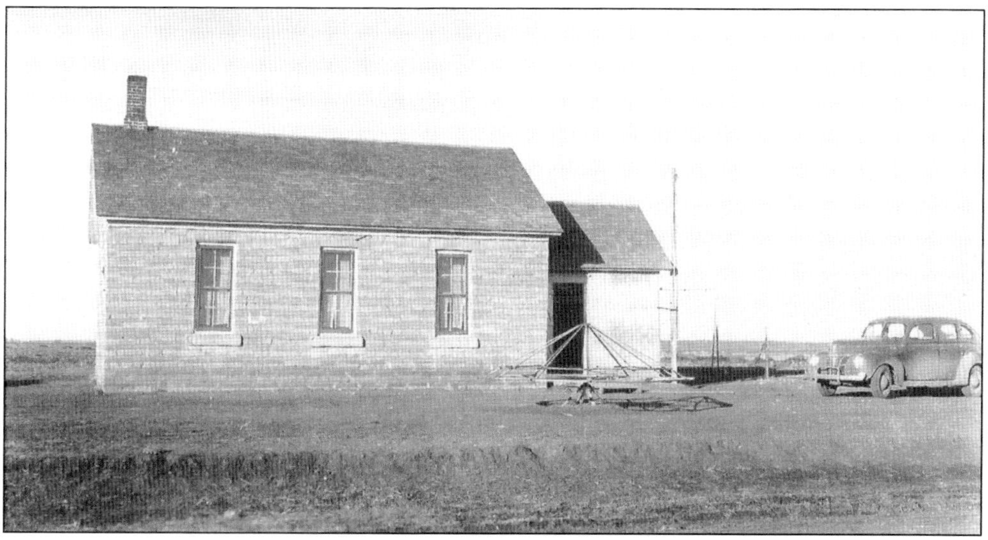

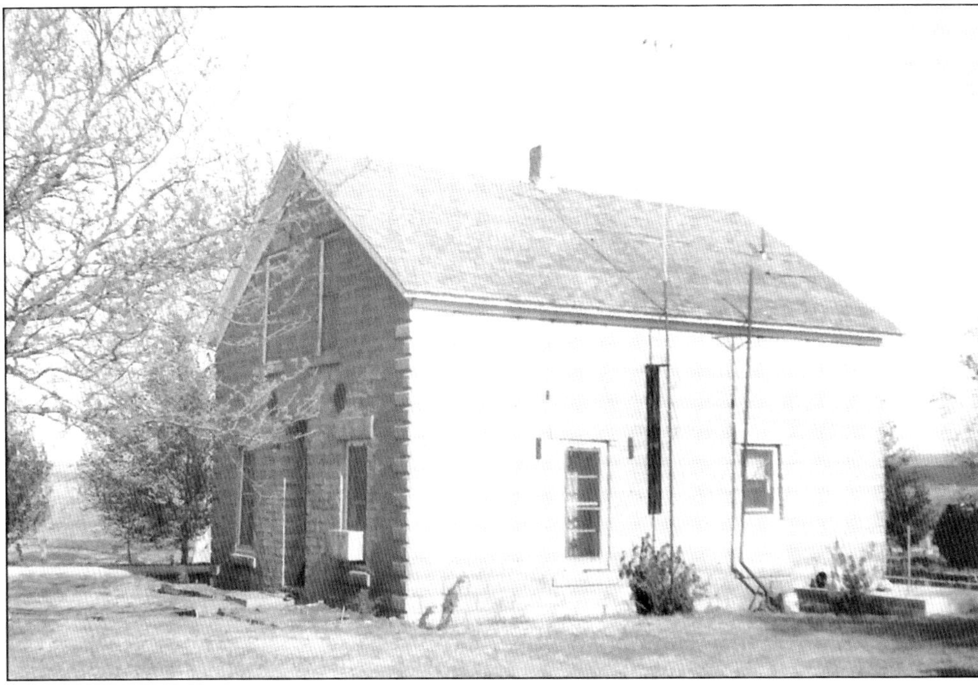

This is another stone residence located in rural Rush County. The exact location of the home is undetermined, but the original photograph, taken in May 1964, is labeled "Bert Nelson's home." The structure appears to retain most of its original character but with a few modern conveniences, including a window air conditioner and television antenna.

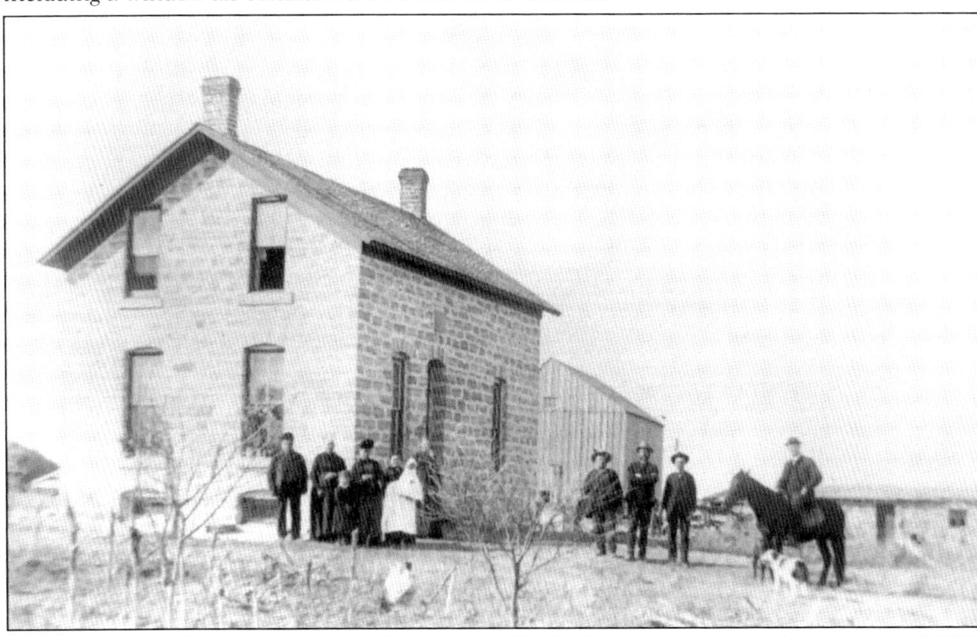

The J.W. Seuser homestead, located in eastern Rush County, is pictured here around 1875. The one-and-a-half-story stone home's rectangular form, full raised basement, and gabled roof (with chimneys at each end) echoes the Colonial style popular on the east coast. This type of construction was not used in imitation but rather for its simplicity.

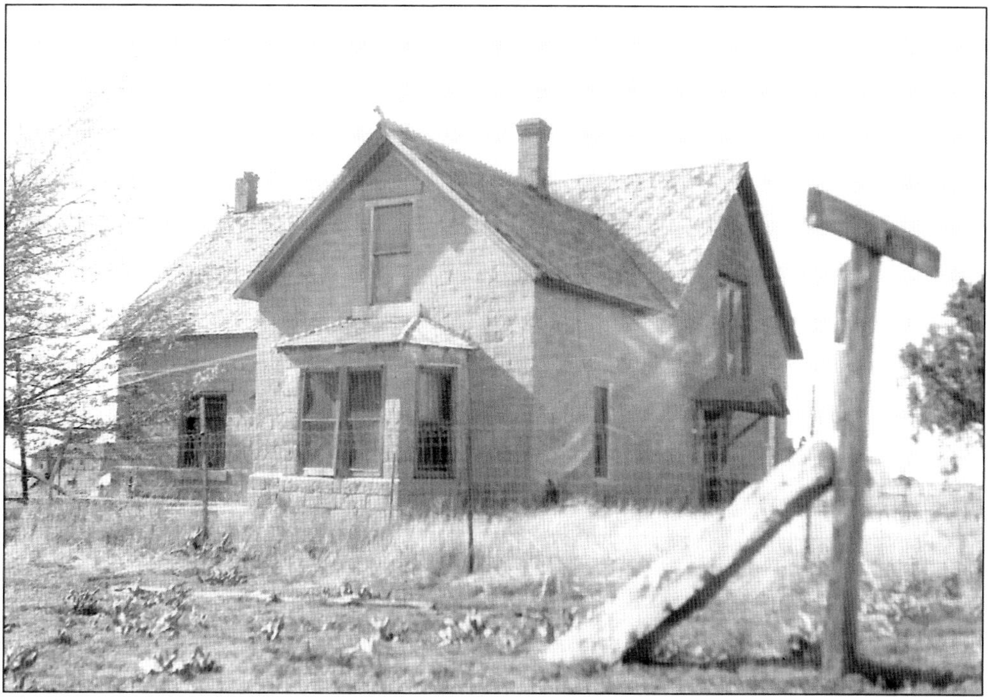

This large stone farmhouse is located near Timken. The protruding box window and large upper-level windows indicate that this was probably once a stylish residence. An extra-long stone post was used as a clothesline support in the same manner as supporting posts used at the corners of fences.

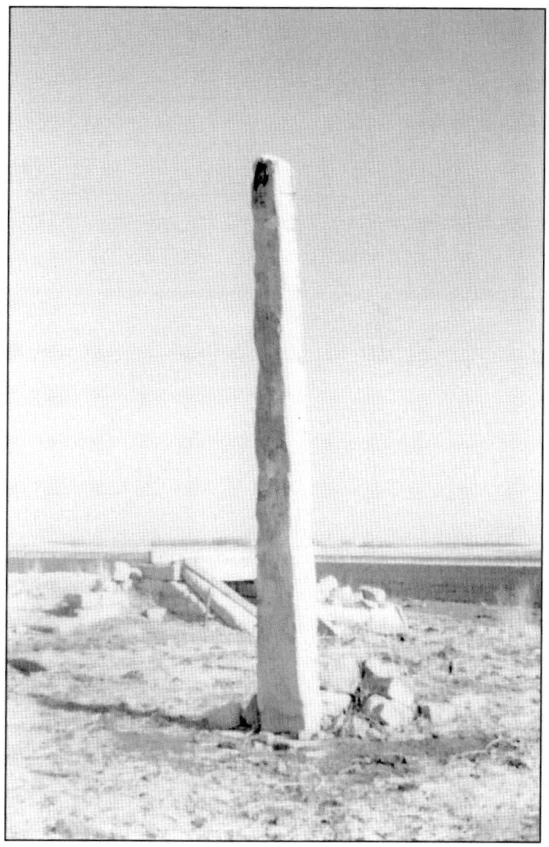

Quarried Post Rock was used to construct telephone poles (such as the one pictured at right), but the rock was also frequently used in the construction of root cellars, underground rooms with arched ceilings used to store vegetables at a constant temperature. Limestone cellars, like the one pictured in the background of this image, maintained a consistently cool and humid environment throughout the year, as well as providing families with protection from storms.

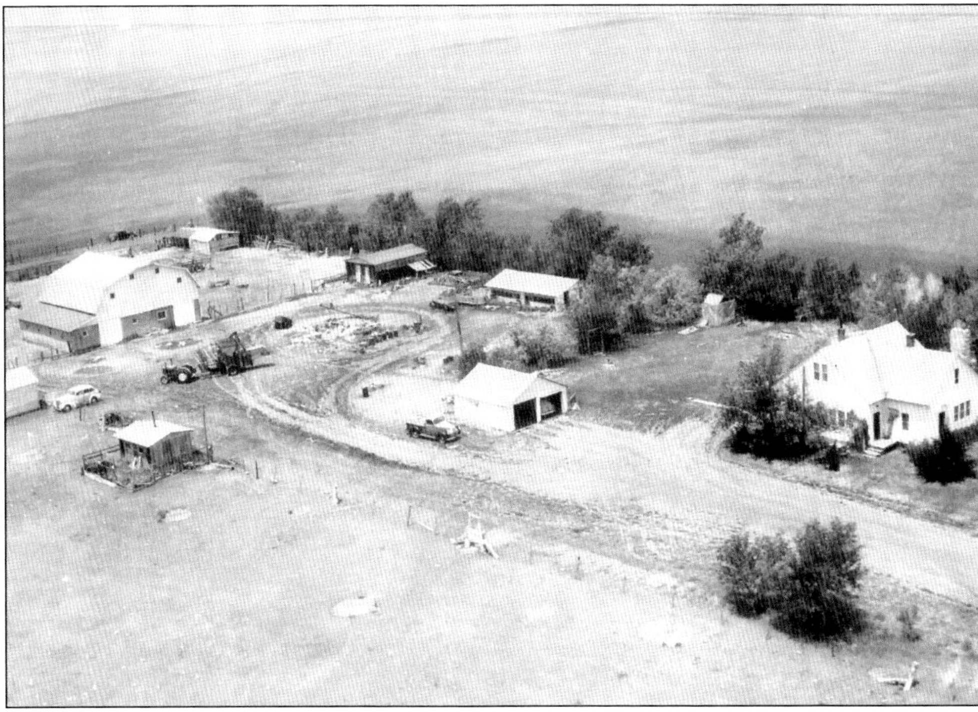

This c. 1940 photograph shows Lloyd and Alta Mellick's farm, which was located one mile north of La Crosse. The uncommon barn (at far left) is a combination limestone-and-wood structure with native limestone on the south bay, a hollow clay tile addition on the north end, and a wooden loft with a gambrel roof. Records show that the house was added to multiple times.

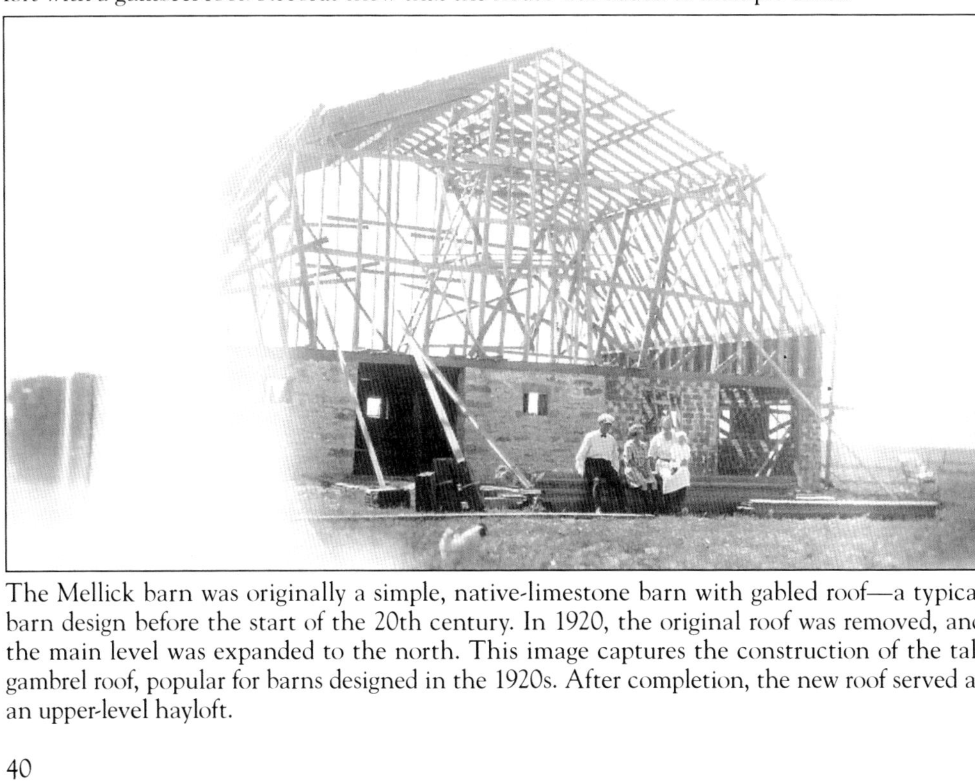

The Mellick barn was originally a simple, native-limestone barn with gabled roof—a typical barn design before the start of the 20th century. In 1920, the original roof was removed, and the main level was expanded to the north. This image captures the construction of the tall gambrel roof, popular for barns designed in the 1920s. After completion, the new roof served as an upper-level hayloft.

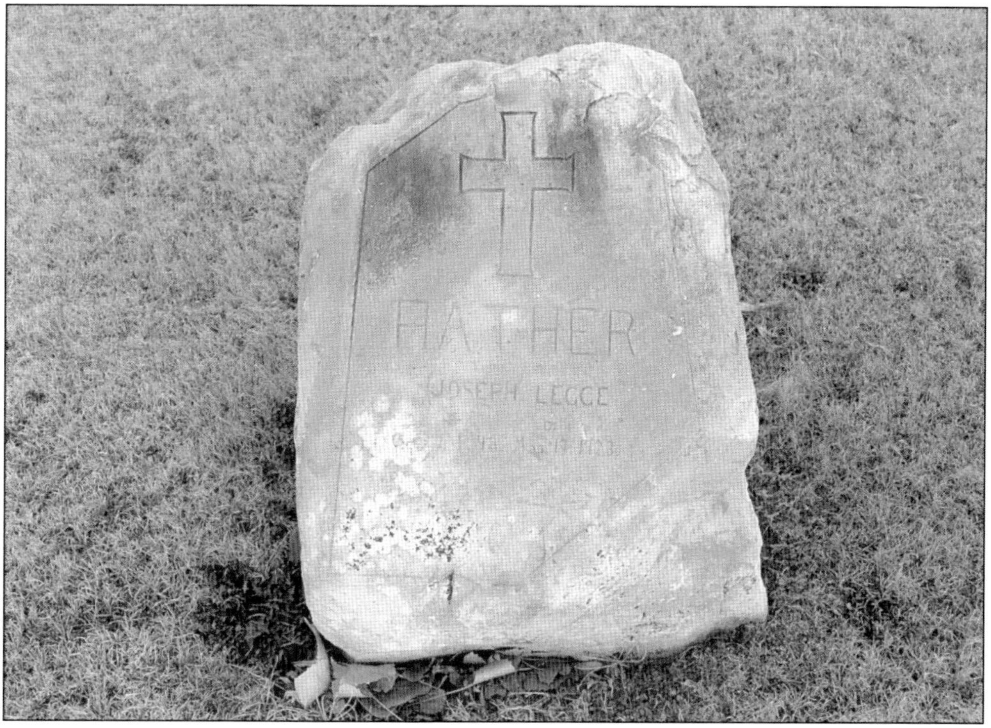

Death is a necessary part of life. To mark burial plots, pioneers made use of what was readily available—native stone. Some markers were simple and engraved by hand. This stone reads, "Father, Joseph Legge, B. Oct. 7, 1848, D. Mar. 19, 1923."

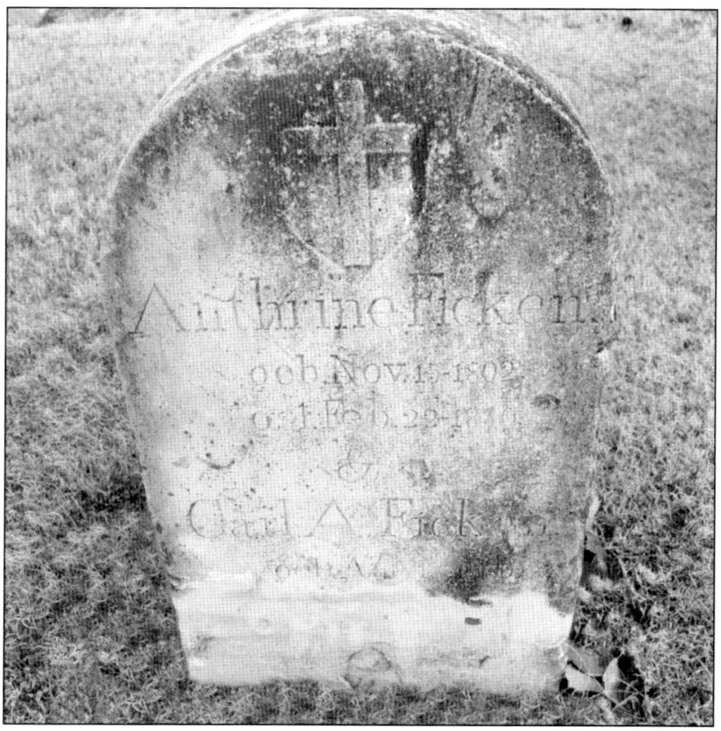

Handmade gravestones could be fairly elaborate. This stone, with engraving in German, is for two graves. The first name records, "Anthrine Ficken, geb ["born"] Nov. 15, 1802, gst ["died"] Feb. 22, 1889." Below it is a second name: "Carl A. Ficken, geb Aug. 18, 1880." The date of death is only partially legible but appears to mention November in the 1890s.

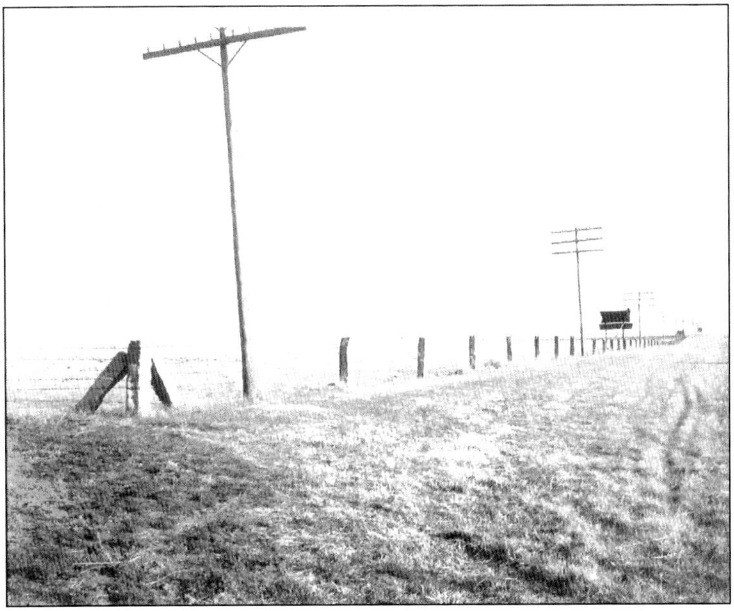

Highway construction in the 1950s required that fence rows be moved back. Many stone posts were replaced with barbed wire stretched across wood posts. This 1964 image captured two sights that were disappearing from the roadside landscape: Post Rock fences and above-ground telephone lines.

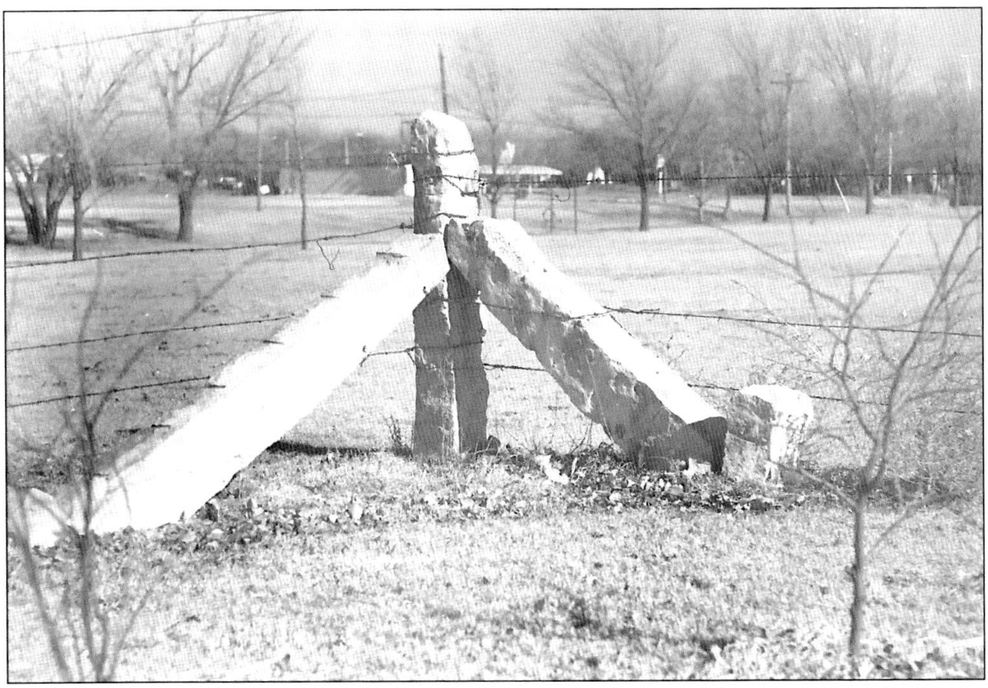

To add strength at the corner of a fence, builders leaned additional posts against the corner post at 45-degree angles to counter the tension from the wires. To add more strength, a short stub post was set at the lower end of the angled post. People later began to use corner posts as yard decorations.

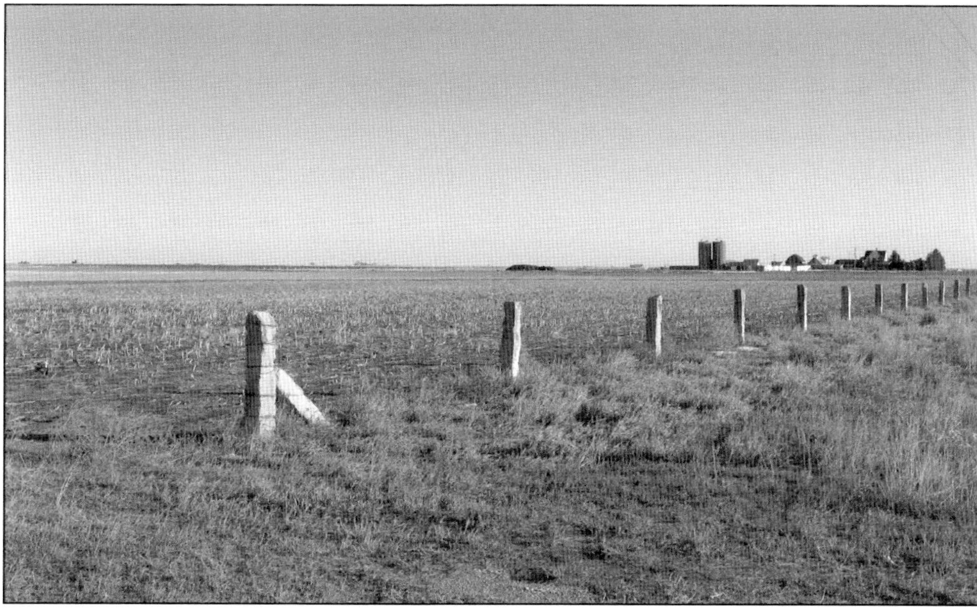

A typical Post Rock fence post is five to six feet in height and ranges in weight from 350 to 560 pounds. Each side of the post was eight to ten inches wide. The posts were set in holes from 18 to 24 inches deep, depending upon the length of the post, and spaced 15 to 30 feet apart.

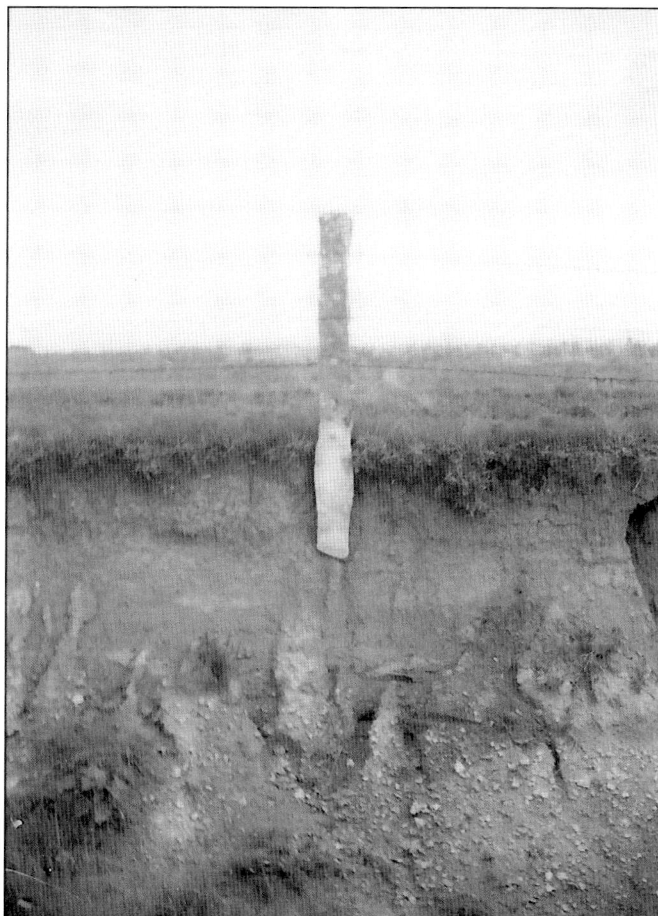

Only about two-thirds of a typical fencepost is visible at the surface. To prevent the post from shifting, it is usually buried about two feet into the ground, leaving about four feet above ground. Generally, if posts are uneven, the larger end is placed in the ground. This unusual image shows soil eroded away from one side of a fence, exposing the full post.

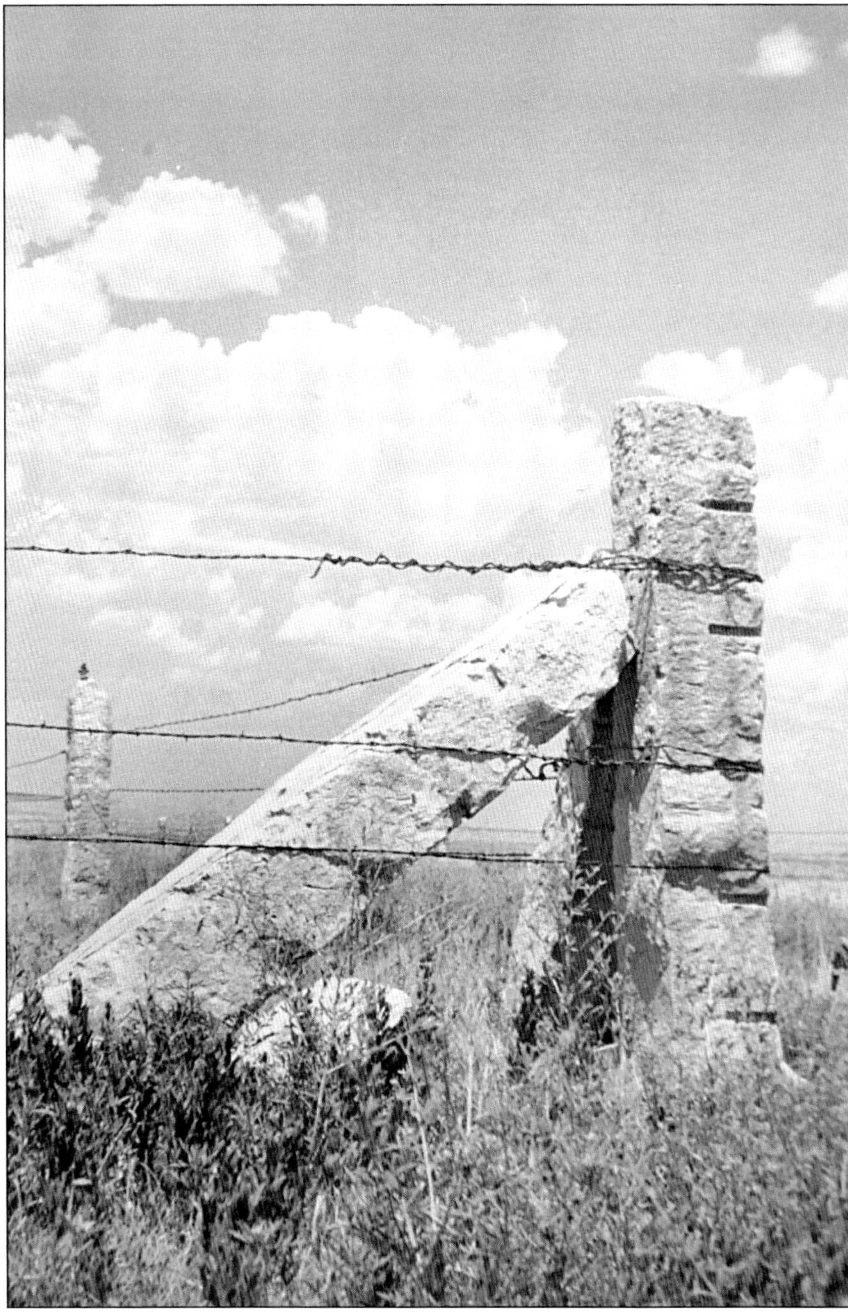

Experts estimate that at one time, over 40,000 miles of stone fence posts dotted the Post Rock Country area, with an average of 165 posts per mile. Most of these fences were constructed in the years between 1870 and 1920. These fences were extremely labor-intensive and took a long time to construct. Sometimes, only six posts could be quarried, loaded onto sleds, moved, and set in place in one day. If a settler was unable to quarry his own posts, they could be purchased at a cost of 6¢ each to 25¢ each. Today, only a few of these stone fences remain—some neglected, others maintained. By the late 20th century, the purpose of using Post Rock in fencing had changed from purely functional to primarily stylistic.

Four

Post Rock Comes to Town

In the late 19th century, Post Rock was the material of choice for local construction projects ranging from simple vernacular homes to ornate commercial buildings. It came into widespread use shortly after early settlers determined that their communities were starting to grow and prosper. At first, most buildings were simple wood-frame structures standing on loose limestone blocks that were placed on the ground. As confidence in the permanence of the communities increased, wood buildings were placed on limestone basements or foundations with permanent mortared joints. Because these wooden buildings were situated side by side (sometimes sharing a common wall), many towns suffered large, tragic losses when a fire started in one of the structures and quickly spread along the block. To increase fire resistance, builders began to use masonry. Because native stone was more abundant and less costly, it became a suitable substitute for brick. For those who chose brick as a primary construction material, native stone provided attractive and contrasting accents.

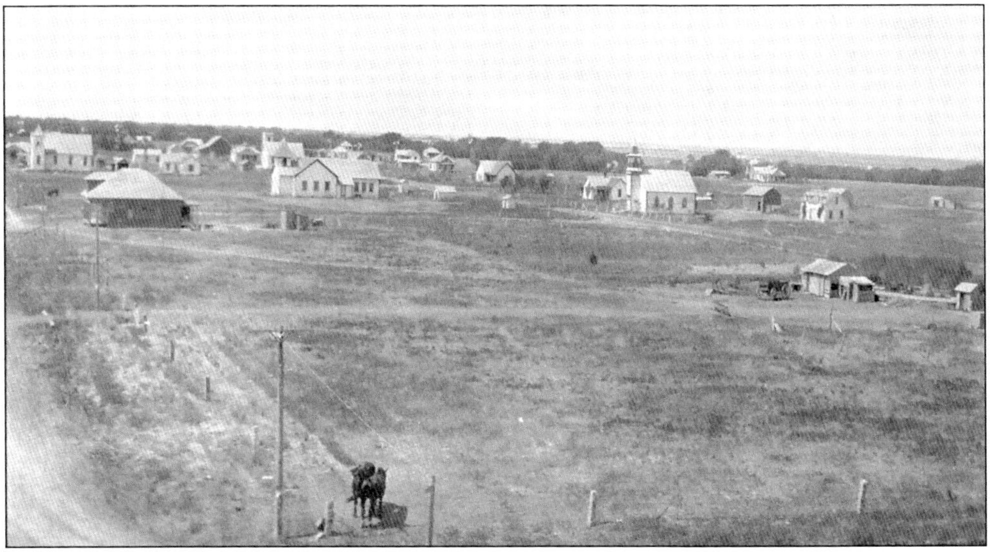

The community of Alexander, located west of Rush County on Walnut Creek, was the first settlement in Rush County. Religion played an important part in the lives of the pioneers, as is apparent in this c. 1909 photograph of Alexander, which shows four churches: German Congregational, German Methodist, Latter-day Saints, and United Brethren.

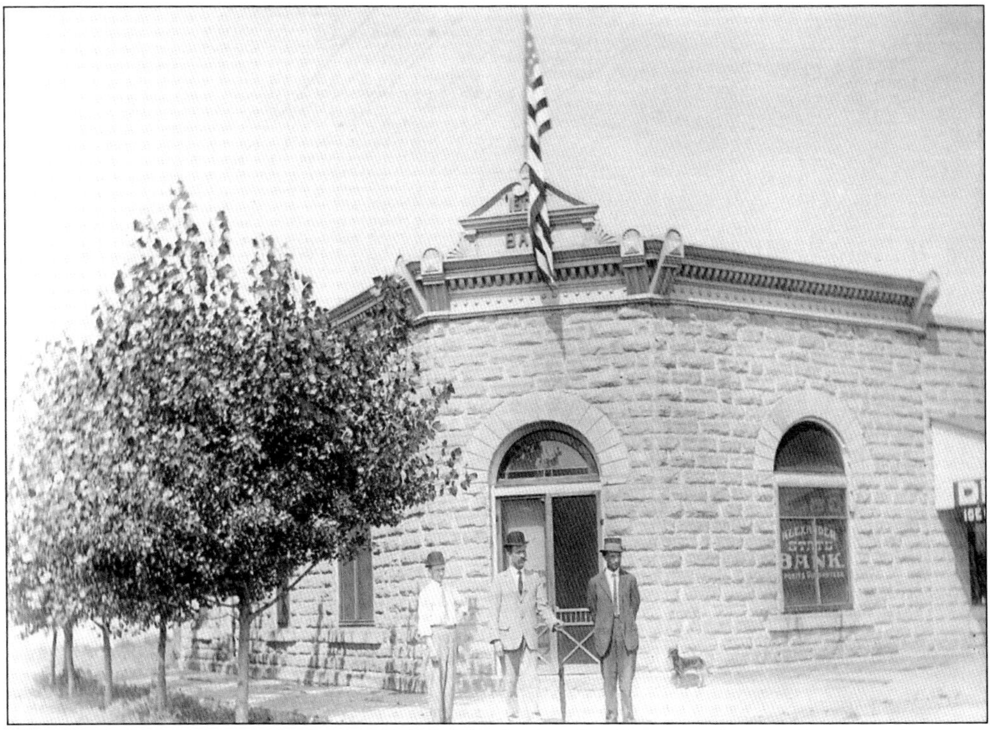

The Alexander State Bank constructed a 25-by-50-foot building in 1909. Its design is almost an exact replica of the Bank of McCracken, located eight miles to the north. The building featured large arched windows, an elaborate metal cornice, and a traditional corner entrance. Pictured in front of the bank in 1913 are R.J. Kueffer (left), S.R. "Doc" Jaynes (center), and bank cashier A.H. Young.

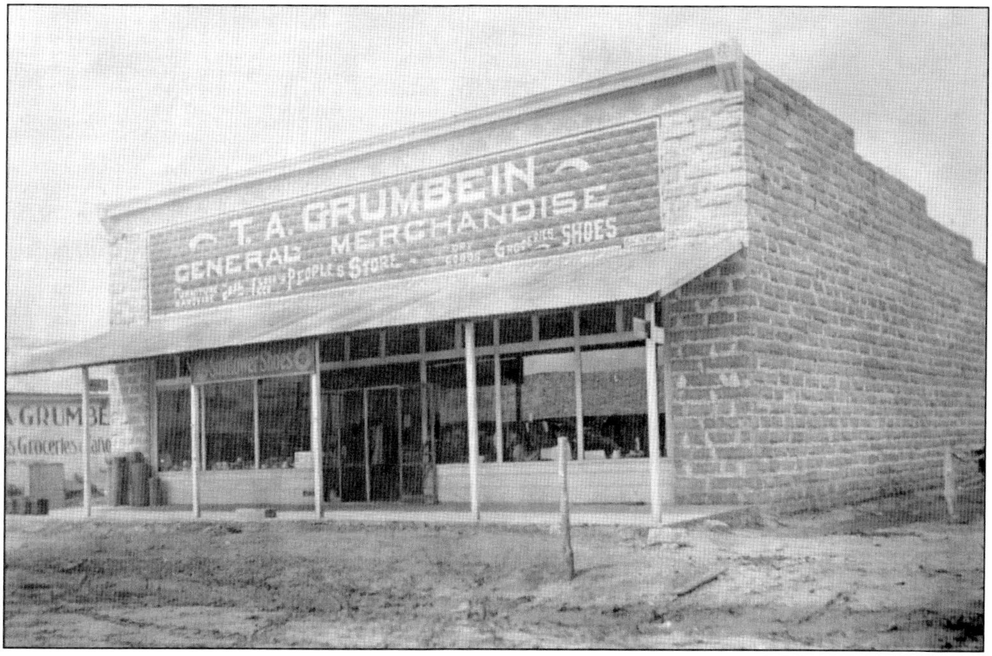

T.A. Grumbein and his wife, Priscilla, moved to Alexander in 1901. They purchased a general store owned by G.E. Brown, and when business flourished, they constructed a larger building out of Post Rock limestone. The Grumbeins spent the rest of their lives in the community, and many of their descendants remained in the area as well.

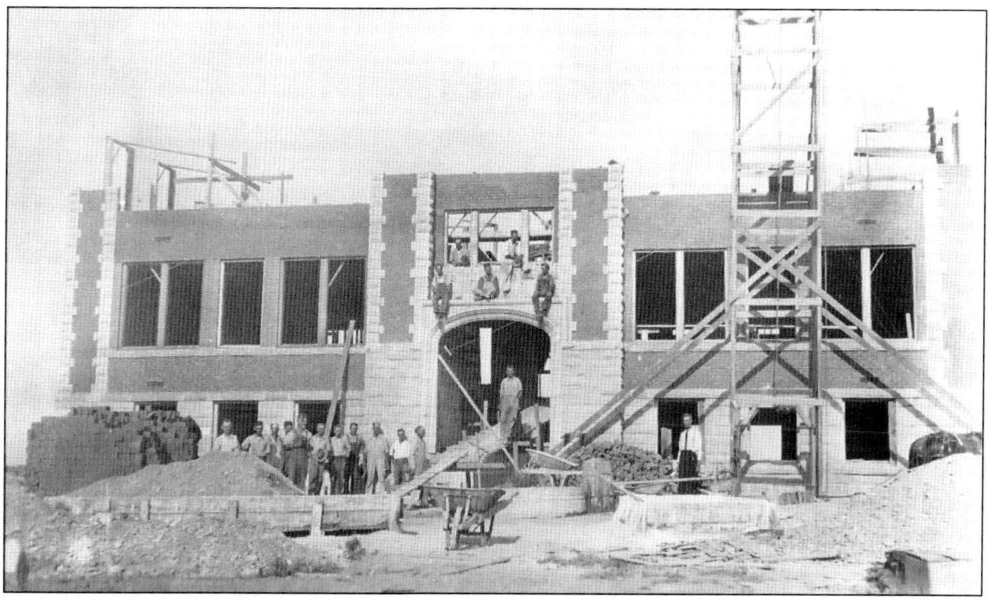

The Alexander School is pictured here on September 14, 1916, during construction. The three-story, raised-basement structure consisted of traditional redbrick trimmed in native limestone. The lower level was reserved for grades one through eight, and high school classes were held on the upper floor.

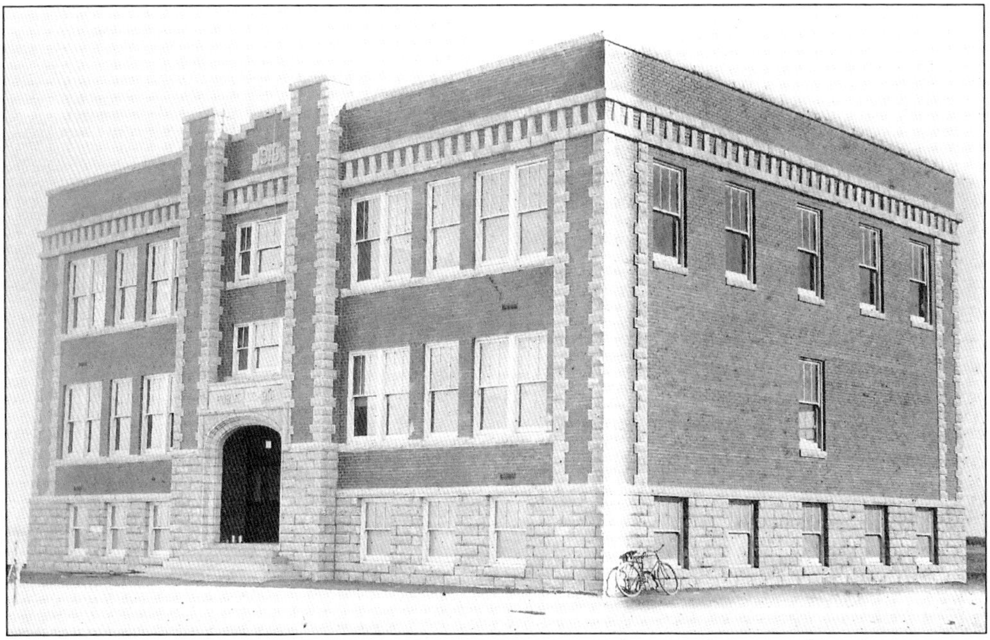

The first Alexander School high school class, consisting of six students, graduated in 1919. In 1930, the district added a gymnasium/auditorium with a full basement. The last high school class graduated from Alexander in 1966, but the building remained in use as a grade school until 1983.

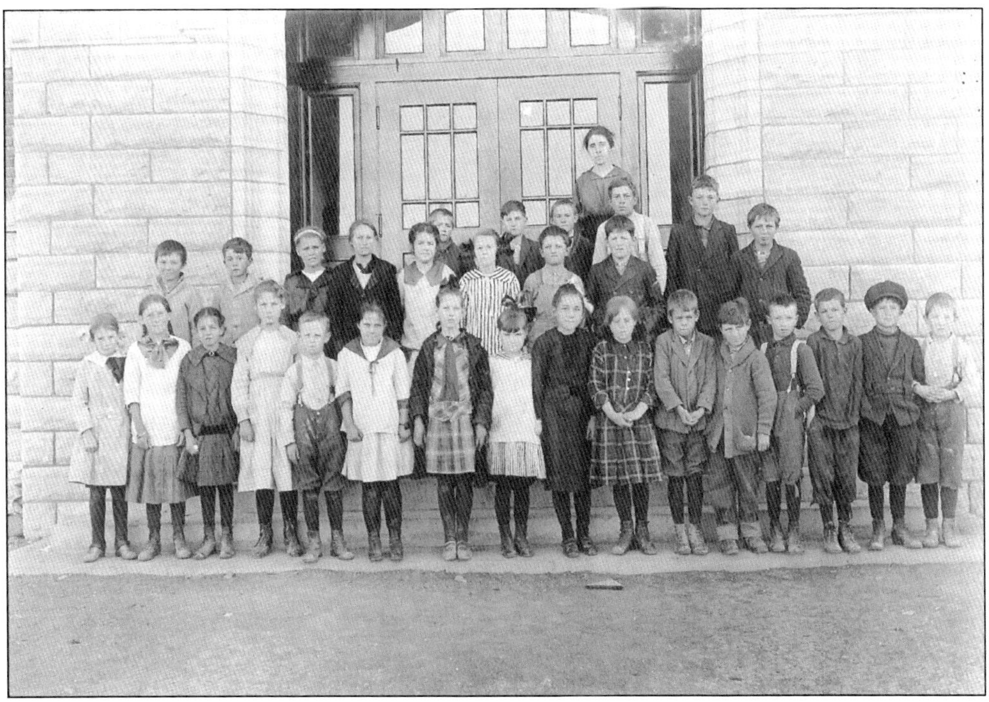

The grade school classes of 1917 stand on the front steps of the Alexander School. This was the first group of students to attend classes in the new building. The teacher standing in the back row is Gertrude Kittle. During its 50 years of operation, 397 students graduated from the high school.

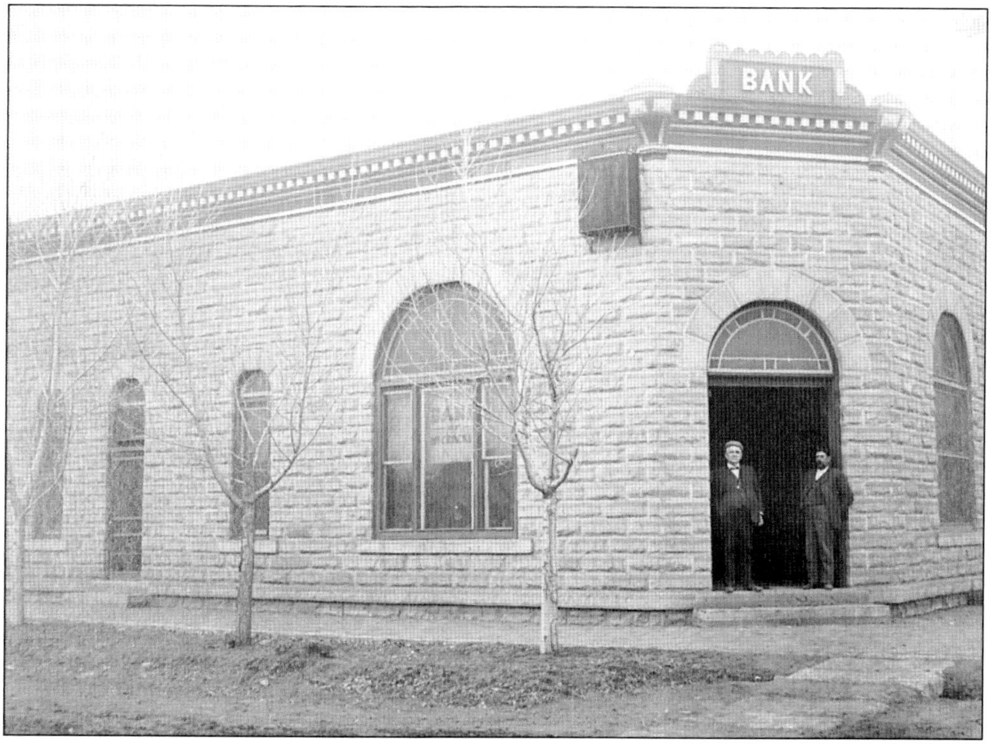

The original Bank of McCracken opened in March 1887 in a small wood-frame building on Main Street in McCracken. In 1901, the bank constructed a more substantial limestone building across the street to the north. Standing in the doorway are Jake Yawger (left), owner of Yawger Ranch (just outside of McCracken), and bank cashier E.S. Chenoweth.

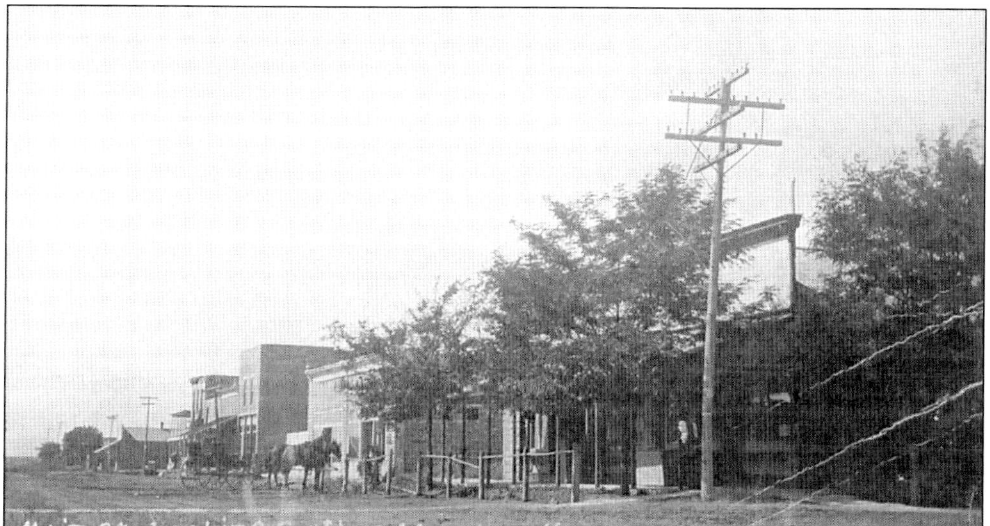

Downtown McCracken was destroyed by fire on two different occasions. In 1905, an entire block on the east side of the street burned. In 1909, fire ravaged the west side of Main Street. This image shows the east side of Main Street after the 1905 blaze. Most of the new buildings had been constructed of stone or other fireproof materials.

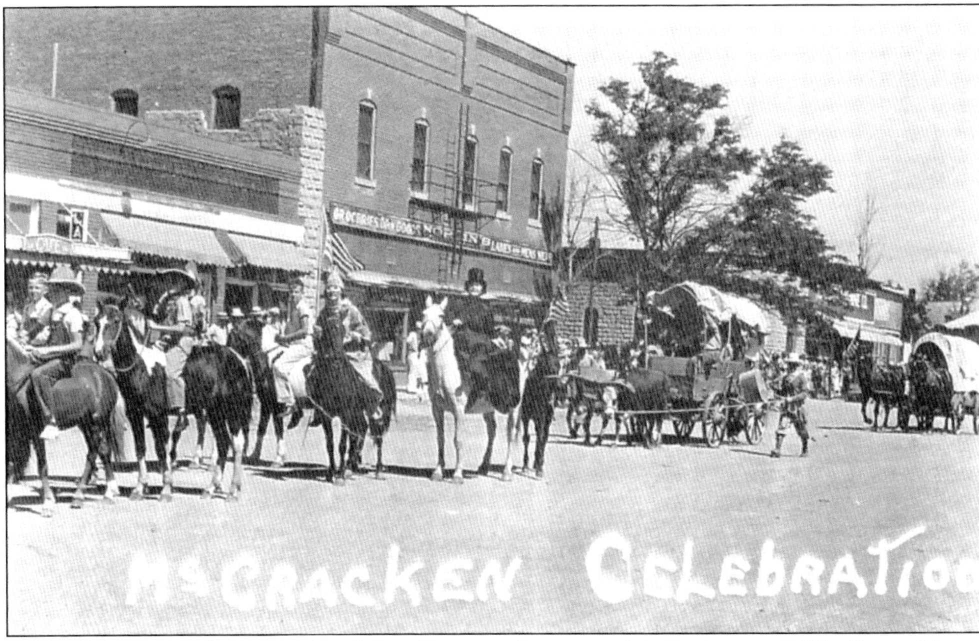

When fire ravaged the west side of Main Street in downtown McCracken in 1909, all wood-frame buildings were destroyed except for C.E. Neal's store, which was located behind a limestone wall. When the Neal store was replaced with a brick building, the firewall was used as part of the new building housing Norlin's store. This is a picture of a 1937 parade celebrating McCracken's 50th anniversary. Note that most of the buildings are constructed of stone and brick.

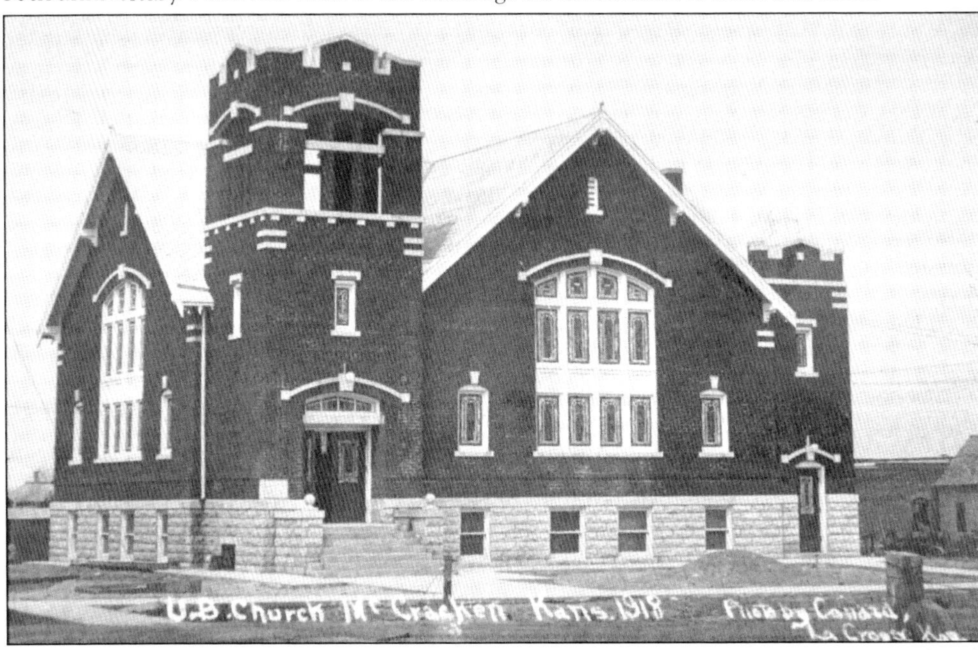

This is the limestone-and-brick Evangelical United Brethren Church in McCracken. The church was completed and dedicated in May 1918 and replaced the frame church constructed in 1893. This church was razed when the congregation combined with the Methodists and constructed a new building on the former site of the McCracken Methodist Church in 1971.

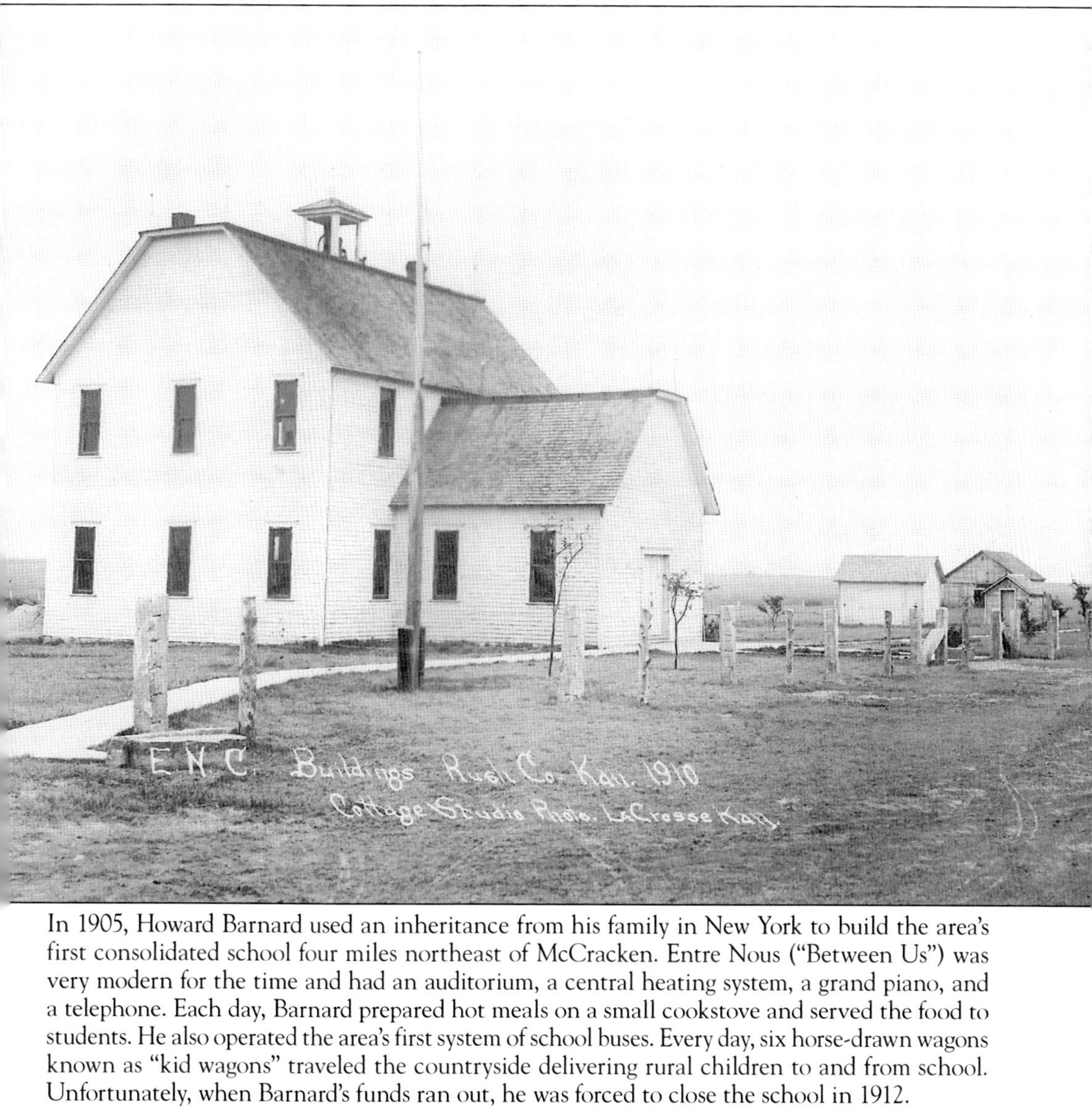

In 1905, Howard Barnard used an inheritance from his family in New York to build the area's first consolidated school four miles northeast of McCracken. Entre Nous ("Between Us") was very modern for the time and had an auditorium, a central heating system, a grand piano, and a telephone. Each day, Barnard prepared hot meals on a small cookstove and served the food to students. He also operated the area's first system of school buses. Every day, six horse-drawn wagons known as "kid wagons" traveled the countryside delivering rural children to and from school. Unfortunately, when Barnard's funds ran out, he was forced to close the school in 1912.

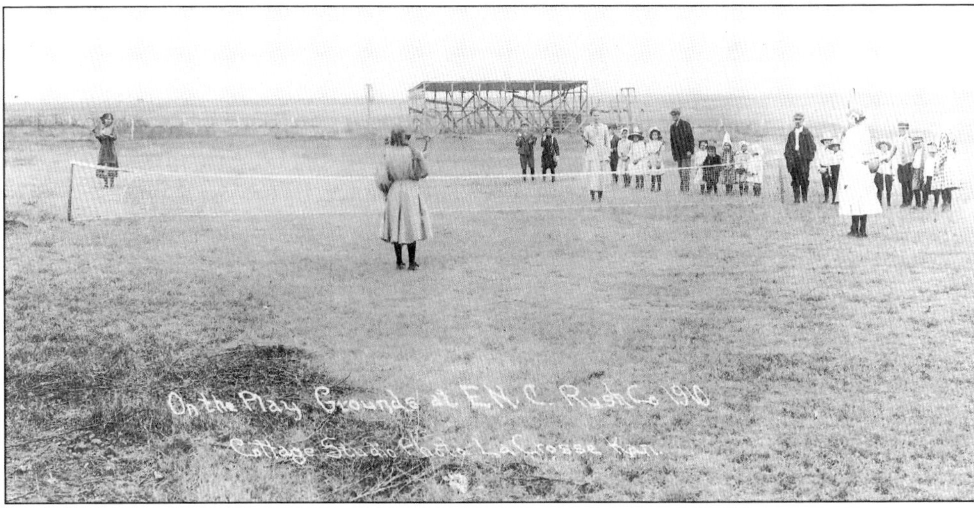

In addition to offering a well-rounded curriculum, Howard Barnard's Entre Nous school provided for the physical well-being of students; it had a sports field with gas lights and bleachers that could accommodate up to 300 spectators. He purchased uniforms and equipment for the school's girls' basketball team (known as the Bloomer Girls).

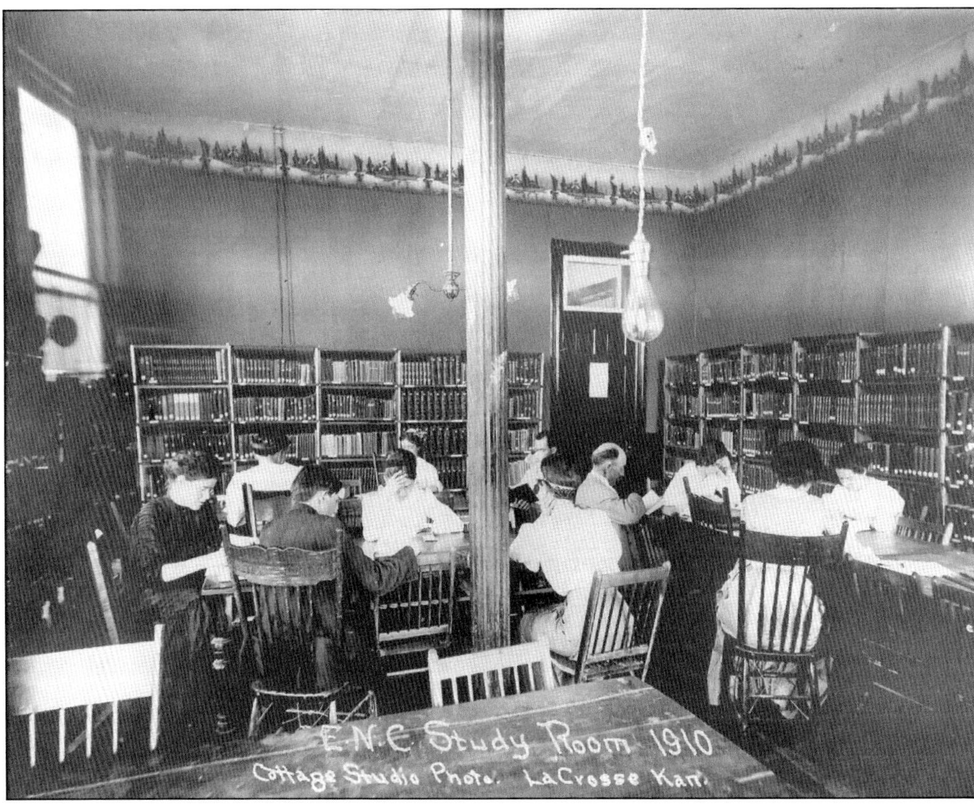

Howard Barnard had a strong respect for books. When he first started teaching in Rush County, it was common for him to go without meals in order to have money for books. When his school closed, he transferred his collection of books to the La Crosse High School and later to the library that bears his name.

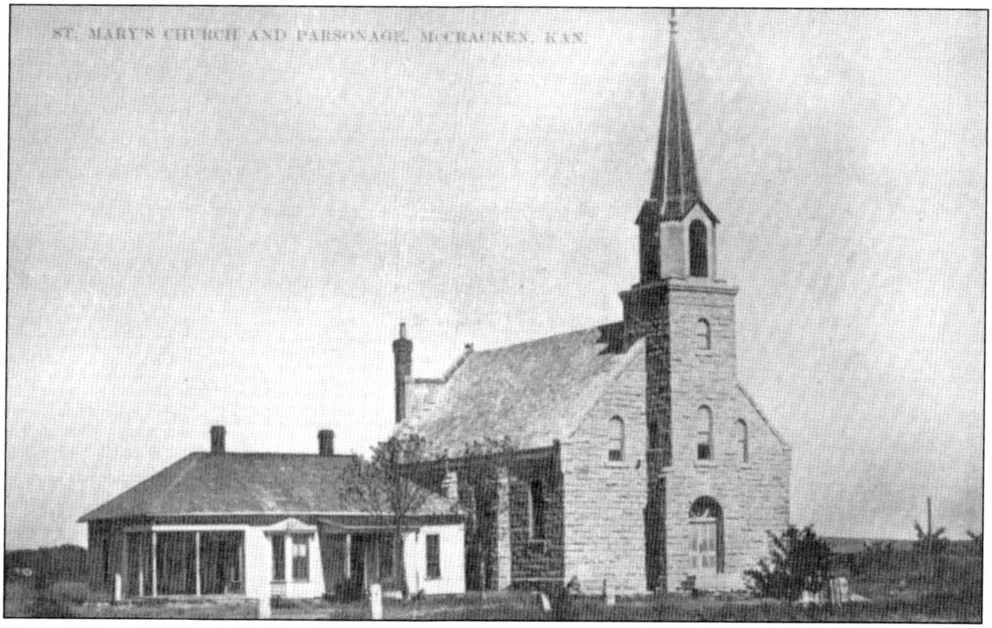

From 1884 to 1886, parishioners of St. Mary's Church held Catholic Masses in a native-stone house west of St. Mary's Cemetery and southwest of McCracken in Ness County. The congregation's first permanent church was a frame building located next to the cemetery. On May 24, 1906, the frame building was replaced with this native-stone church.

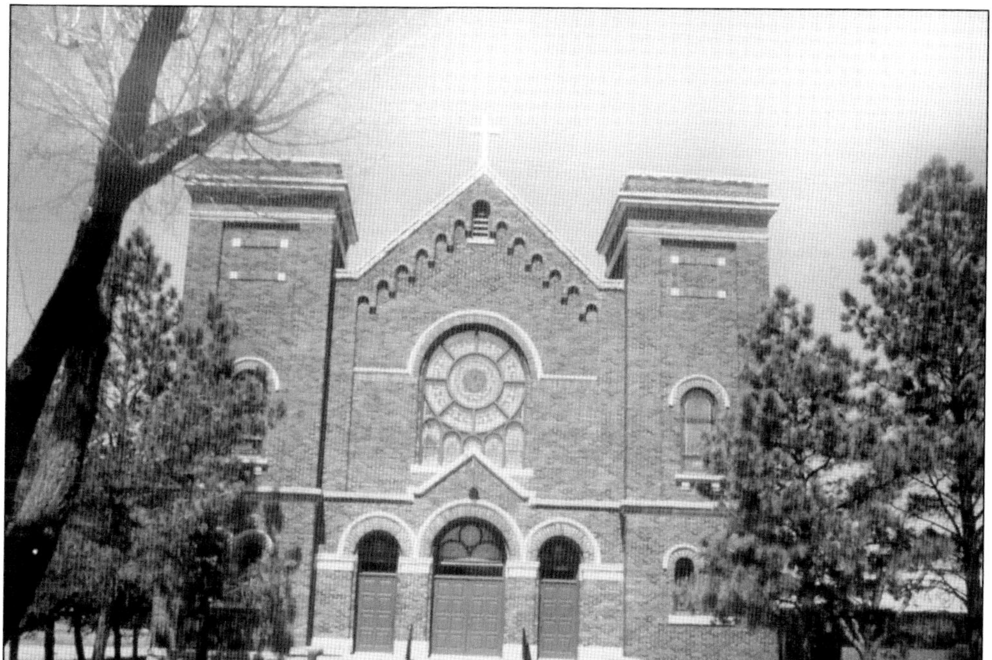

On July 7, 1922, the rural St. Mary's Church was dismantled, and the stone was reused for the basement and foundation of a new church located in the northwest part of McCracken. During construction, the congregation celebrated Mass in the basement of the unfinished church. The new church was completed and dedicated in May 1926.

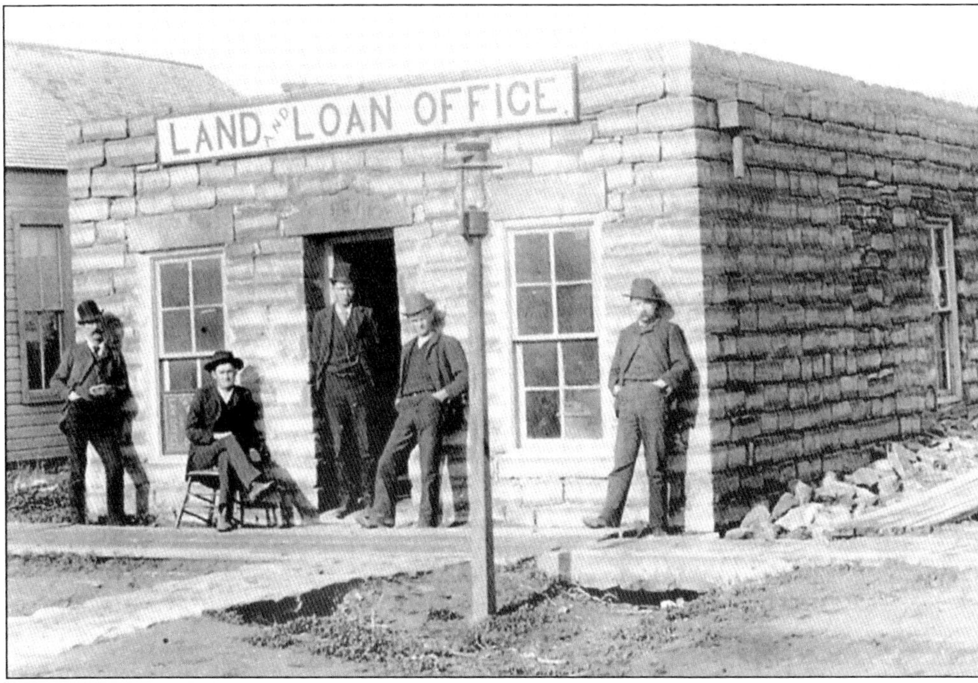

One of the earliest buildings in La Crosse was a two-room stone structure known as the "Hole in the Wall" because it had a small front window with a removable sash that allowed voters to hand in their ballots during local elections. It was also used as a law office and a secret meeting place during the 1886–1888 battle between La Crosse and Rush Center over which town would be the seat of Rush County. F.H. Davis tore down the building in 1889.

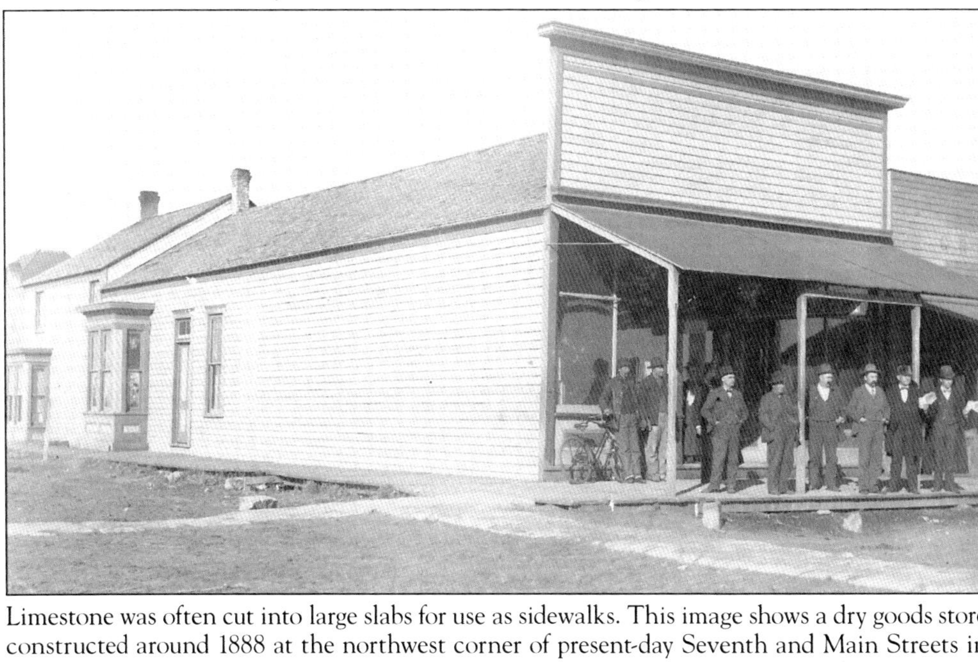

Limestone was often cut into large slabs for use as sidewalks. This image shows a dry goods store constructed around 1888 at the northwest corner of present-day Seventh and Main Streets in La Crosse. Note the limestone sidewalks extending across both streets from the front corner of the building.

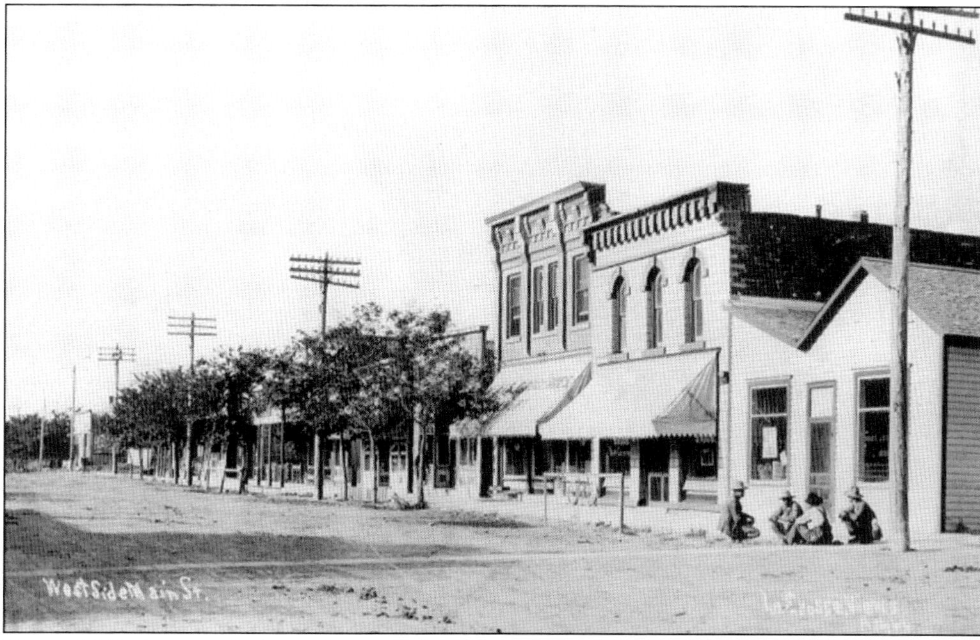

This c. 1900 photograph shows the west side of Main Street between Seventh and Eighth Streets in La Crosse. The two-story edifice at far right is an ornate limestone building with arched windows and a decorative cornice. It was constructed sometime before 1886 by A.C. Snow. From 1886 until 1888, the upper floor intermittently housed the county offices while Rush County was in the midst of a bitter county-seat war between La Crosse and Rush Center.

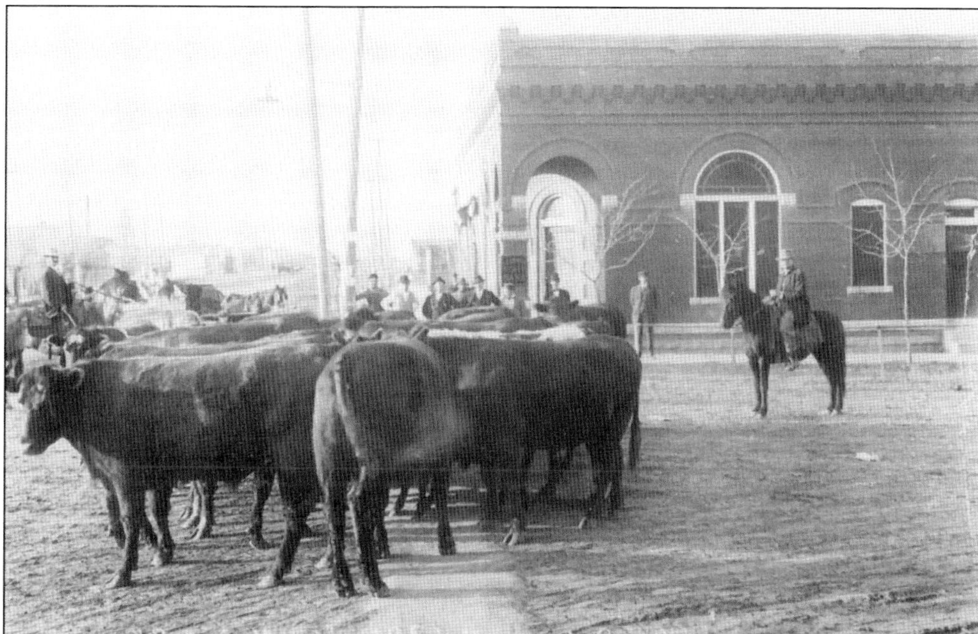

In this c. 1910 photograph, cattle belonging to J.C. Schiedeman are being driven through downtown La Crosse on the way to market. During this era, it was common to see horses, cattle, and other livestock in the middle of town in small farming communities in Post Rock Country.

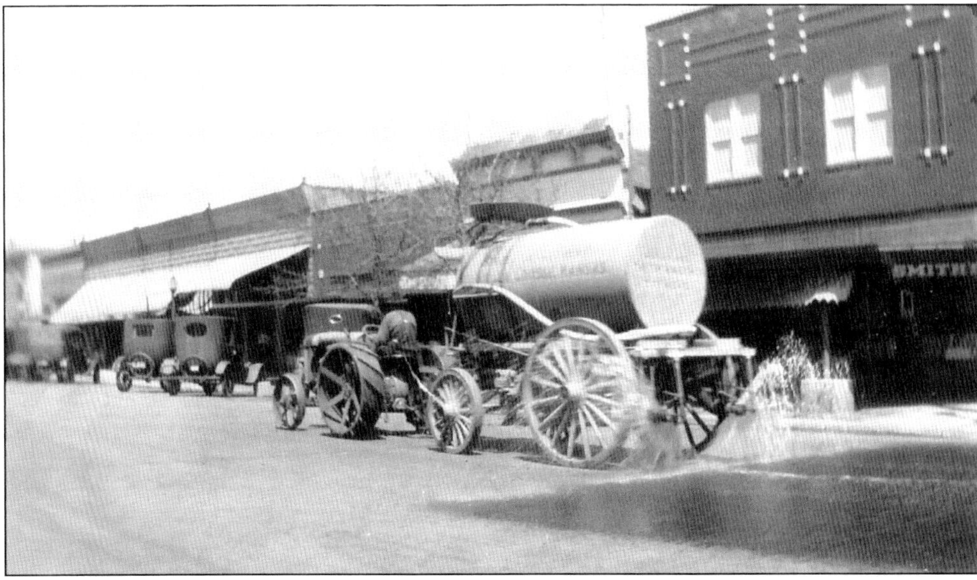

With automobiles becoming the primary means of transportation, it was common in the 1930s to see the newly paved brick street in downtown La Crosse being watered to control dust. In the background, buildings along the east side of Main Street between Seventh and Eighth Streets exemplify three types of construction material: wood, stone, and brick.

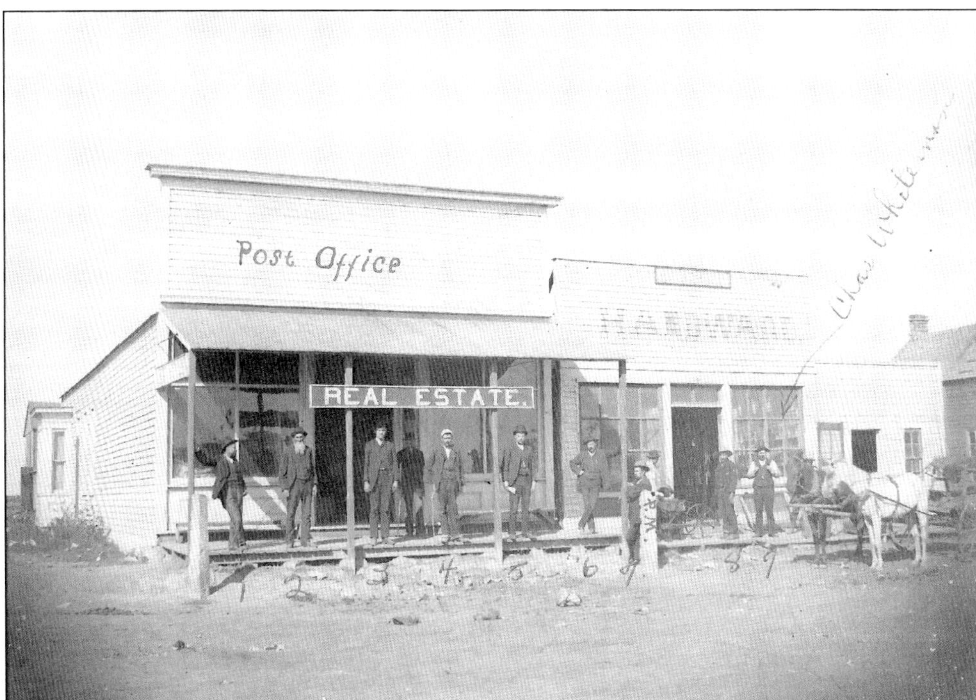

Post Rock served a variety of uses in the late 1800s. Here, stones are being used as hitching posts in front of a row of buildings on the west side of Main Street between Seventh and Eighth Streets. The building with the "Real Estate" sign later served as the La Crosse post office and, for many years, as a bakery.

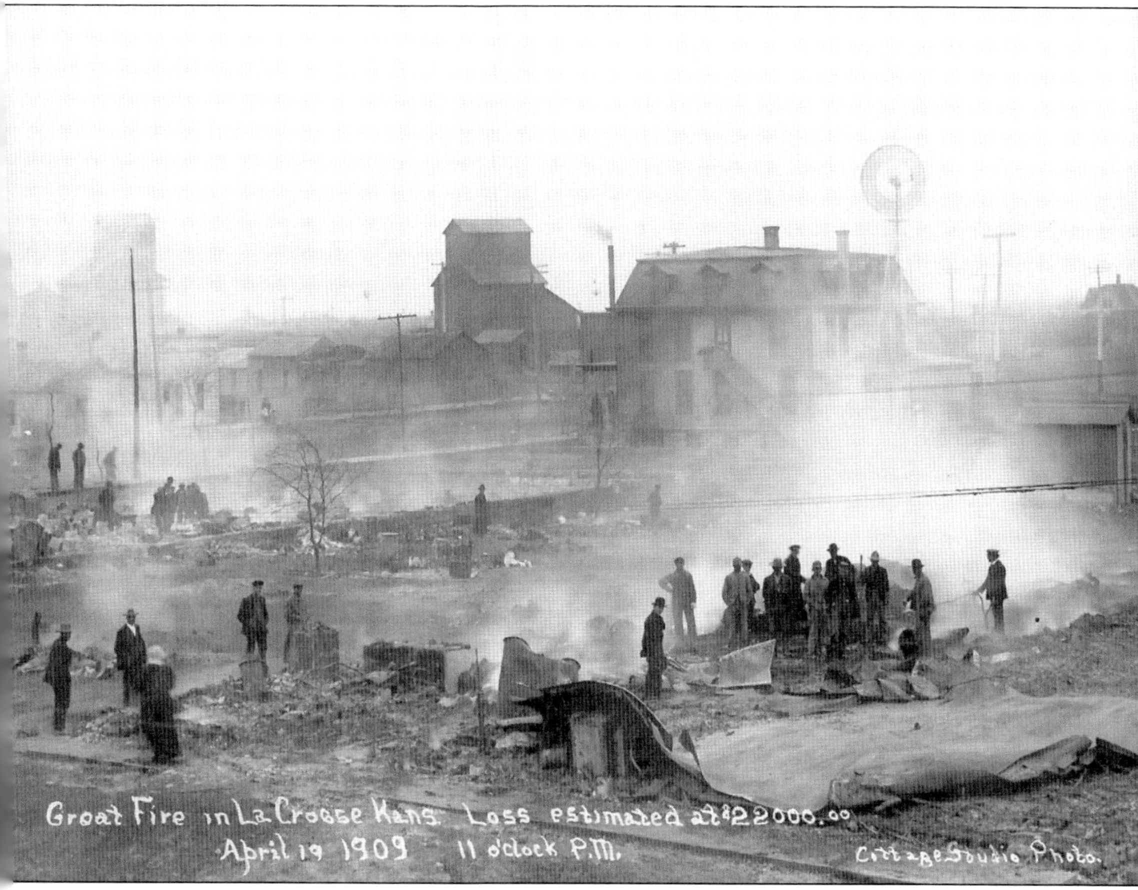

On April 10, 1909, a fire that started in a nearby livery stable destroyed the majority of a city block in downtown La Crosse. Businesses lost included the Maine Livery Stable, the opera house, Fred Cook's general store, Lippert Grocery, Lou Robinson's restaurant, and the Greenleaf & Sowers meat market. The brick-and-limestone La Crosse State Bank building, which stood immediately to the left of the burned foundations, and the Windsor Hotel were the only structures spared. Because historical records confirm the existence of the bank building at the time, it may be assumed that the photographer deliberately omitted the building from this photograph in order to highlight the extent of the fire damage.

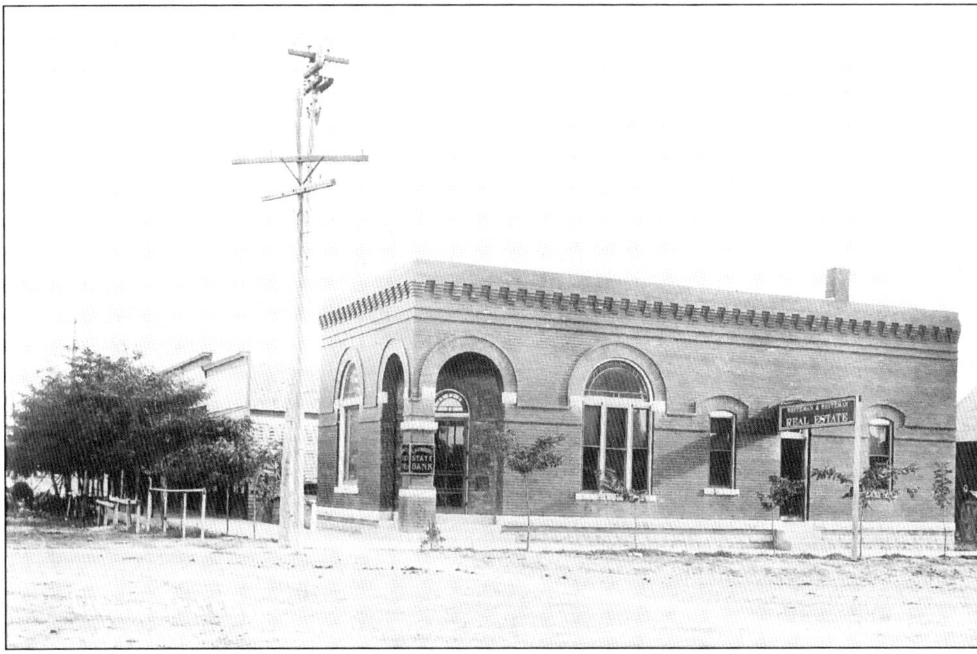

Although smaller and more unassuming than the First National Bank, the La Crosse State Bank also utilized native stone to accent its building. Three other banks in Rush County followed an identical design: the Bison State Bank in Bison, State Bank of Liebenthal, and Citizens State Bank of McCracken. The above photograph is of the bank building shortly after its construction in 1905. The tree-lined row of stores in the background of the above photograph was completely destroyed in a fire on April 10, 1909. Following the fire, the frame structures were replaced by more fire-resistant brick structures, as shown below.

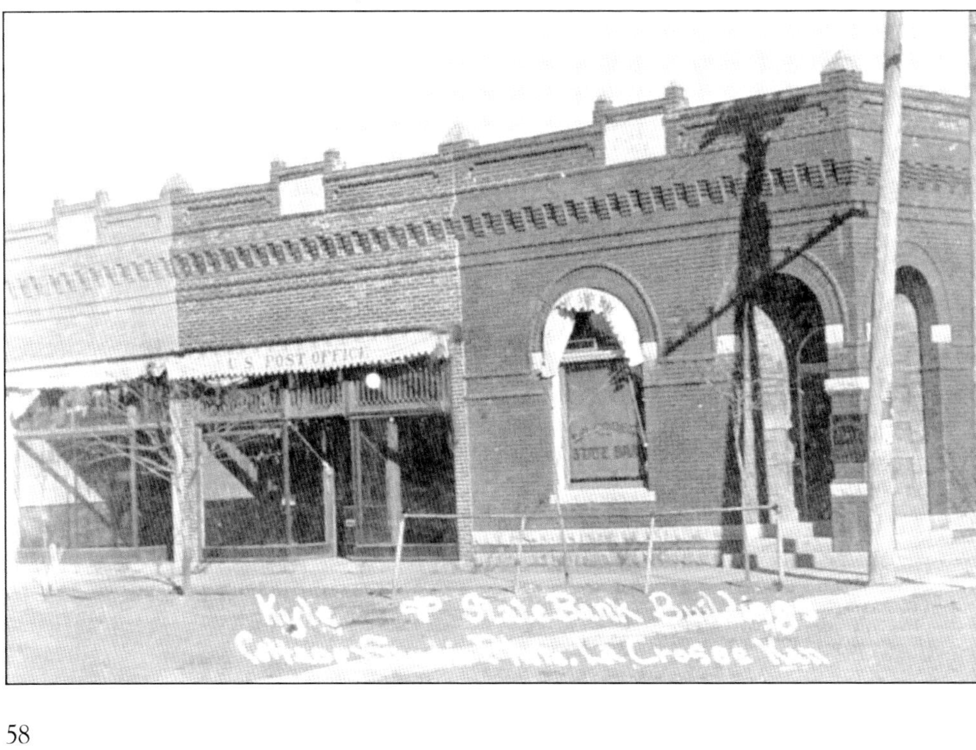

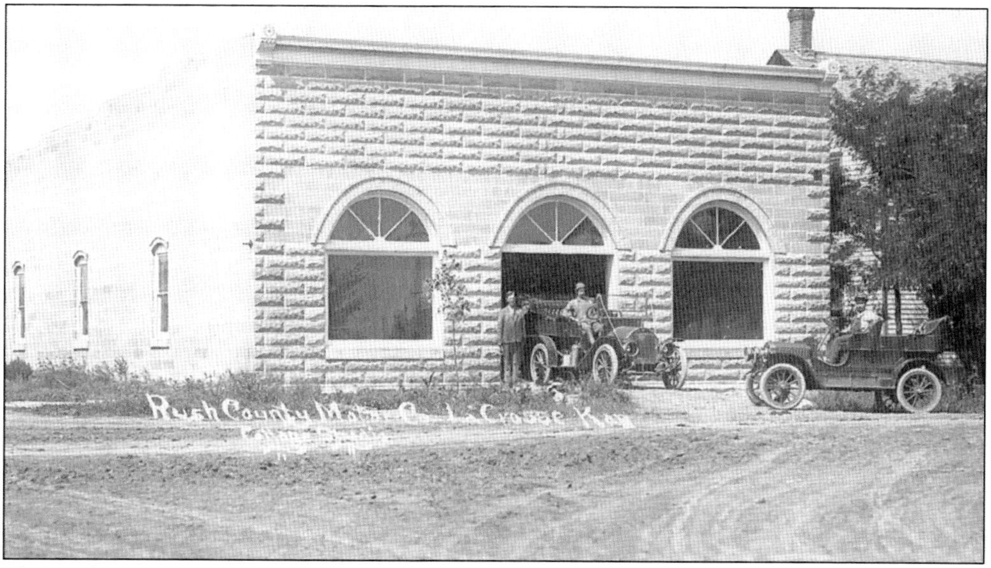

The Rush County Motor Company building stood on the northwest corner of Sixth and Main Streets adjacent to the National Hotel. The rear section of the building was constructed of native limestone, and the remainder was cement shaped to replicate stone. The facade was later replaced with traditional brick. In the late 1950s, this building housed the L&W Motor and Implement Company.

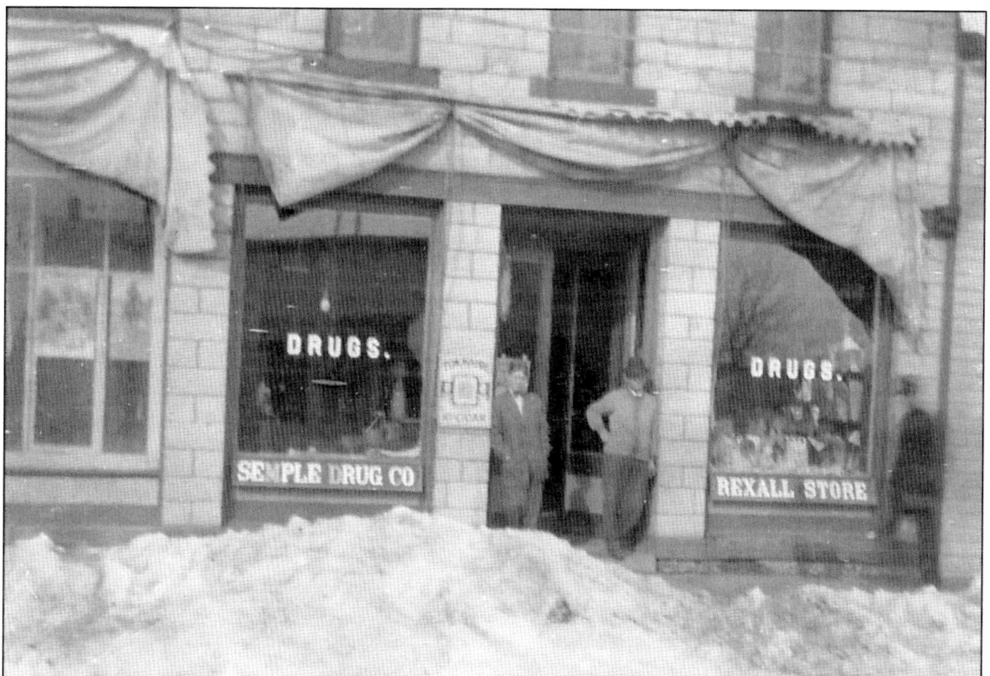

The Semple Drug Co. store is pictured here around 1900. The store carried a diverse line of goods in addition to pharmaceuticals. In 1897, they advertised schoolbooks, holiday goods, albums, various attire, and toilet cases. The following year, they advertised musical instruments as well as miracle cures such as a kidney treatment, blood purifiers, and blood makers.

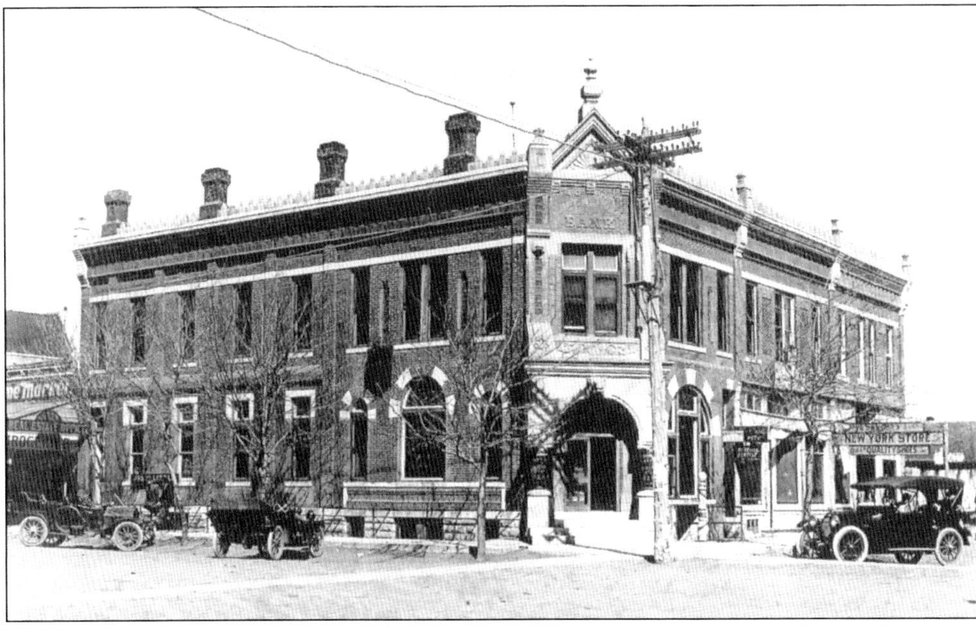

The First National Bank received its charter in 1889. The two-story building, with raised basement, had a brick exterior with a native-stone foundation and native-stone accents over the arched windows and doors. During 10 years of operation, the bank absorbed the two other banks in La Crosse. After falling into insolvency, it was reorganized in February 1898 as the Farmers & Merchants State Bank.

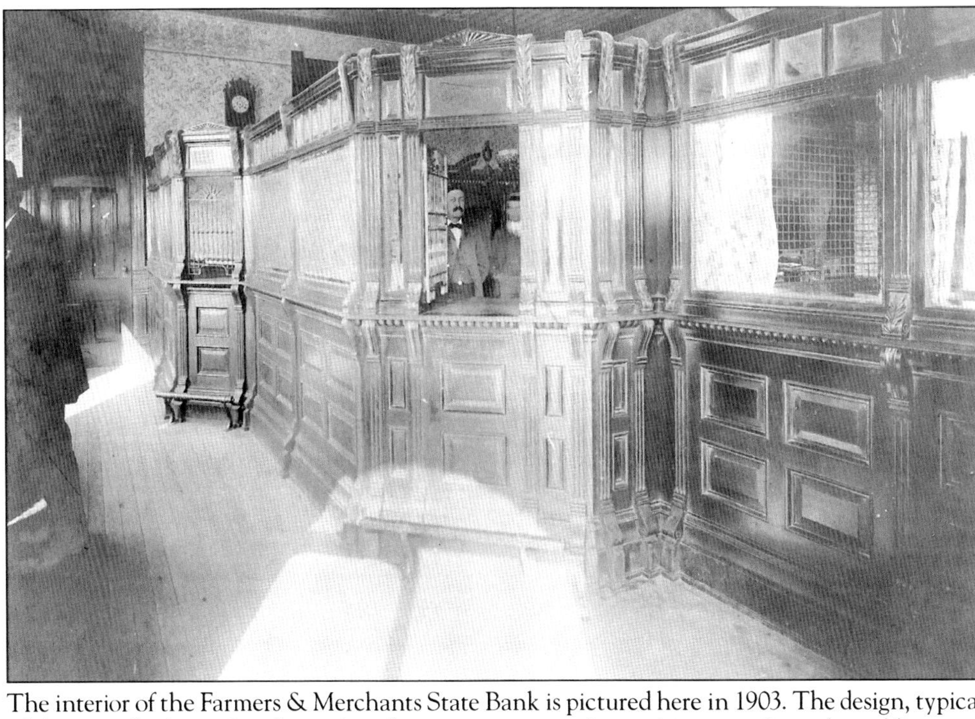

The interior of the Farmers & Merchants State Bank is pictured here in 1903. The design, typical of the time, had wood and metal enclosures separating the working area from the public areas. Bank president H.W. Grass (left) and an unidentified man are standing in the window.

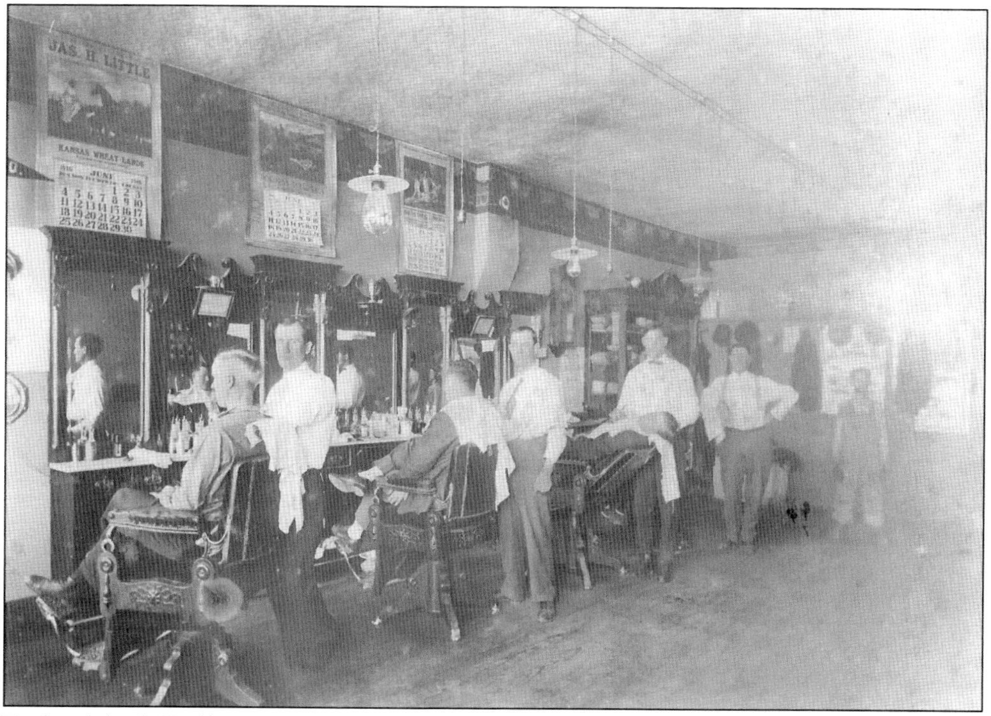

Fred and Andy Wolfe operated a barbershop in the basement of the Farmers & Merchants State Bank building. This June 1916 photograph shows Fred Wolfe standing at the first chair with Fred Vaughn (in the chair). The other men in the photograph are unidentified.

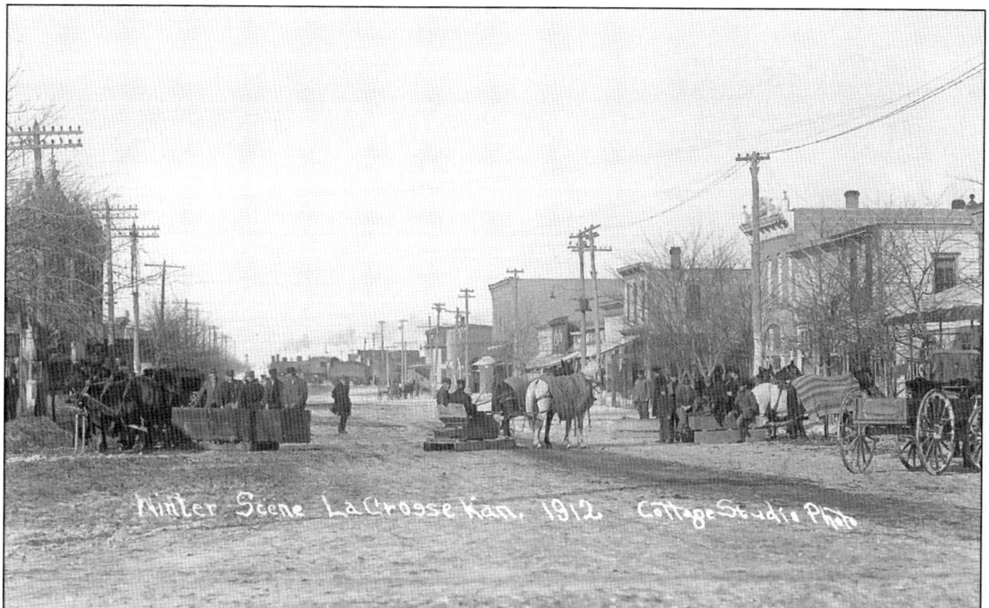

Winter snows could be harsh in Post Rock Country. In town, people tended to make the best of the situation. This almost romantic 1912 "winter scene" gives the impression of cold weather with its blanketed horses and makeshift sleds. The men on the sleds are preparing to "quarry" ice from the creek beds and bring it back into town in blocks on the sleds.

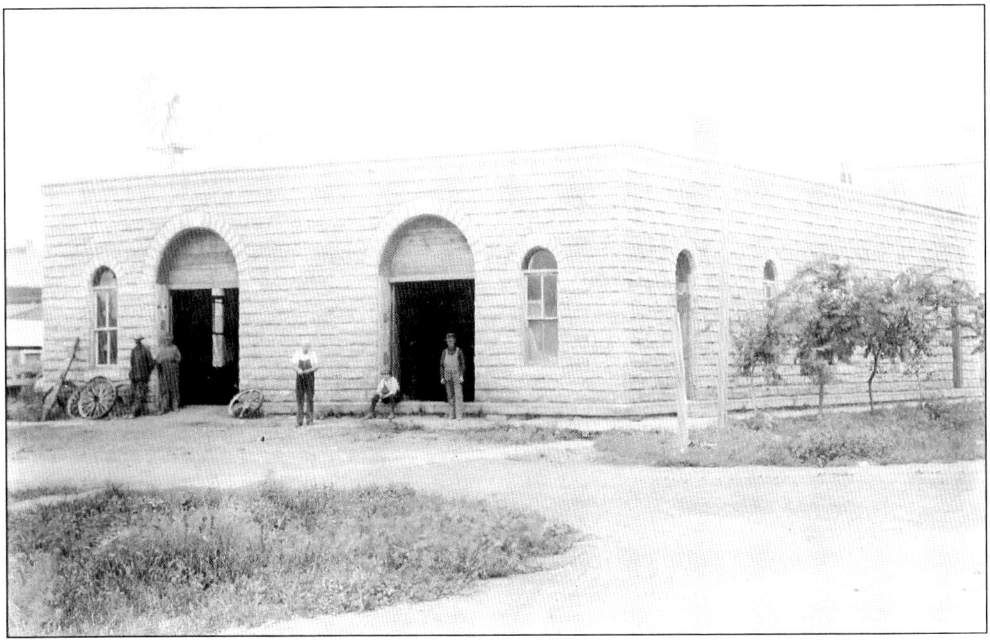

In the 1880s, C.H. Benbow constructed this limestone building on the corner of Ninth and Peace Streets in La Crosse to house his blacksmith and machine shop. The structure's exterior was quite ornate for its purpose. It features pitch-faced stone, arched doors and windows, and native-stone sidewalks on the north and east sides. The interior was simple and unfinished and had dirt floors. It was divided into two rooms and designed to accommodate large machinery brought in for repairs. The building was sold to the city of La Crosse to be used as the city workshop. Today, it is one of the few 19th-century buildings in La Crosse that has remained virtually unchanged.

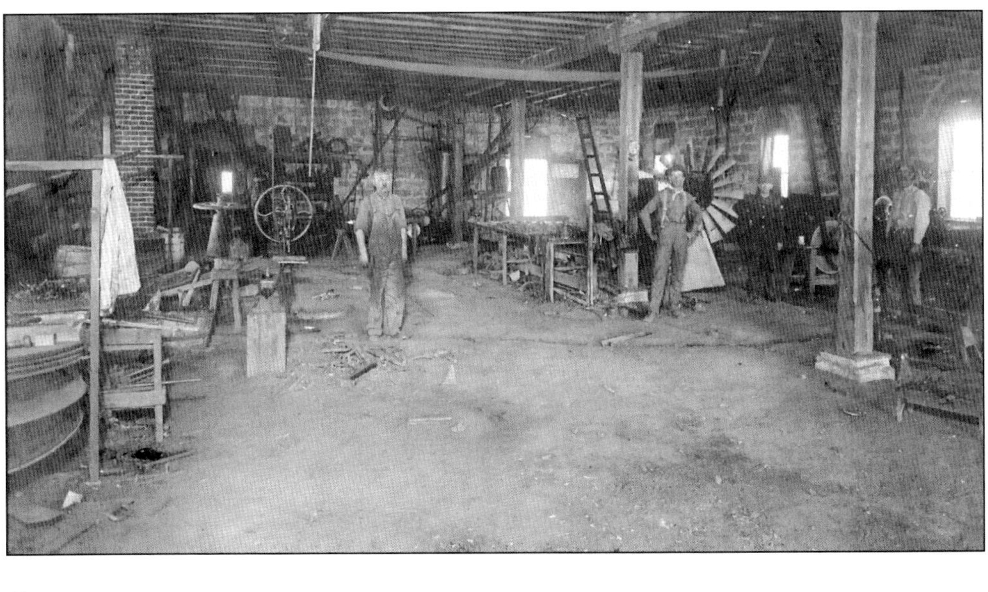

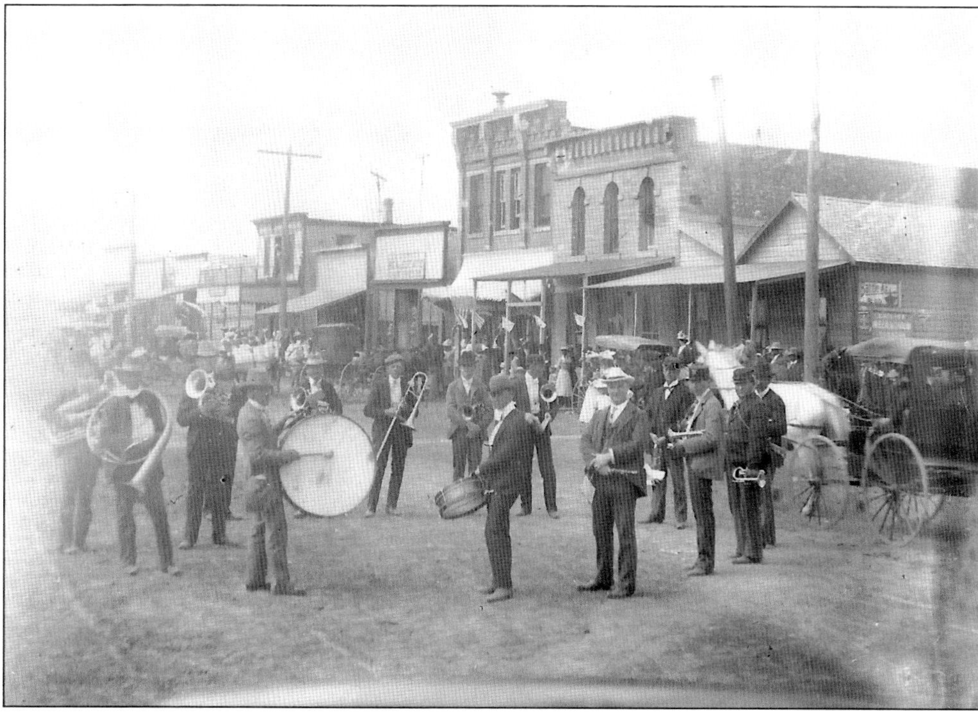

This c. 1910 picture shows the town band gathering for a performance on Main Street. Spectators in the background are waving flags, leading to the assumption that this may be a Fourth of July celebration. The two-story buildings in the background are constructed of Post Rock.

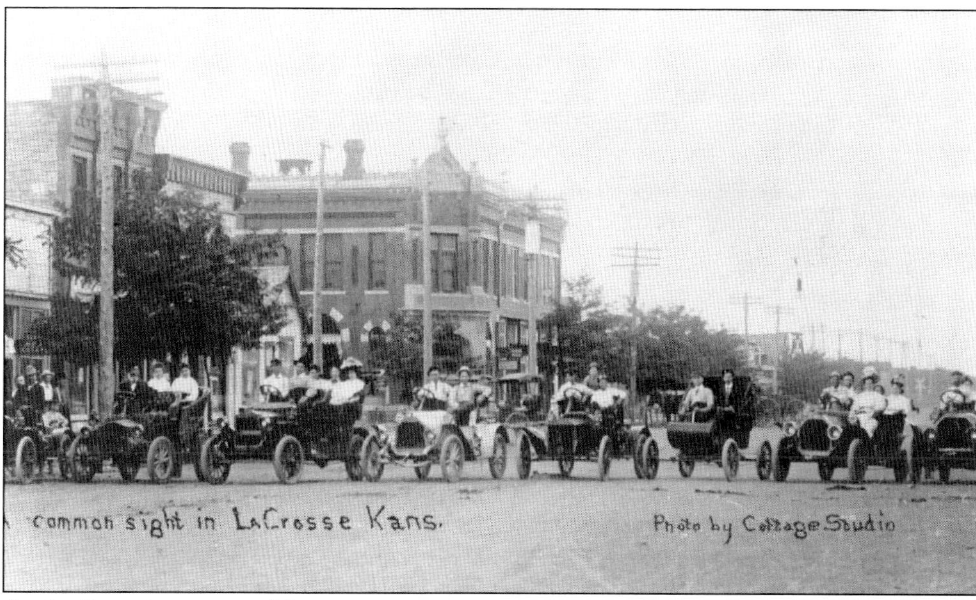

As the "horseless carriage" became more common, car races down Main Street became a part of the social lives of La Crosse residents. Many of the participants shown here were wives or daughters of town leaders. The second car from the left contains Dr. and Mrs. Ferguson and a woman identified as Miss Muzzy. In the third car from left are Pearl Shiney, Mame Turk, Marie Bellport, and Effie Ferguson. The driver of the third car from the right is Gus Bellport.

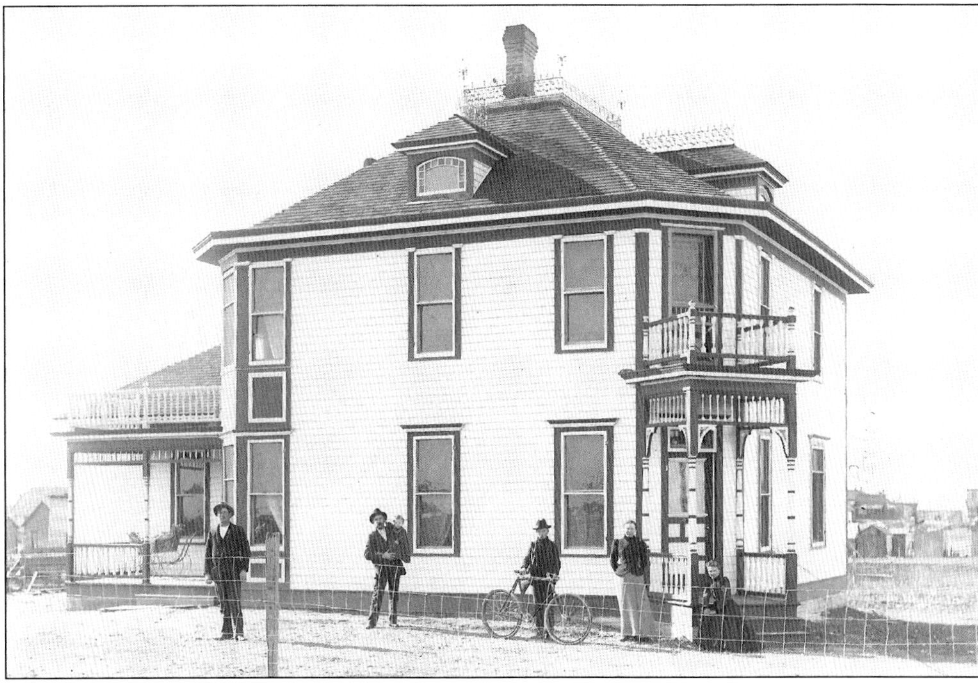

The house of John J. Forney, located on the southwest corner of Eighth and Washington Streets, was a fine example of a city home built on a limestone foundation; it featured a distinctive corner entrance, large windows, and a widow's walk—a flat, fenced area at the peak of the roof.

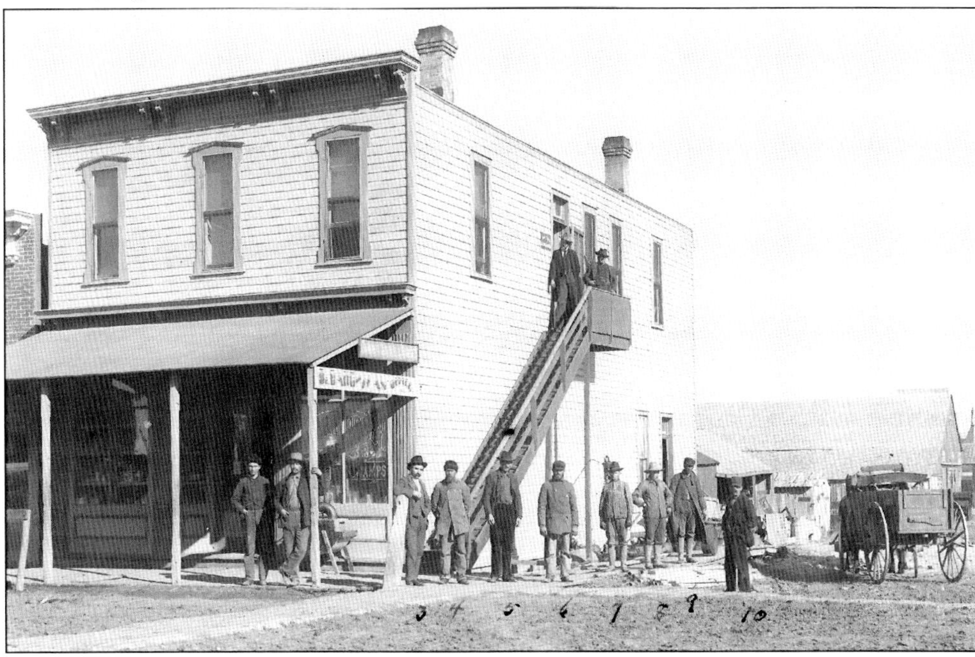

This is another photograph that shows the limestone walks that crossed the streets at each of the downtown intersections on La Crosse's Main Street. This 1895 picture shows the John J. Forney hardware store at the northeast corner of Eighth and Main Streets. The man in front at the top of the stairs is identified as Dr. Baughman.

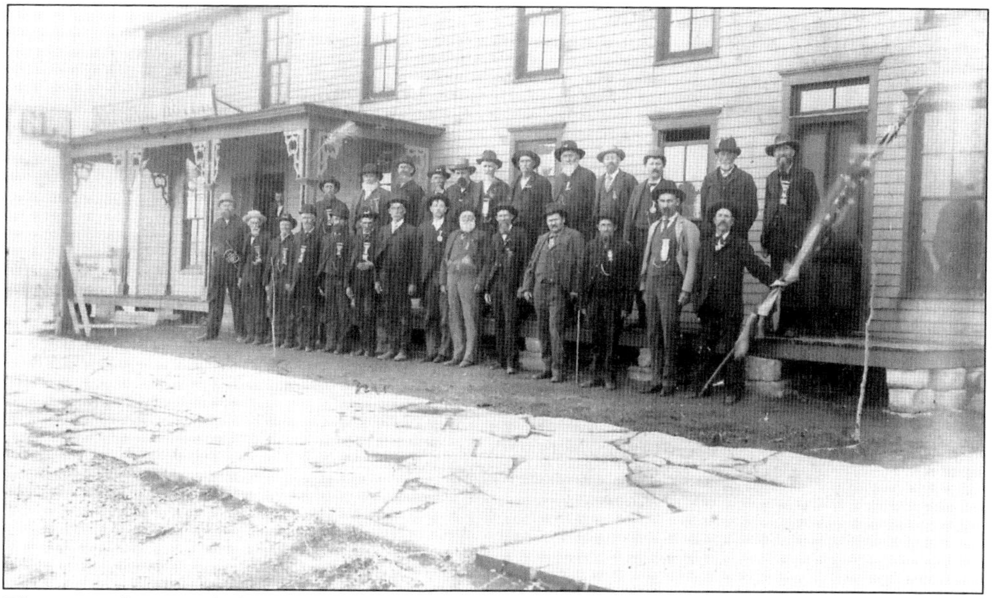

This 1892 photograph features local Civil War veterans standing in front of the National Hotel. Many of these men were founders of the community. The National Hotel was the first hotel in La Crosse, and its foundation is built from Post Rock stacked on the ground. A stone sidewalk is visible in the foreground. This building was destroyed by fire in 1916. At the time of the fire, La Crosse had no public water system.

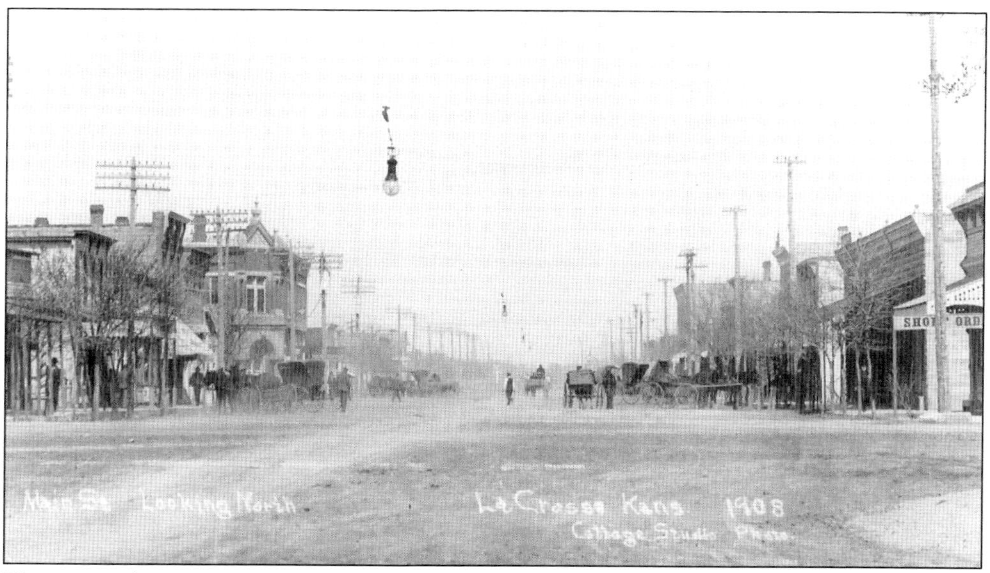

This image shows Main Street in La Crosse in 1908. The two-story Farmers & Merchants State Bank (at left) was the most prominent building on the busy road. In 1907, a 25-foot addition to the north of the bank was constructed to match the existing building. For over 100 years, the upper floor of the bank housed the Masonic lodge and several other fraternal groups.

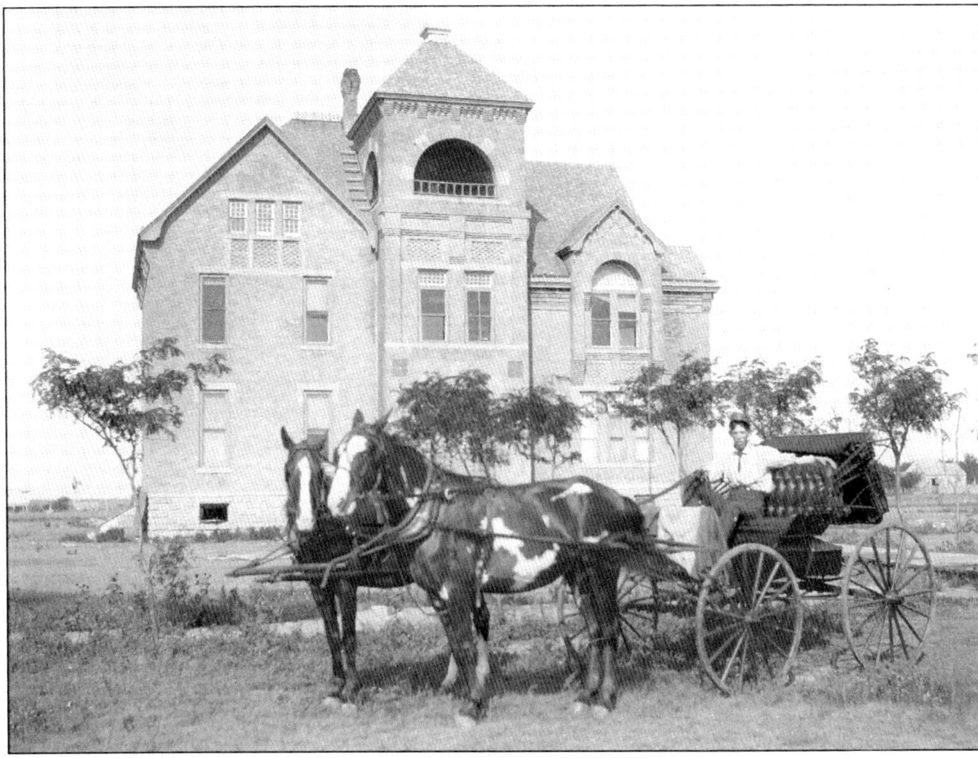

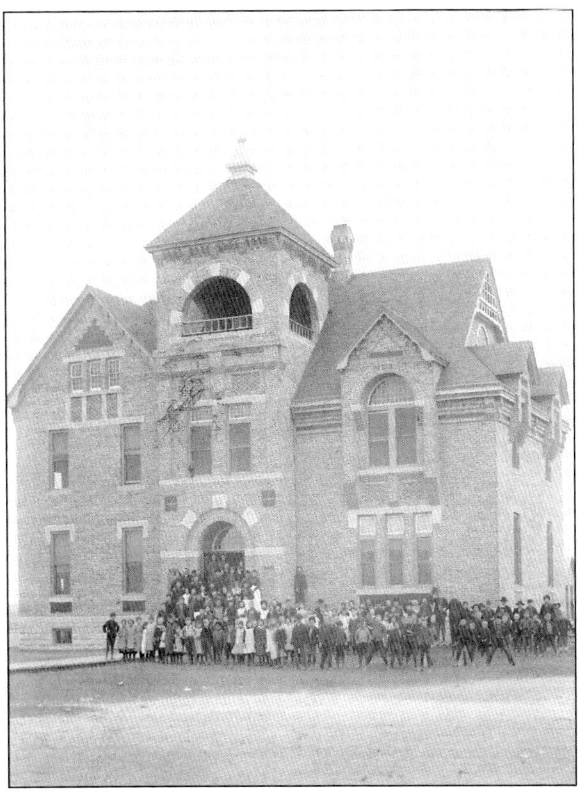

The first permanent school in La Crosse, the Normal School, was built in 1890 and reflected the Romanesque architecture of the Rush County Courthouse with a native-stone foundation and brick exterior accented with native stone. The first floor housed classrooms for the grade school, and high school classes were held on the second floor. The first class graduated in 1893 with three students: Clark Chapman, Nellie M. Hallock (Bunn), and Andrew W. Wilson.

Students and teachers are shown in front of the Normal School in 1892. All grade levels attended classes in the same building until a high school was constructed on the north part of the school block. In 1929, a new grade school was constructed in the same block behind the 1890 building. Materials from the original school were used to construct the city auditorium.

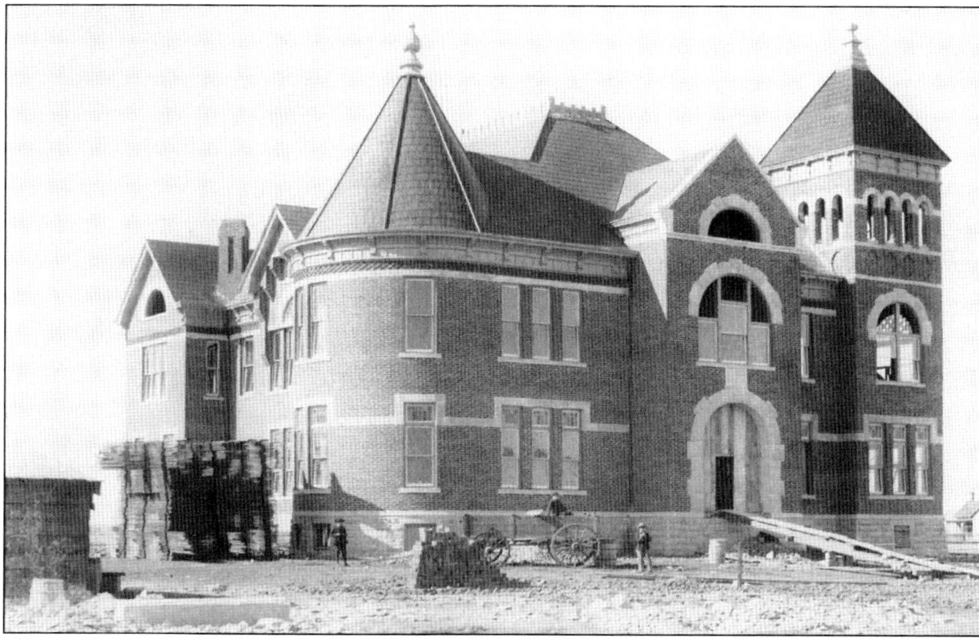

The Rush County Courthouse was constructed in 1888–1889 following a fight between La Crosse and Rush Center for the county seat. For years, county records were literally moved back and forth between the two communities, which led to the coining of the phrase "courthouse wheels." After the battle was settled and La Crosse named the permanent county seat, government offices moved to this courthouse.

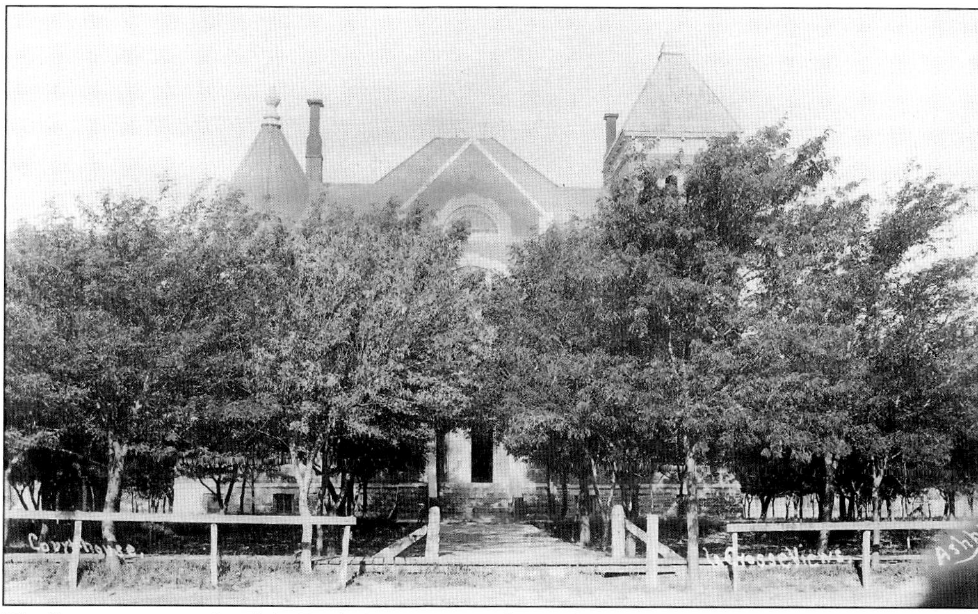

The Romanesque style of the Rush County Courthouse features a circular tower on the southeast corner, a square tower on the northeast corner, and native-stone arches over stained-glass dormers. In the early part of the 20th century, the building was nearly obscured by trees. By mid-century, most of the trees had been removed. This building is now listed in the National Register of Historic Places.

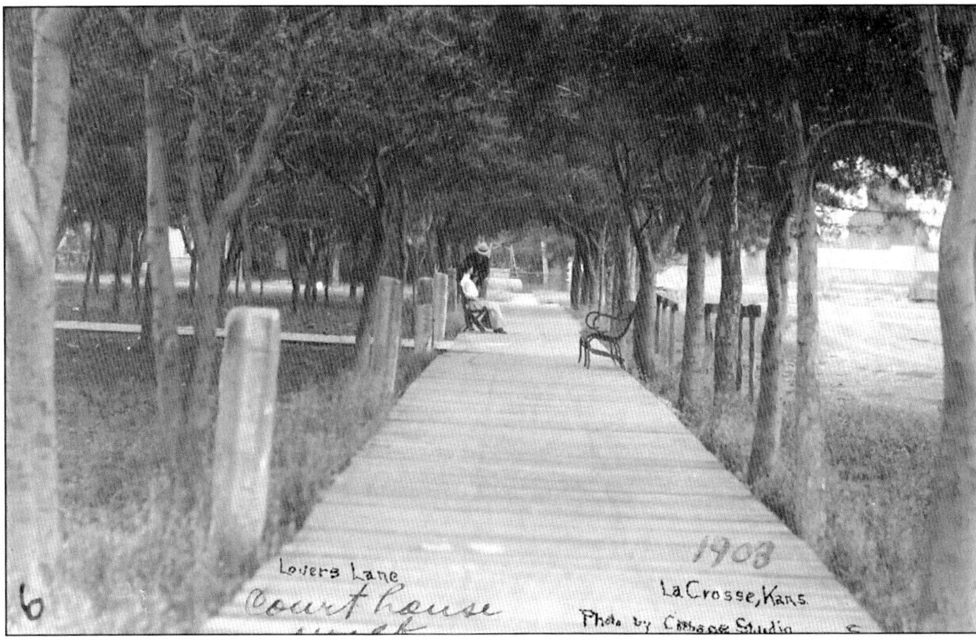

For the first couple of decades in the 20th century, dense trees lined the boardwalk along the front of the Rush County Courthouse. Native-stone fence posts, park benches, and electric lights framed what became known as "Lovers Lane." This photograph was taken around 1903.

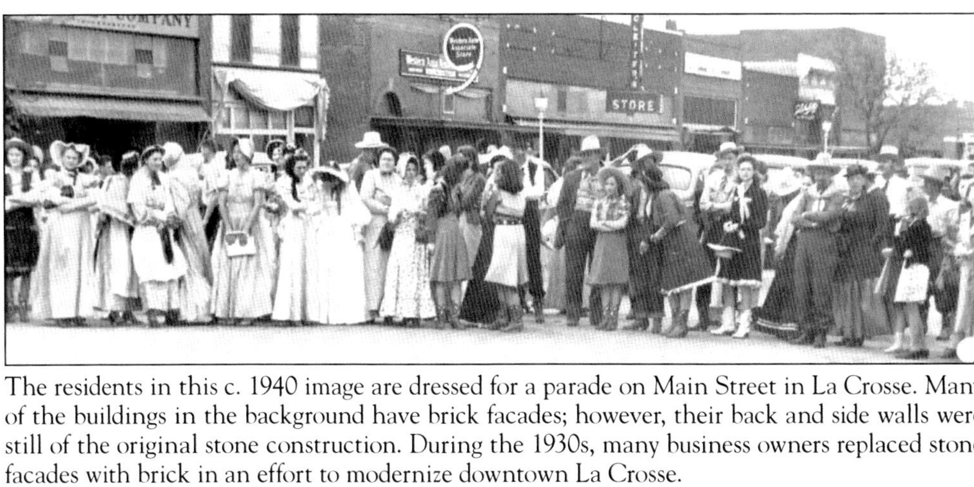

The residents in this c. 1940 image are dressed for a parade on Main Street in La Crosse. Many of the buildings in the background have brick facades; however, their back and side walls were still of the original stone construction. During the 1930s, many business owners replaced stone facades with brick in an effort to modernize downtown La Crosse.

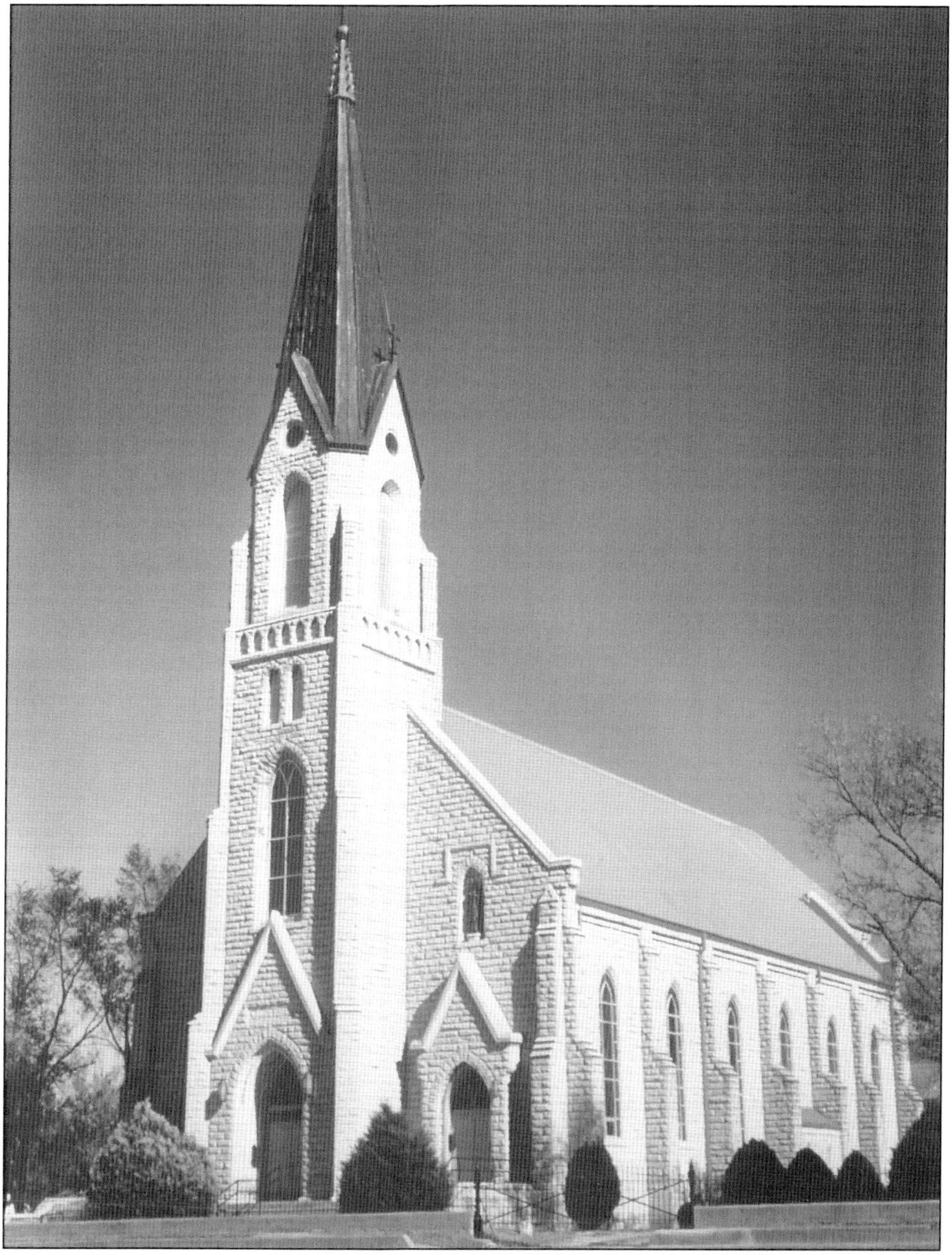

Liebenthal, the first of the Volga German settlements in the area, welcomed settlers on February 22, 1876, and they constructed their first native-stone church—St. Joseph's Kirche—in 1877. It measured 48 feet long by 28 feet wide and had a 15-by-15-foot sacristy. On November 22, 1902, a cornerstone was laid for a new St. Joseph's, and the 148-foot-long-by-56-foot-wide church was dedicated on May 28, 1905. Rev. Rudolph Stollenwerk supervised construction, and stonework was done by local residents. A total of 2,260 loads of stone and 600 loads of sand were used in construction. German artists created the stained-glass windows at a cost of $2,000. The estimated total cost of construction was $75,000—an incredible amount of money to spend in a small settlement in western Kansas.

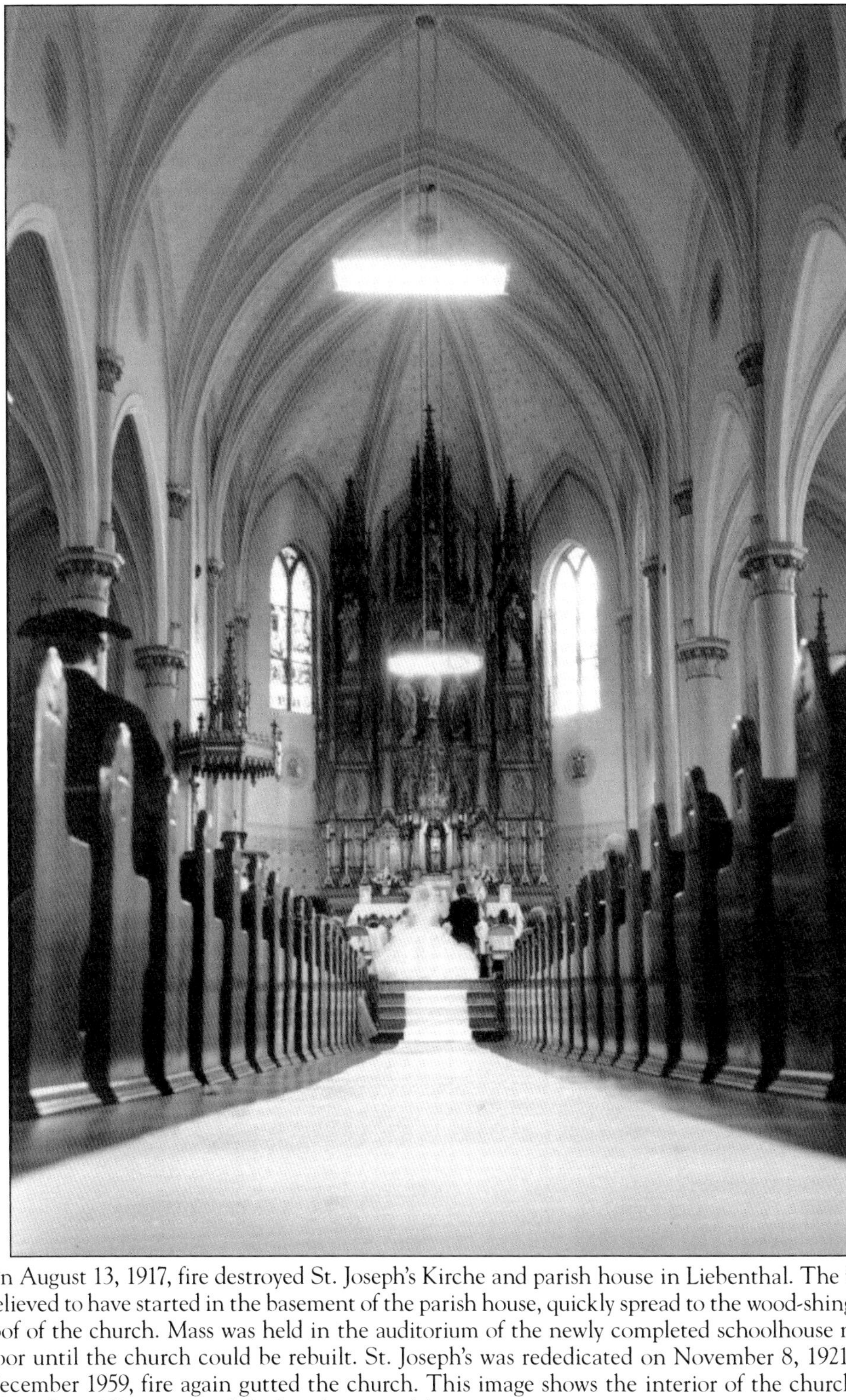

On August 13, 1917, fire destroyed St. Joseph's Kirche and parish house in Liebenthal. The fire, believed to have started in the basement of the parish house, quickly spread to the wood-shingled roof of the church. Mass was held in the auditorium of the newly completed schoolhouse next door until the church could be rebuilt. St. Joseph's was rededicated on November 8, 1921. In December 1959, fire again gutted the church. This image shows the interior of the church in November 1959, one month before the second fire.

The church built its first parochial school in 1890. In addition to educating children, the school held classes to help German pioneers to learn to read, write, and speak English. A stone school was constructed east of the church in 1917. St. Joseph's School has a full basement, classrooms on the main level, and a large auditorium/gymnasium on the second floor. School consolidation and declining attendance forced it to close in 1968.

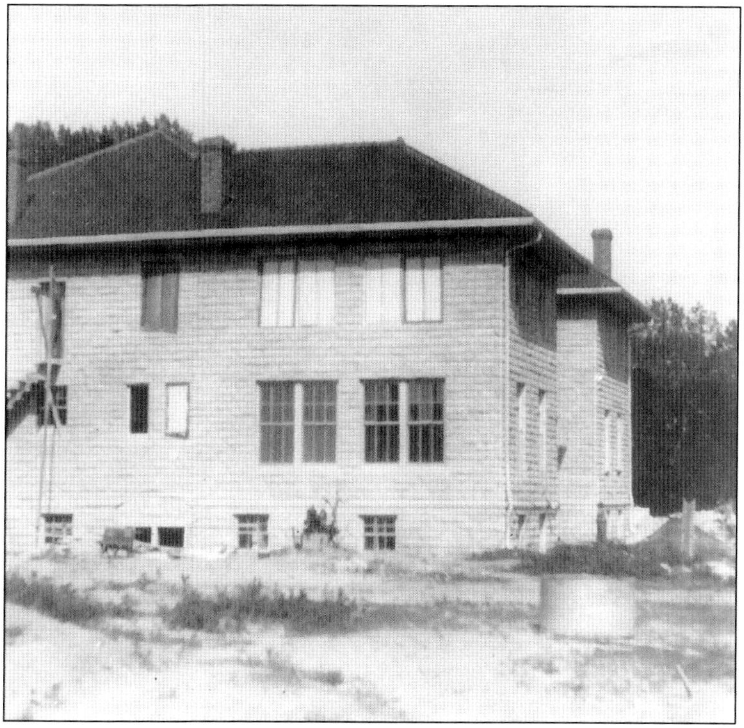

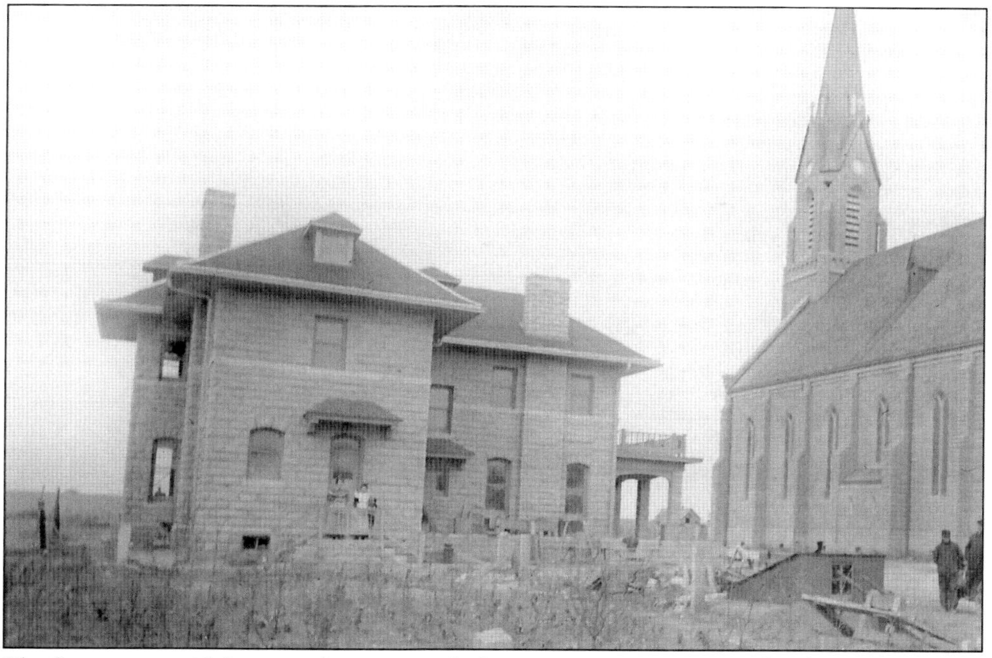

The first stone parish house is shown around when construction was completed in 1910. In 1917, fire gutted both the house and the church. Because its walls were dangerously weakened, the parish house was razed, and a new limestone building was completed in 1918. When fire struck the church again in 1959, the parish house was spared, suffering only minor smoke damage.

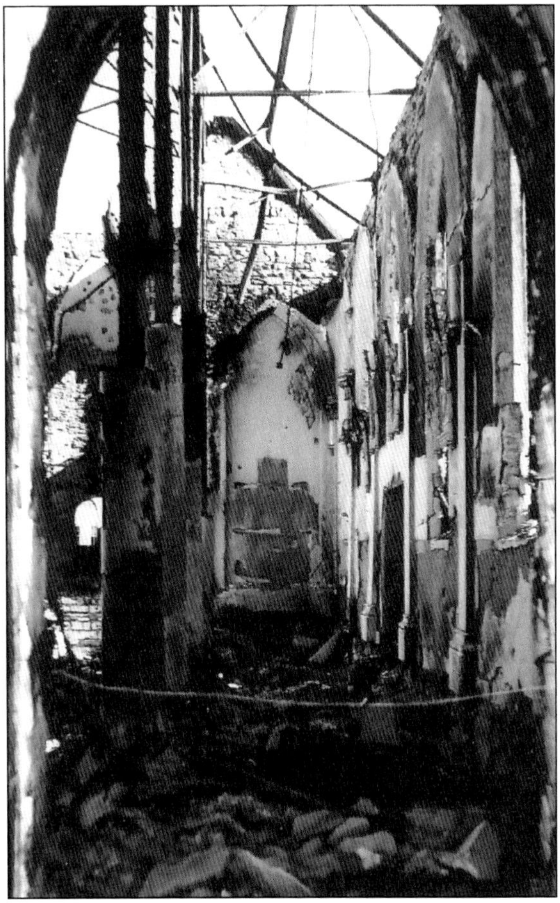

In December 1959, a second fire gutted the 60-year old St. Joseph's Kirche, which had suffered a devastating fire in 1917. This time, the fire was believed to have started as a result of faulty wiring. After serious consideration, the parishioners decided to rebuild again within the existing walls as a tribute to those who labored diligently to quarry and construct the stone walls that miraculously survived two conflagrations.

The St. Joseph's Kirche church and parish house are shown below following reconstruction after the 1959 fire. After the second devastating fire, the congregation, taking into consideration the declining population of the area, debated whether to rebuild the church. Parishioners finally agreed to rebuild as a tribute to their forefathers, who had made great sacrifices to construct the church.

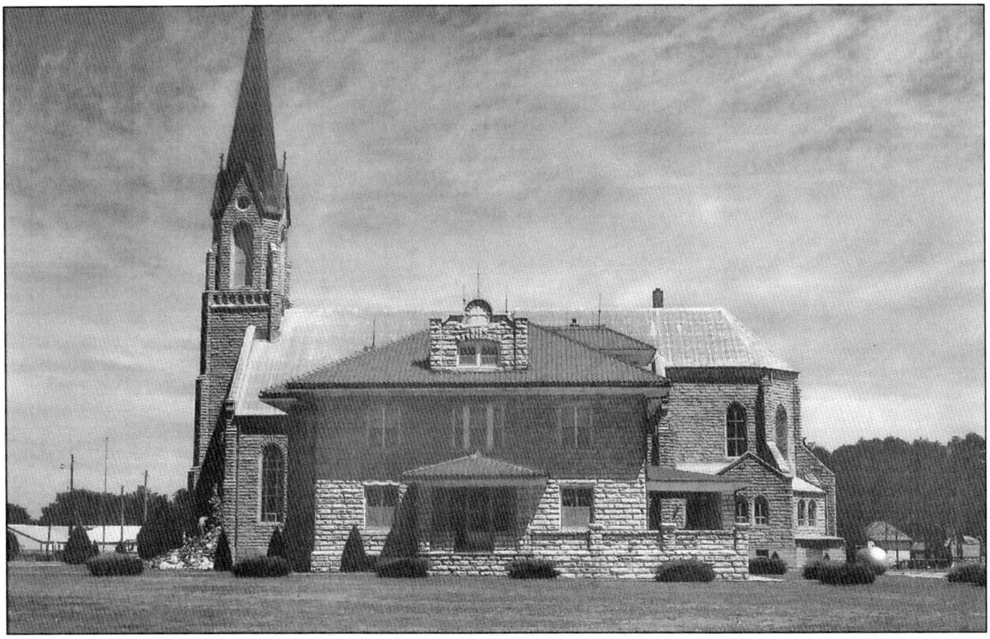

This Post Rock limestone garage is located in the northeastern part of Liebenthal. Constructed in 1939, during the latter part of the Great Depression, its design is quite elaborate for its time and purpose. Its narrow width and extra height suggests that it was designed for a buggy or tall vehicle.

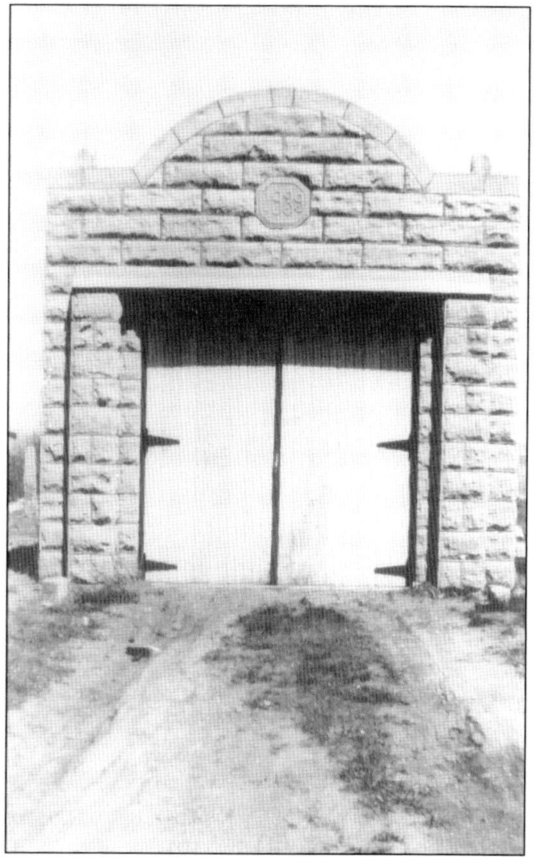

This small house is one of the oldest homes in Liebenthal. The Volga German settlers modeled homes after the *semelanka* in their home country. A *semelanka* was a two- or three-room dwelling with a gabled roof and central chimney—an official plan devised by the Colonists Welfare Office in the Volga-German region of Russia. The front did not face the street; instead, gabled ends were pointed to the street, and the front faced toward a courtyard.

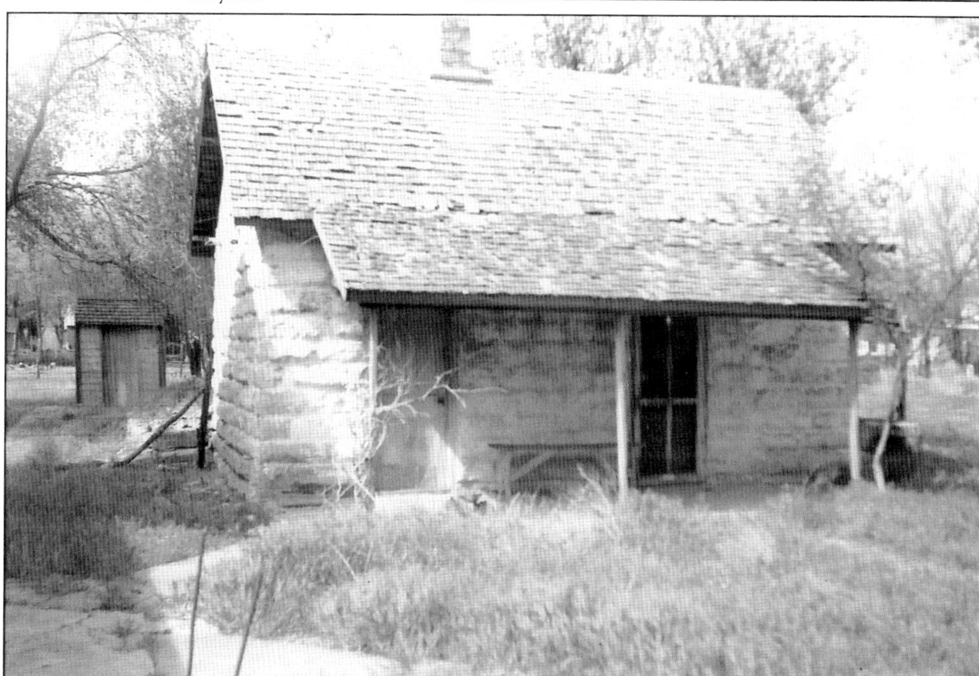

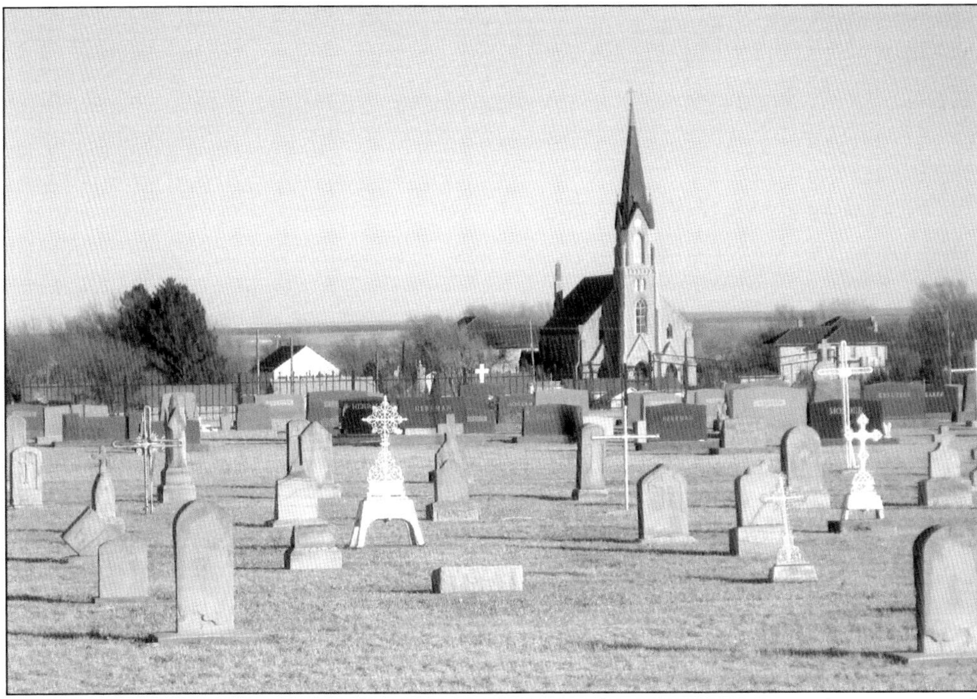

Because money was scarce among the pioneers, the first Volga German grave markers were simple wooden crosses. However, wood did not stand up to the harsh Kansas winds, so blacksmiths crafted elaborate iron crosses from scrap metal. In the Post Rock region, the availability of Post Rock provided another alternative. In Liebenthal, the cemetery exhibits a variety of iron, stone, and traditional granite headstones.

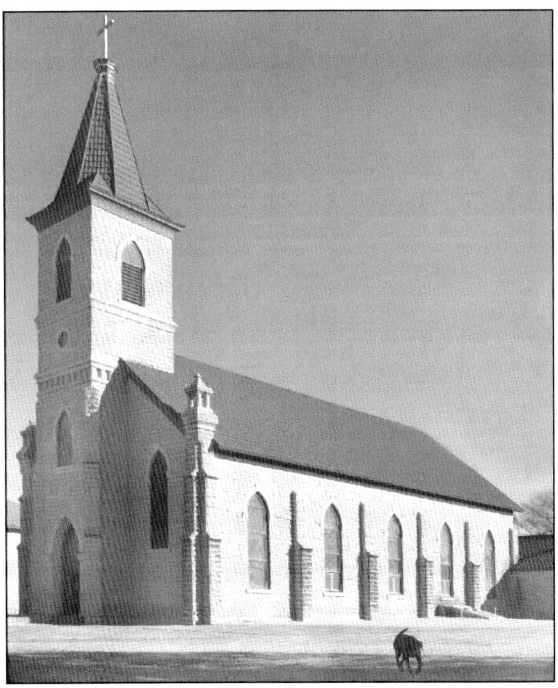

In the fall of 1876, a dispute arose among St. Joseph's Kirche parishioners in Liebenthal about the location of a new church. A number of settlers became angry and moved their houses four miles to the north and one mile west along the banks of the Smoky Hill River, naming the new community after their former home of Schoenchen, Russia. In 1900, the new community commenced construction on St. Anthony's Church under the direction of Fr. Emmeran Kausler, who did some of the masonry work himself. All adult male parishioners pledged to donate one day each week to quarry, dress, and move the stone. The church was twice damaged by fire. Flames erupted from a faulty floor furnace in the 1920s, damaging the front of the building. A second blaze damaged the rear of the building in 1932. Each time, the church was rebuilt.

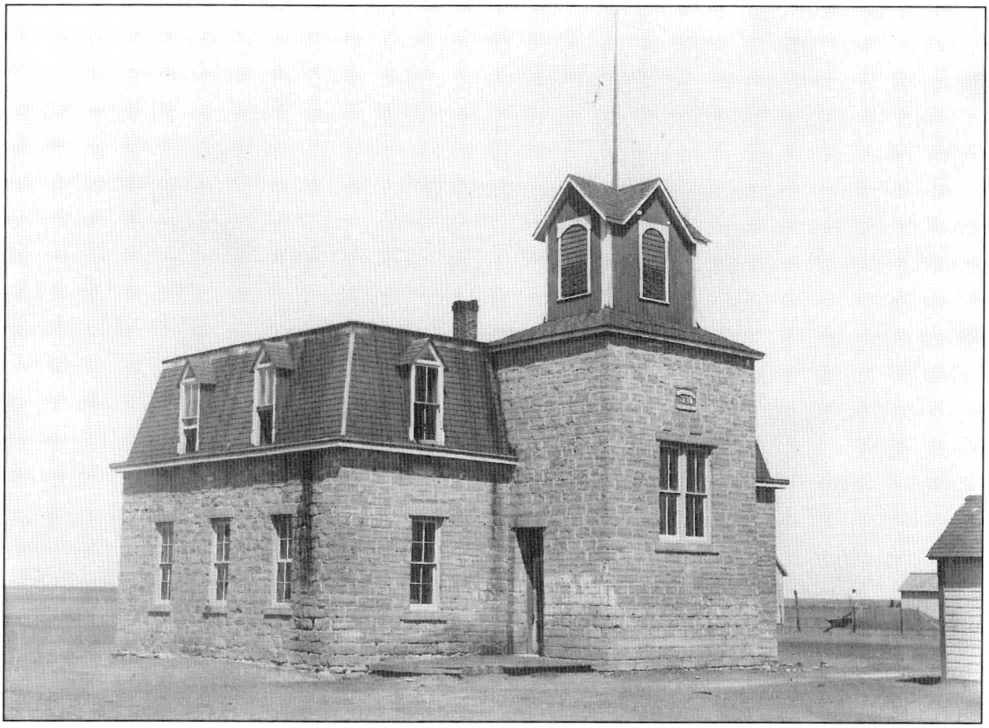

School District No. 1 was organized in the fall of 1874 in Rush Center. The school was a one-room building constructed from stone quarried near the town. In 1880, it was enlarged to two rooms on the first floor and a large, unfinished room on the second floor. In 1909, the district replaced the building with a four-room, two-story brick school.

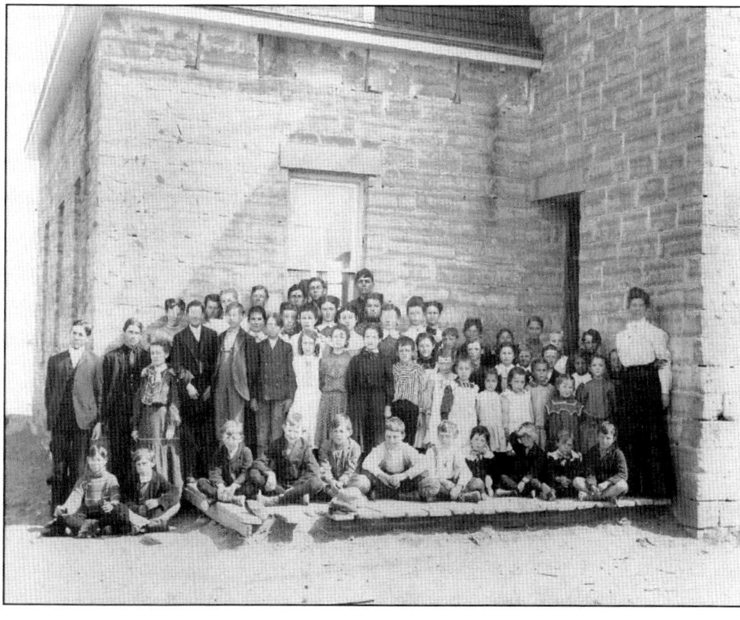

Students from District No. 1 in Rush Center are pictured here on the last day of school in 1905. The teachers are Ernest Kirkpatrick (far left) and Alice Guldin (far right). Four years later, the 35-year-old building, which had undergone major structural modifications, was declared unsafe and then condemned.

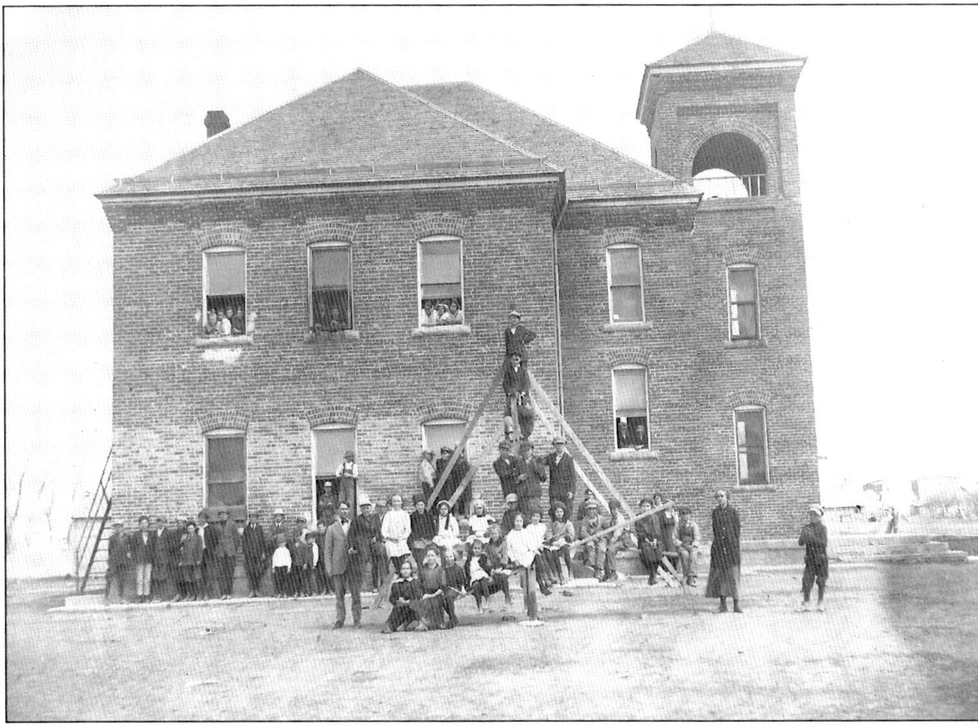

In 1909, the district hired John Butler to build a four-room, two-story brick-and-limestone school to replace the old stone Rush Center School building that had been declared unsafe. The new school featured a tall bell tower above the front entrance. This building was completed in the summer of 1910, and the first classes were held that fall.

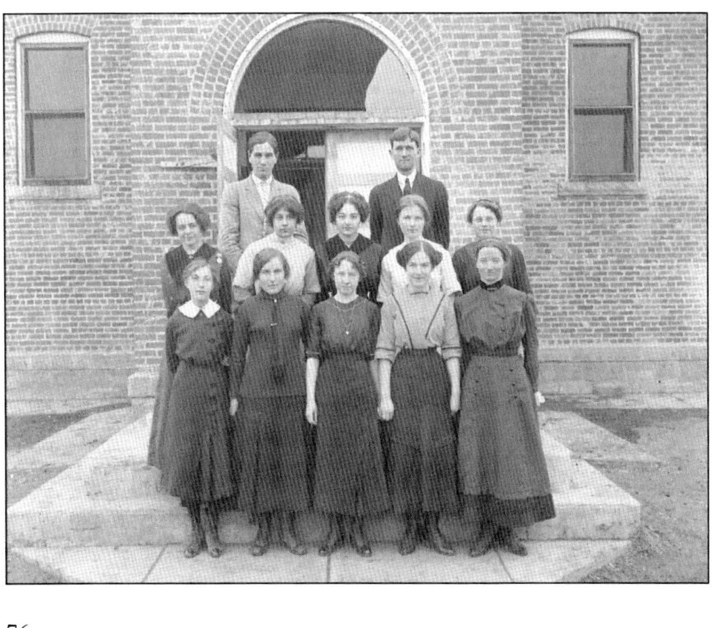

This c. 1911 image shows one of the first high school classes in the new Rush Center School. From left to right are (first row) Edith Scandrett, unidentified, Florence Bates, Nellie Hallett, and Rose Lyman; (second row) Flossie Scranton, Lois McKinney, Fern Scranton, Bessie Burns, and Marie Schrader; (third row) Charles Ott and Bill Rankin.

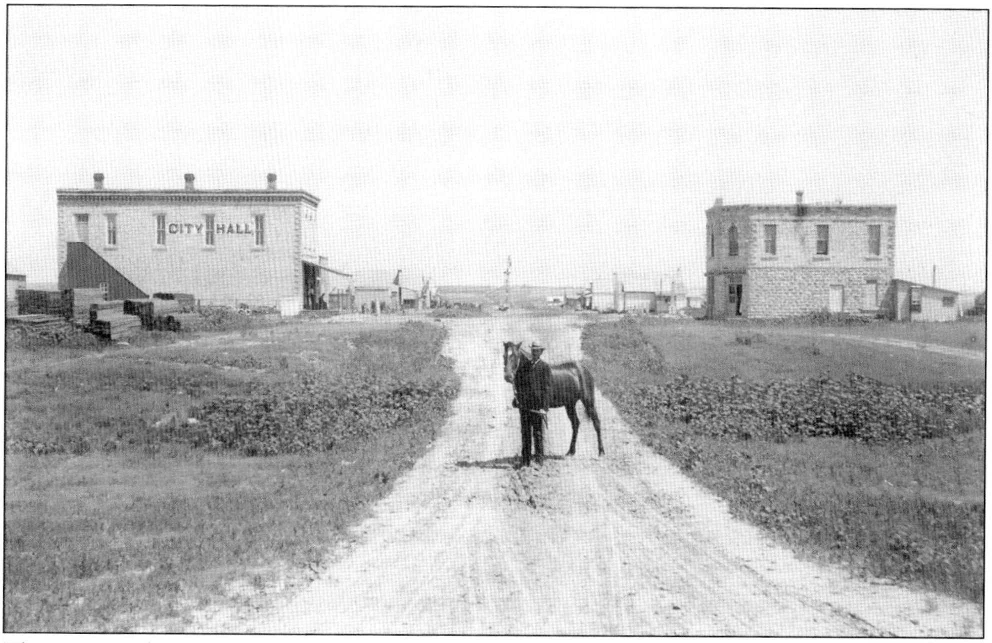

The area now known as Rush Center was established as Walnut City in 1871. When Rush County was established in 1874, Walnut City was named as the county seat, and the population of the town exploded to nearly 1,500 people. At the same time, the name was changed to Rush Centre (the spelling changed to "Center" in 1895) because of its location in the center of the county. With hopes of the city being the county seat, town leaders and businessmen erected several substantial buildings in the downtown area. In 1876, the county was resurveyed, and the southern tier of Rush County townships was transferred to Pawnee County, placing La Crosse at the center of the county. When La Crosse was named the permanent county seat in 1888, many of the wooden structures in Rush Centre were picked up and moved four miles north to La Crosse, and the stone buildings were abandoned or dismantled.

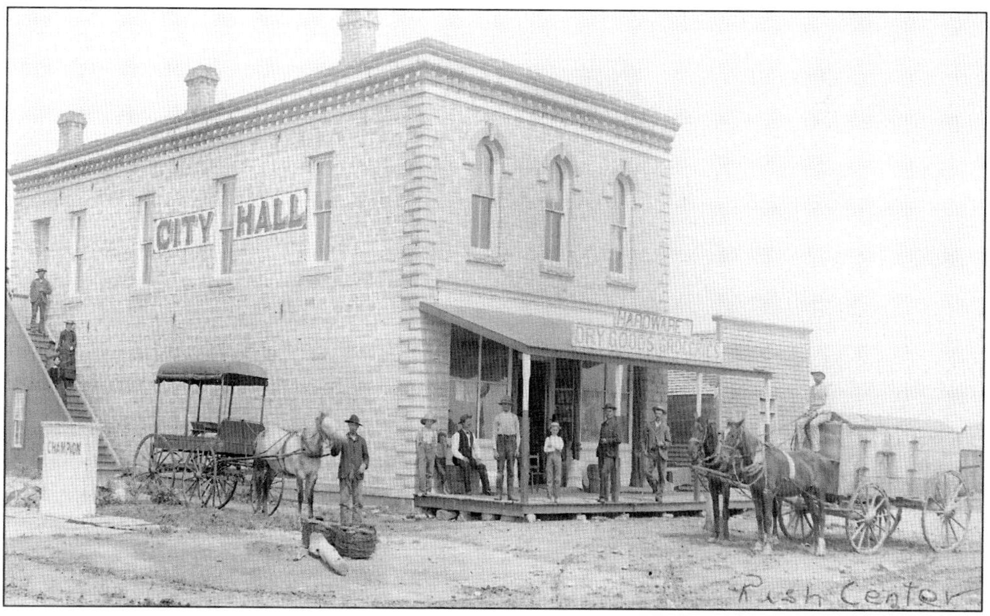

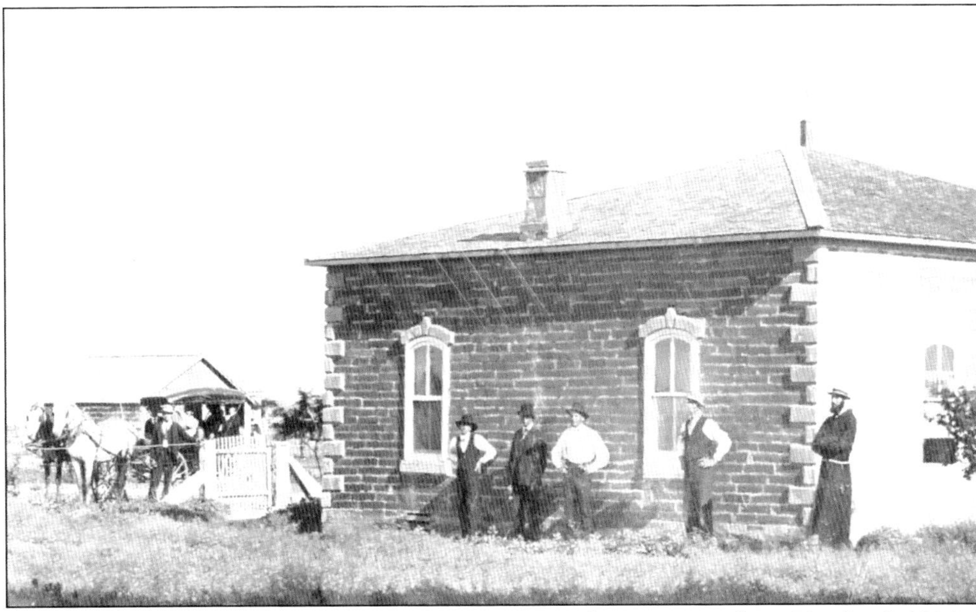

When the first Volga German settlers arrived in Post Rock Country in the 1870s, they held Mass outdoors at the foot of a makeshift cross until they were able to construct a more permanent facility. Many parishes constructed simple buildings that often doubled as schools. This building near Pfeifer was used as an early church by Volga German settlers.

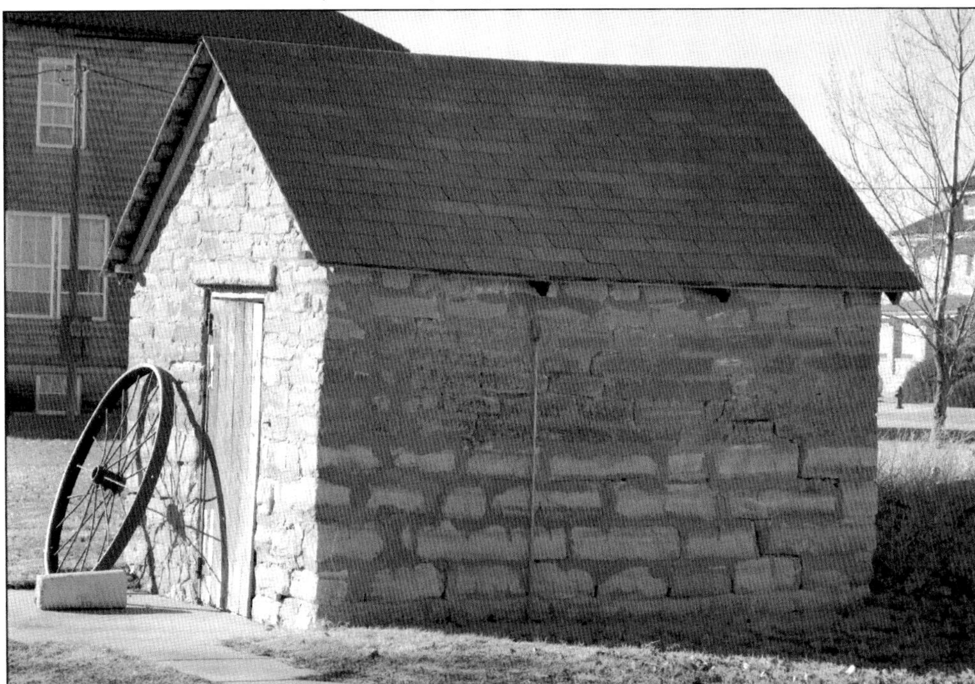

Small outbuildings, like this one located in Liebenthal, were common in the Volga German communities. The building shows early construction that was updated later with the addition of modern shingles and electricity. Judging from the variations in the stone, the building was likely constructed in two separate sections—upper and lower.

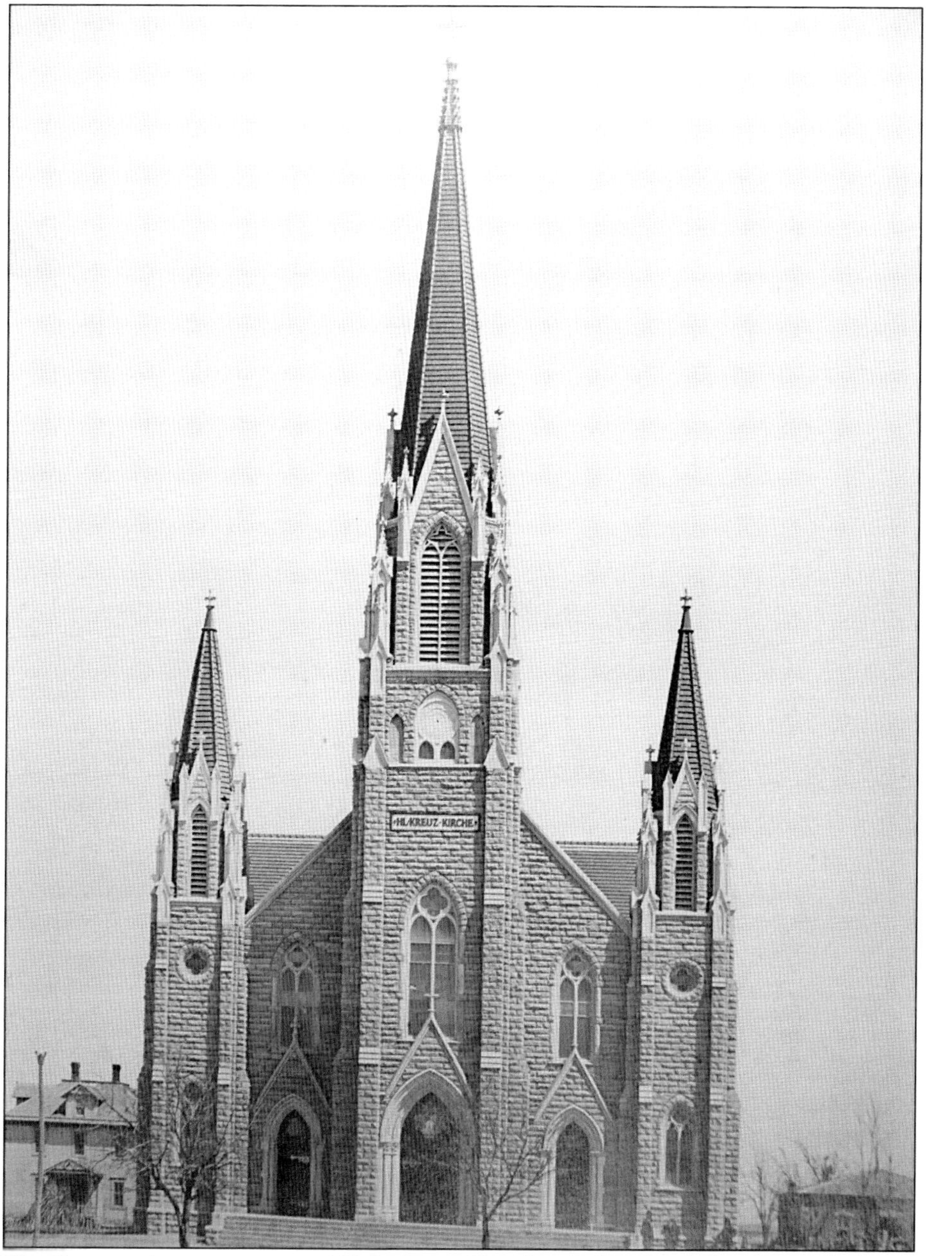

In Ellis County, the cornerstone of Holy Cross Church, Pfeifer's third church, was laid in 1916 under the direction of Fr. Peter Burkard. A fundraiser was initiated to finance the new church. Each family was assessed 2¢ for every bushel of wheat sold. The "two cent" church, as it became known, was completed and dedicated on May 3, 1918. Families who lived in Rush County objected and were promised that if they decided to build their own church, their money would be returned. In 1912, a group of 17 families received $3,000 from the fund to build a church just across the county line to the south and establish the town of Loretto. The main spire of Holy Cross Church rises 165 feet, with side spires measuring 100 feet in height. The church is built in the shape of a cross; its main structure is 50 feet wide, and transepts protrude 12 feet on each side. Stone quarried for the second church in 1887 was reused for interior walls and as a foundation for the altar.

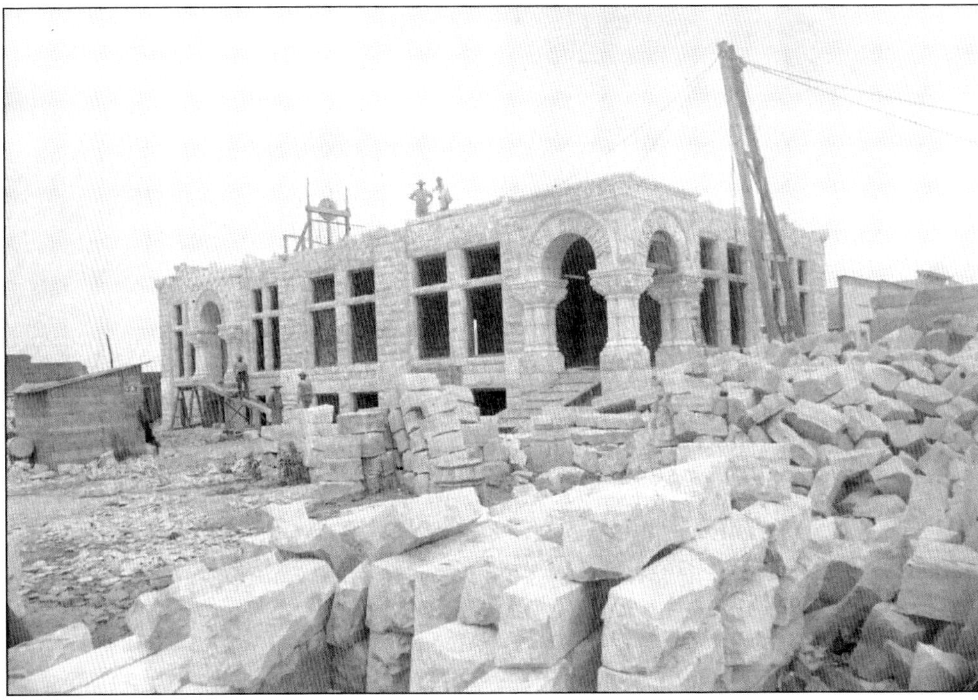

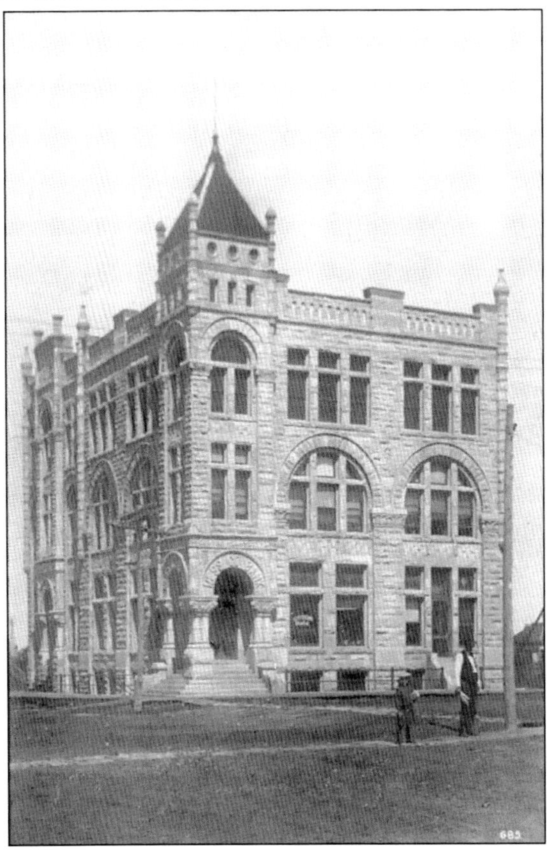

The 18,000-square-foot native-stone building that housed the Ness County Bank in Ness County was designed by the architectural firm of Holland & Hopkins of Topeka. William Ruff of Ness City was awarded the contract for construction in November 1888, and Daniel J. Rogers of Newton was subcontracted to do the stonemasonry. Ground limestone was used in the mortar instead of sand to coordinate the color with the adjoining stone. The building has 30 rooms and features 13-foot ceilings, an elevator shaft, four vaults, and brass doorknobs bearing a sunflower design. Initial cost was estimated to be $34,000, but records indicate that final costs were more than double that amount. Today, the building, known as the "Skyscraper of the Plains," is listed in the National Register of Historic Places. Since 1984, it has been owned by the nonprofit Ness County Bank Building Foundation, Inc., and now houses a gift shop, community rooms, and the Ness City Chamber of Commerce offices.

Trustees of the First Methodist Church of Hays in Ellis County planned to construct a new native-stone church at the corner of Ash and Seventh Streets before 1920. The church struggled with finances, however, and held services in the basement of the incomplete building for many years. Construction resumed around 1944, and with a generous donation from the Hadley family, the building was finished and dedicated in 1949. (AC.)

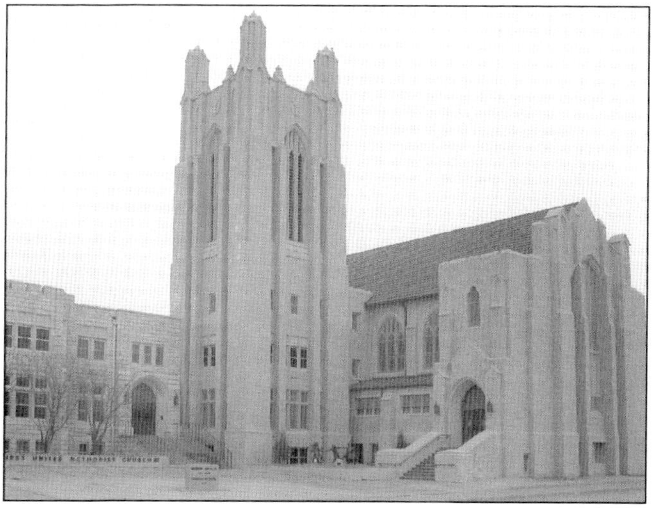

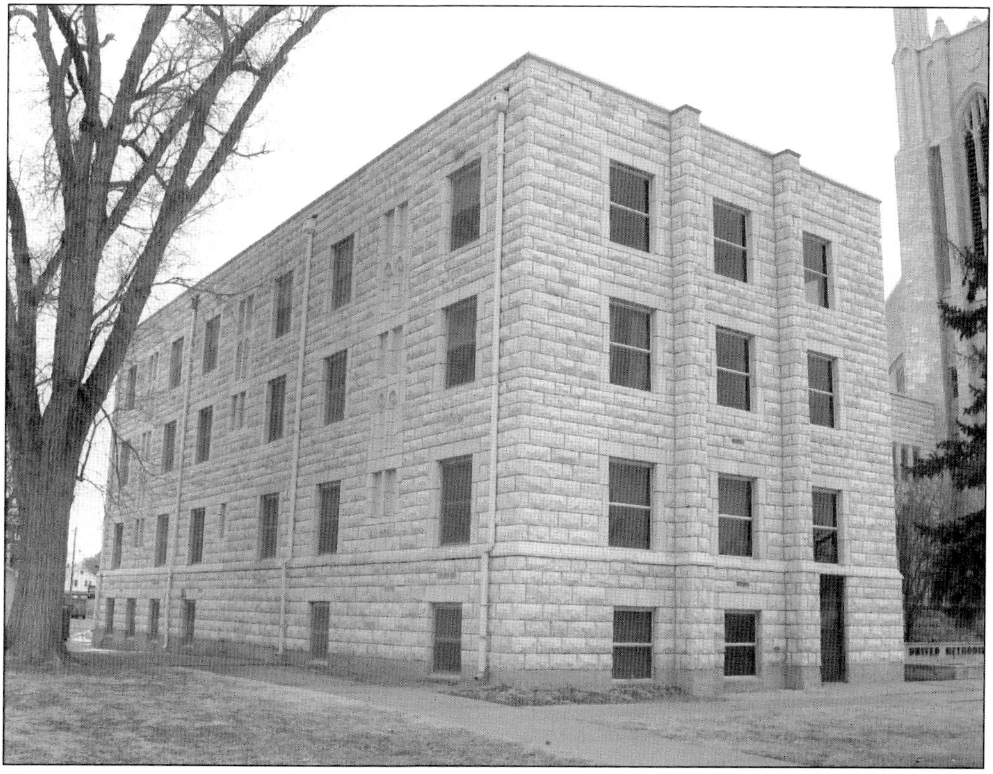

The education wing of the First Methodist Church was initially a girls' dormitory for Fort Hays Kansas State College, located three blocks to the west. When the college constructed additional dormitory space, this became an educational wing. The multiple stages of the church's construction are shown in the two different types of stone used to create the building's walls. (AC.)

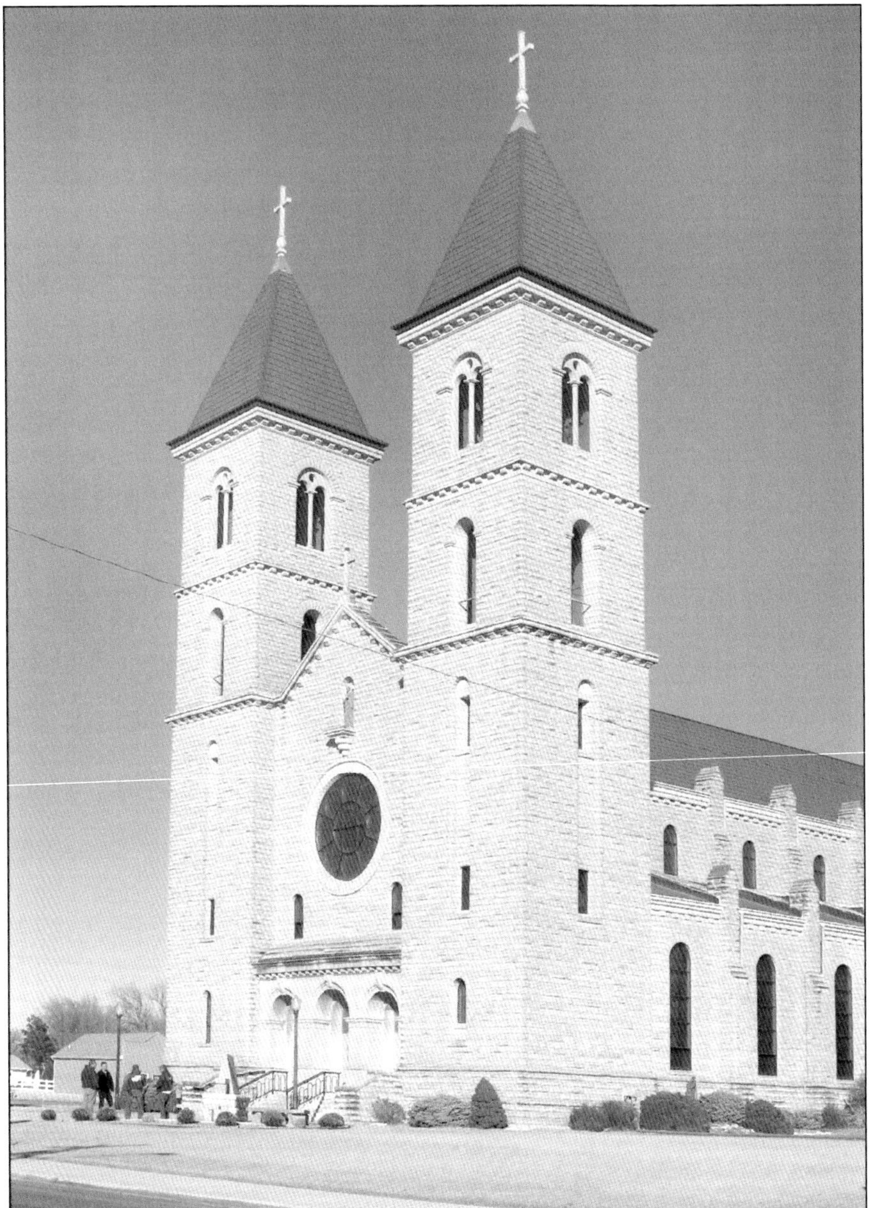

St. Fidelis Church in Victoria (in Ellis County) is a magnificent example of Post Rock Romanesque architecture. The original settlers of Victoria arrived from England in 1872. In 1876, a group of German-Russian immigrants established the town of Herzog adjacent to Victoria. When the British settlers found the environment too harsh, they returned to England, leaving the town in the hands of the Volga Germans. The church was completed in 1911 and is constructed of native limestone quarried seven miles south of Victoria. It was designed by church architect John T. Comes of Pittsburgh, Pennsylvania. The building, which is in the form of a cross facing to the west, is 220 feet long, 110 feet wide at the transepts, and 75 feet wide at the nave. The ceiling is 44 feet high, and the two towers extend 141 feet into the sky. At the time of its construction, it was the largest church west of the Mississippi. The building, referred to as the "Cathedral of the Plains," is now listed in the National Register of Historic Places. (AC.)

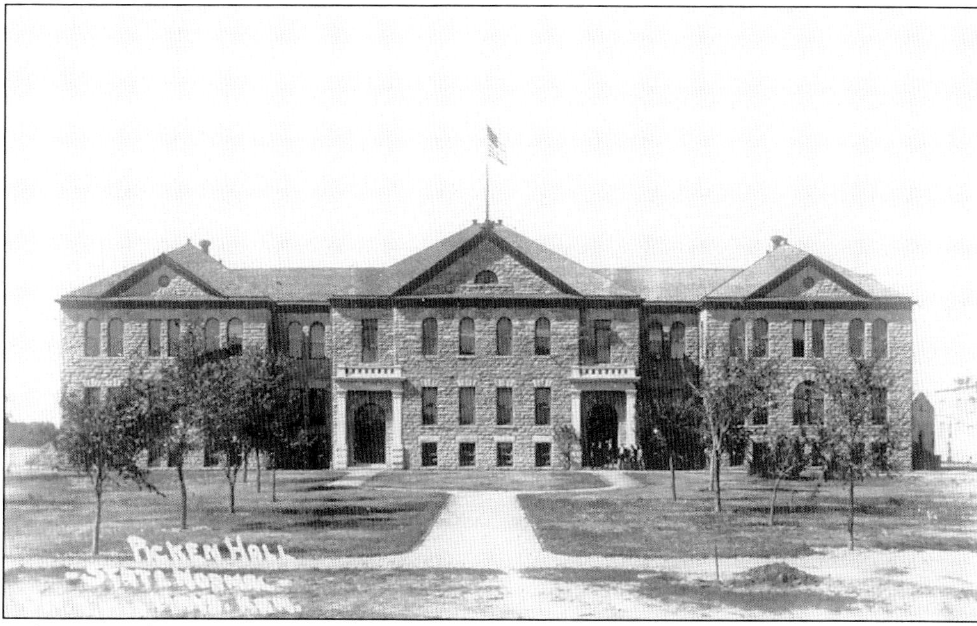

Picken Hall, the first building on the campus of Fort Hays State University, was constructed in 1904. Like most campus facilities, it is constructed of native limestone. At that time, the college was known as the Western Branch of Kansas State Normal School; it was later known as Fort Hays Kansas State Normal School. This 1915 photograph shows the east elevation of the building.

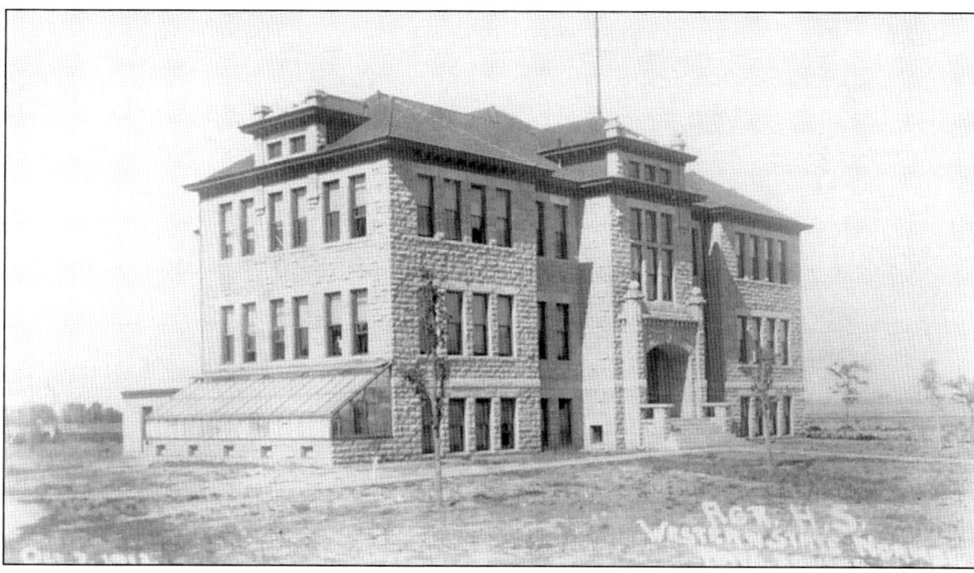

Rarick Hall, located on the campus of Fort Hays State University, was constructed in 1912 using native limestone. The building was first known as the Hays Model Agricultural High School. In 1914, the name was changed to the Industrial Building. In 1952, the name was changed to Rarick Hall. It was demolished in 1978.

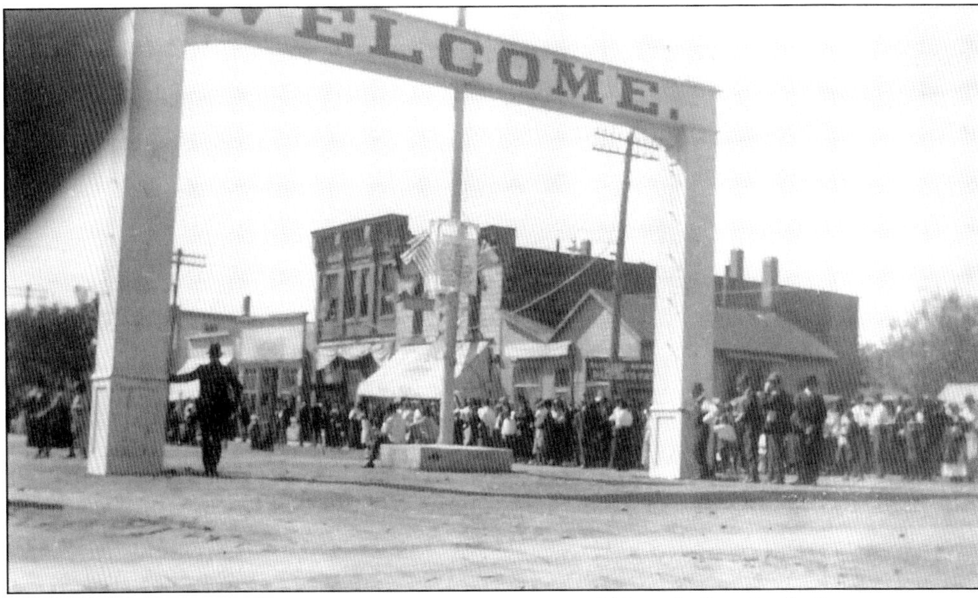

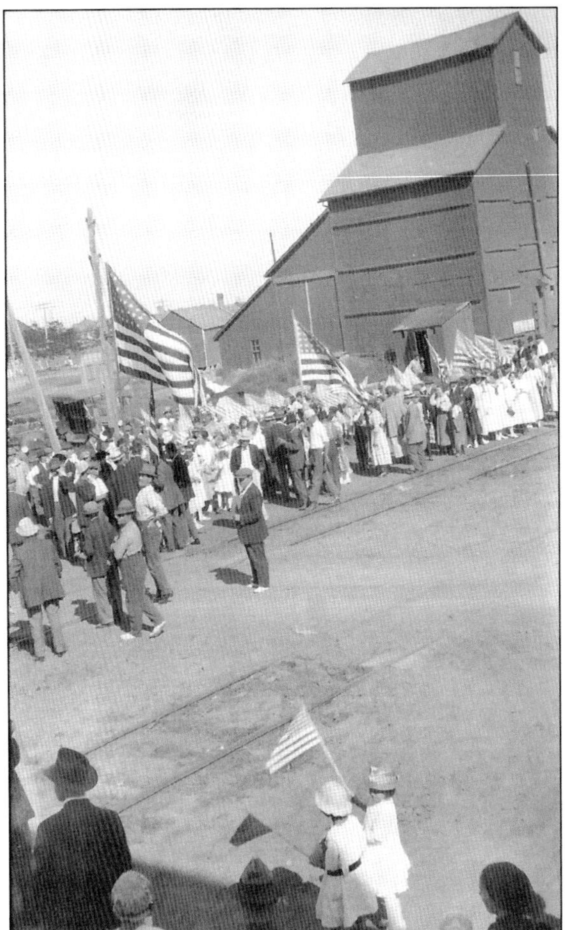

Although Post Rock Country may have seemed far away from the battles of World War I, the camaraderie exhibited among its people was most apparent during wartime. In the above photograph, a massive arch has been constructed across Main Street in La Crosse to welcome soldiers returning from the war. Much of the modernization of the Post Rock buildings in the background of the picture began in the years following World War I. The next period of modernization occurred in the late 1940s after the end of World War II. In the image at left, citizens eagerly await the train that will soon be bringing soldiers home to La Crosse.

Five

The Works Progress Administration

The Works Progress Administration (WPA) was established in April 1935 as an agency of the federal government. A product of Pres. Franklin D. Roosevelt's New Deal, its main purpose was to combat unemployment caused by a national economic depression that started in 1929. The WPA cooperated with state and local governments in the field of public works and community service, with projects that included the construction of more than 664,000 miles of highways, 285 airports, water and sewage systems, tunnels, parks, playgrounds, and over 120,000 public buildings.

During the 1930s, WPA workers quarried and used Post Rock in the construction of bridges and public buildings in Rush County. The WPA erected a number of structures in central Kansas, including schools, libraries, shelter houses, and bridges.

In its seven years of operation, the WPA provided employment for over 8.5 million Americans and returned over $10.5 billion into the economy. In 1939, the government changed the organization's name to the Works Projects Administration, and the agency was liquidated in June 1943.

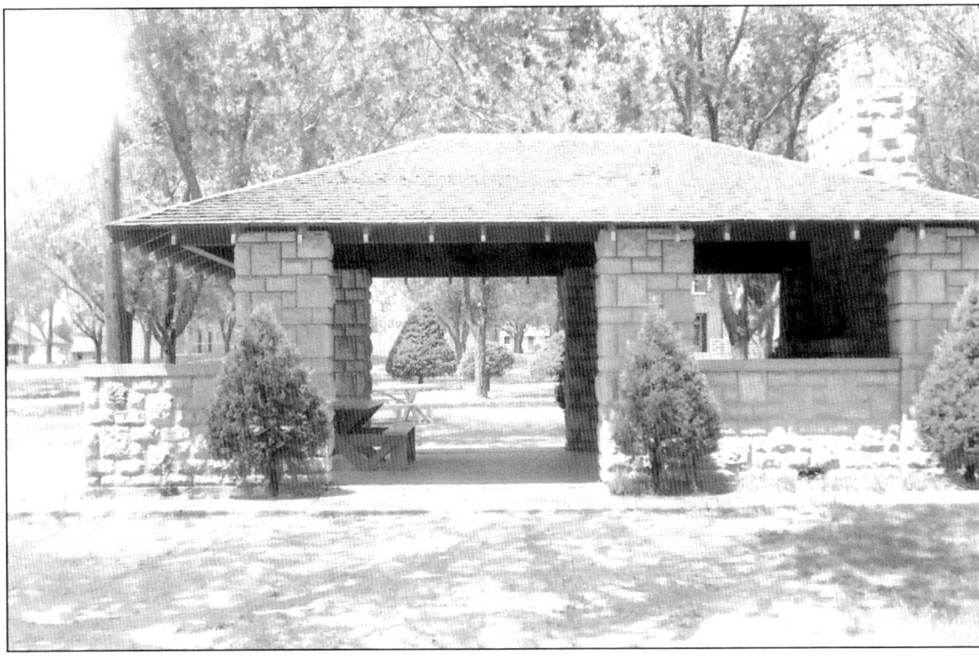

The WPA constructed two identical shelter houses in the La Crosse City Park in 1941. Each features a large fireplace, room for up to four picnic tables, and open side walls with a low roofline to provide protection from the elements. These buildings were some of the last WPA projects completed in La Crosse before World War II.

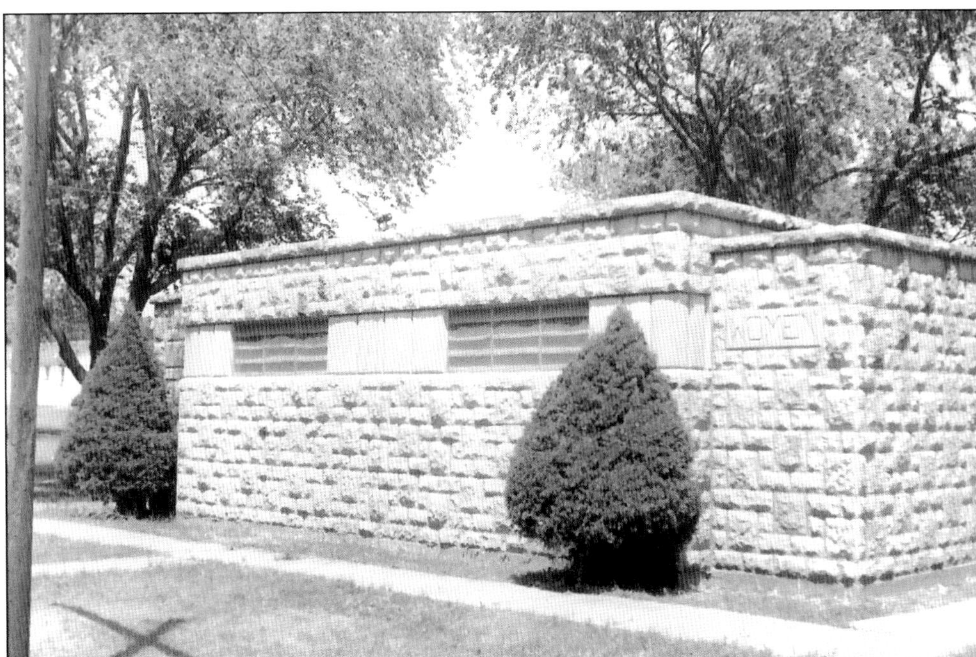

This restroom building, one of the four main Post Rock limestone structures in the La Crosse City Park, was one of the few "sanitary" outdoor public restroom facilities in La Crosse. Doors for each gender are on the ends and protected by privacy walls, with the entrance on the street side.

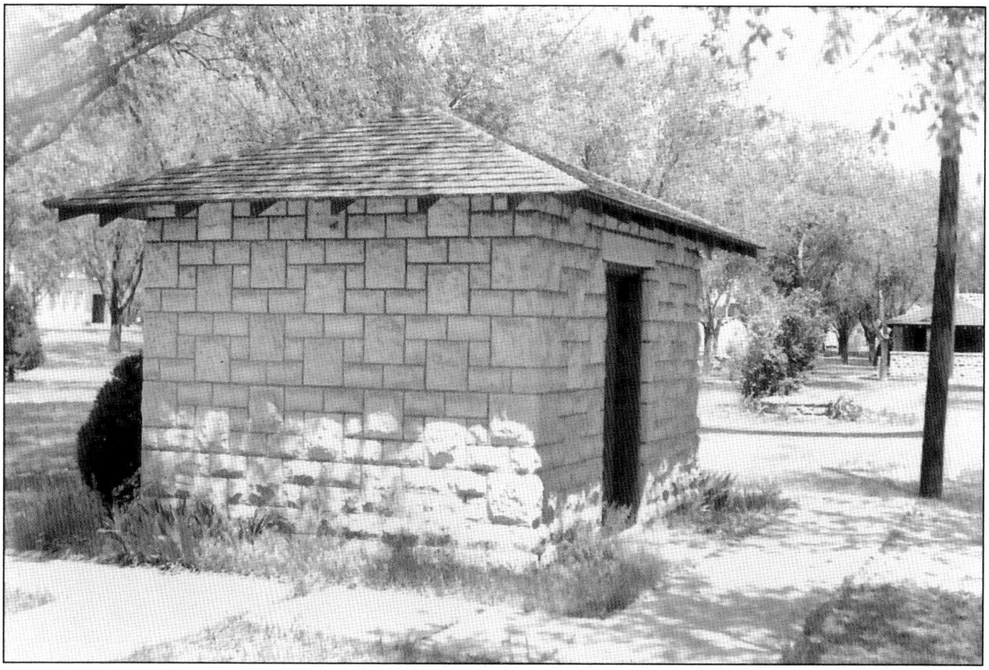

The La Crosse City Park is situated on two city blocks at the south end of Main Street. The design of the park includes two semicircular sidewalks with a fountain placed at the convergence of the arches. Equipment for the pump that powered the illuminated limestone-encircled fountain was housed in this building. In later years, the fountain was converted to a planter and the pump house used to house equipment for a sprinkler system.

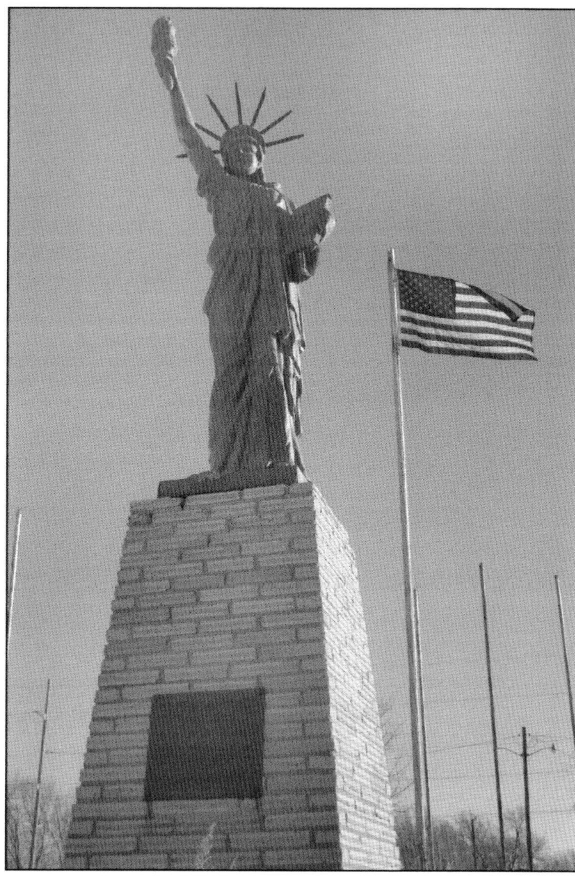

In 1950, in commemoration of their 40th anniversary, the Boy Scouts erected this replica of the Statue of Liberty in the La Crosse City Park as a "pledge of everlasting fidelity and loyalty." Scouts placed more than 200 of these in communities throughout 39 states. The statue is supported by a base of flagstones carved from Post Rock limestone. (Photograph by the author.)

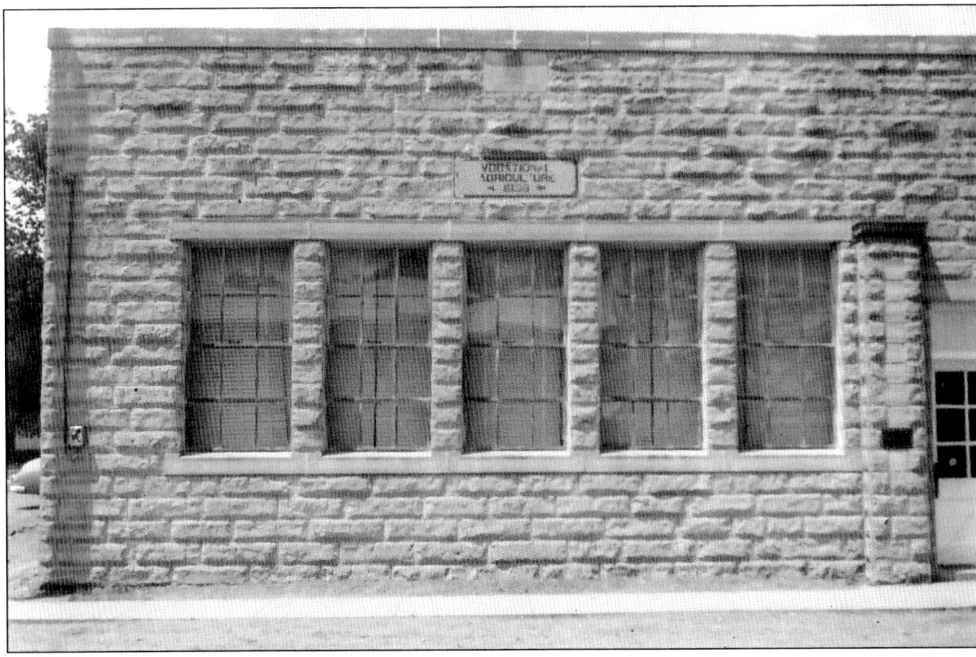

In 1936, WPA workers constructed this building to house vocational agriculture classes for La Crosse High School, located adjacent and to the north of this building. This structure contained a wood shop and welding areas. When the district built a new high school in 1957, the building was remodeled to house locker rooms and a music room for the elementary school.

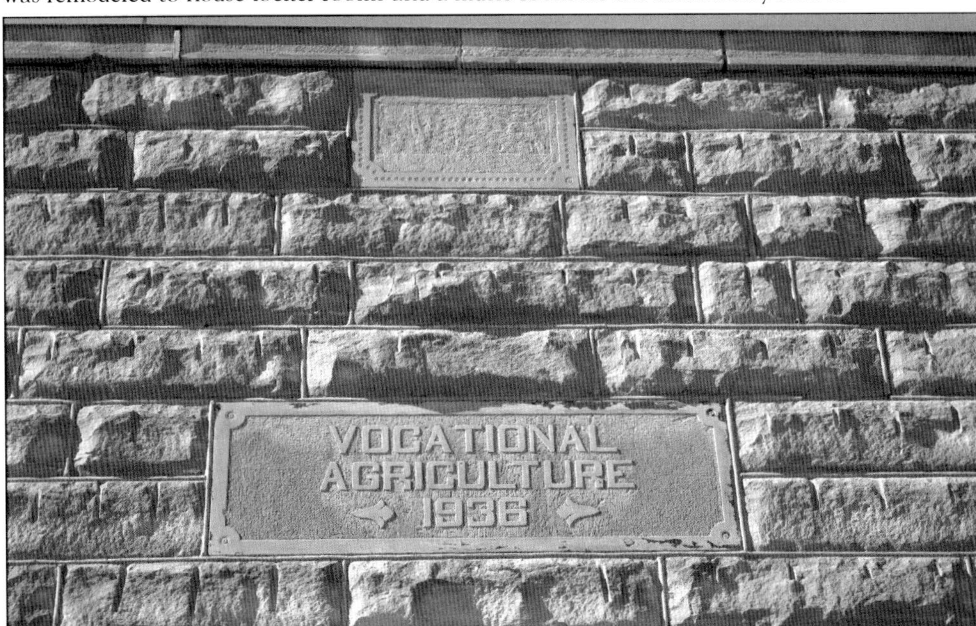

The WPA provided threefold services for small communities like La Crosse—it provided jobs for the unemployed, gave individuals an opportunity to learn new skills, and allowed government agencies to construct buildings at low costs. This limestone date plaque is located at the top of the east wall of the former La Crosse High School vocational agriculture building.

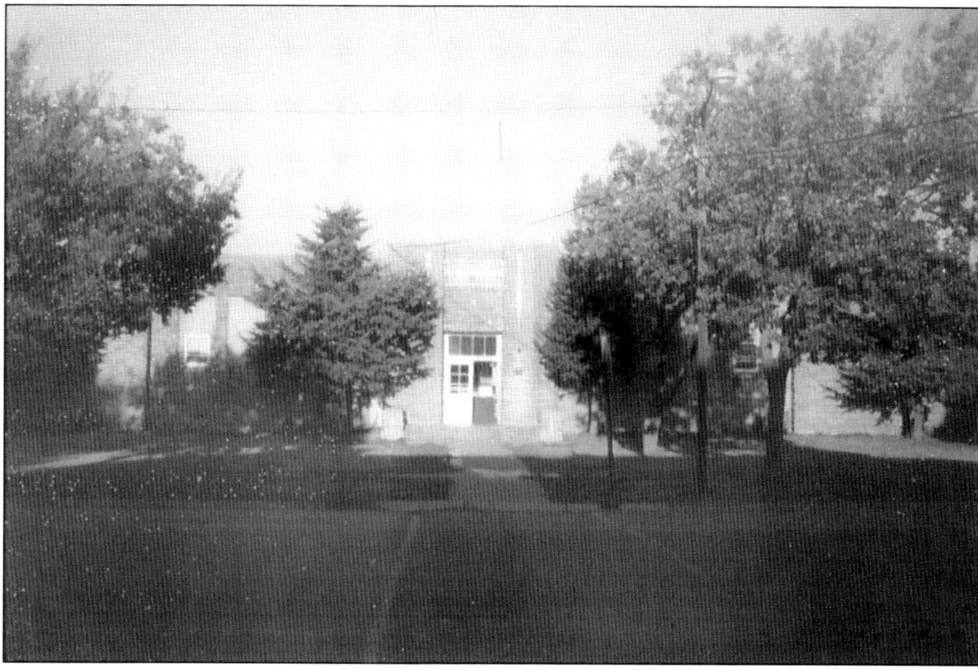

In 1937, WPA workers began construction on a new limestone grade school in Bison on the site of an old two-story frame building that had been used as a combination grade school and high school. The new building was completed and first occupied on February 28, 1938. After school unification in the 1960s, the building was used as a junior high school; it later became Otis-Bison Middle School.

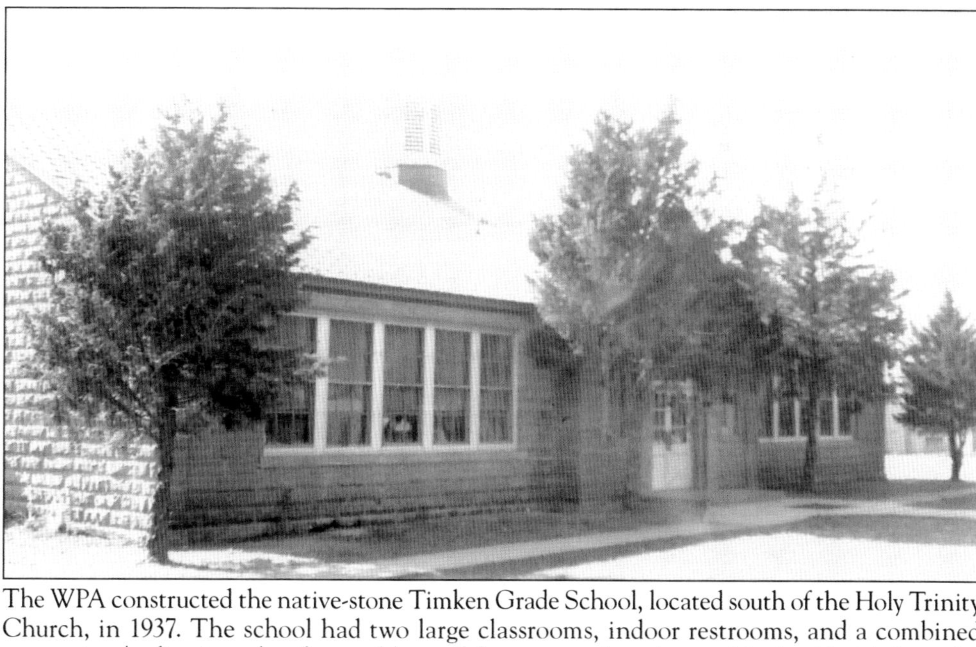

The WPA constructed the native-stone Timken Grade School, located south of the Holy Trinity Church, in 1937. The school had two large classrooms, indoor restrooms, and a combined gymnasium/auditorium that featured beautiful stone carvings (created by Joe Tuzicka) on the large columns that frame the stage. In 1945, a two-room wing was added to the north side of the building. A wing on the south side houses a kitchen and lunchroom.

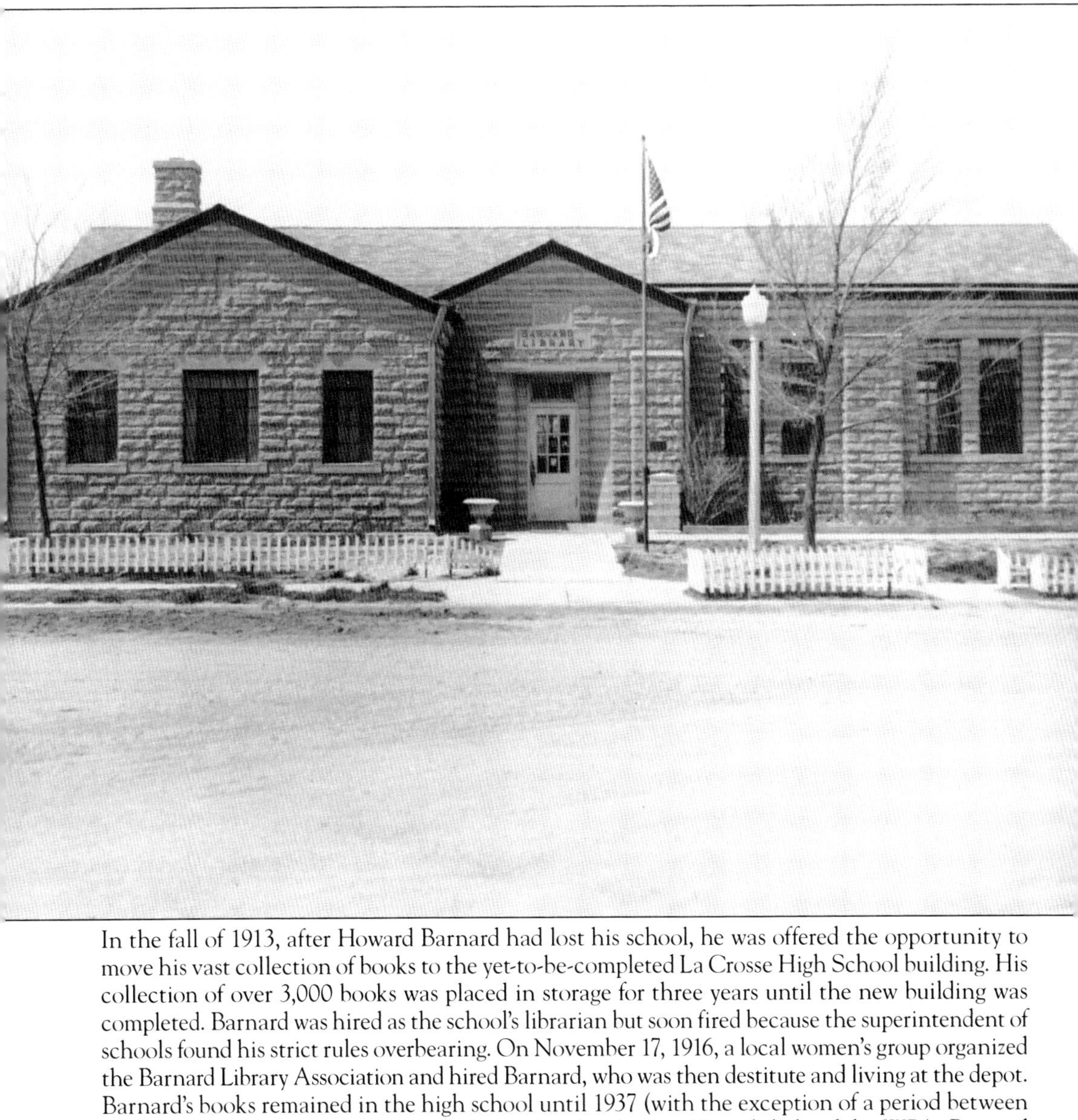

In the fall of 1913, after Howard Barnard had lost his school, he was offered the opportunity to move his vast collection of books to the yet-to-be-completed La Crosse High School building. His collection of over 3,000 books was placed in storage for three years until the new building was completed. Barnard was hired as the school's librarian but soon fired because the superintendent of schools found his strict rules overbearing. On November 17, 1916, a local women's group organized the Barnard Library Association and hired Barnard, who was then destitute and living at the depot. Barnard's books remained in the high school until 1937 (with the exception of a period between 1919 and 1924 when Barnard was teaching elsewhere). In 1937, with help of the WPA, Barnard was honored with a new stone building. At the dedication of the Barnard Library, schools were closed, the community held a parade, and hundreds of Barnard's former pupils cheered.

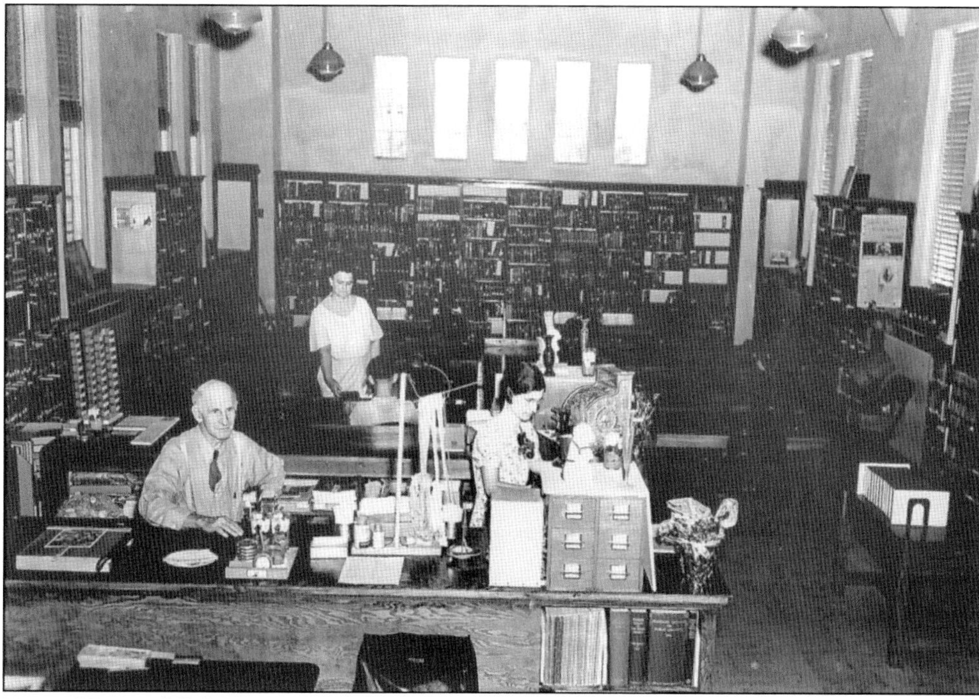

Howard Barnard (left foreground) served as librarian for the Barnard Library Association from 1923 until his death in 1948. He was known for his extremely strict rules regarding library etiquette. There was absolutely no talking in the library, and books were to be handled with the utmost respect. Violation of these rules could result in a slap with a ruler or expulsion from the library.

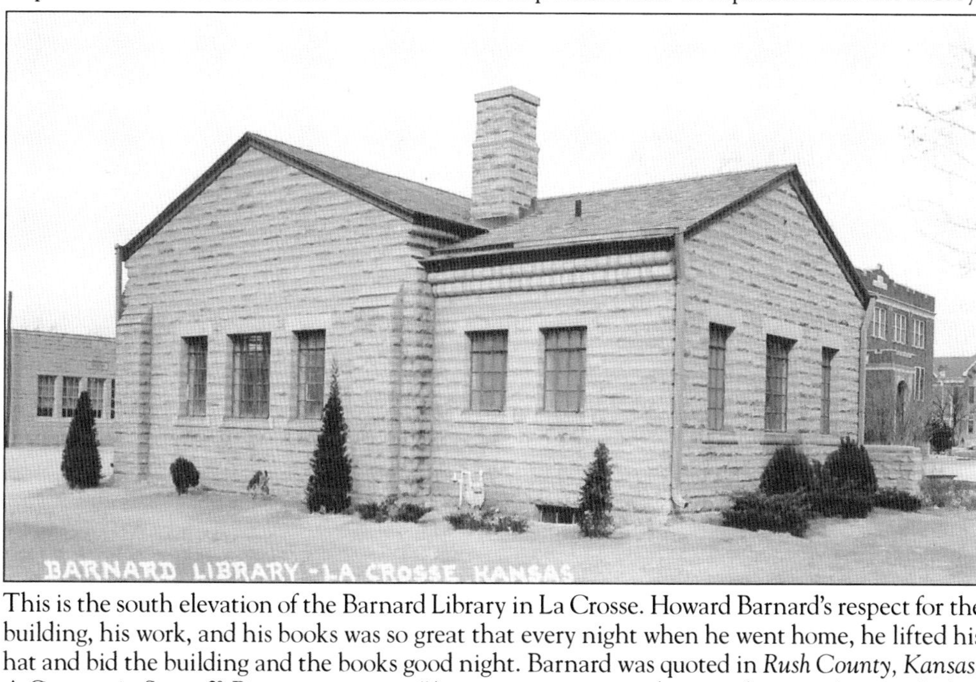

This is the south elevation of the Barnard Library in La Crosse. Howard Barnard's respect for the building, his work, and his books was so great that every night when he went home, he lifted his hat and bid the building and the books good night. Barnard was quoted in *Rush County, Kansas: A Century in Story & Pictures* as saying: "At my age, one never knows what may happen before morning, and I wouldn't want to leave before saying good-bye."

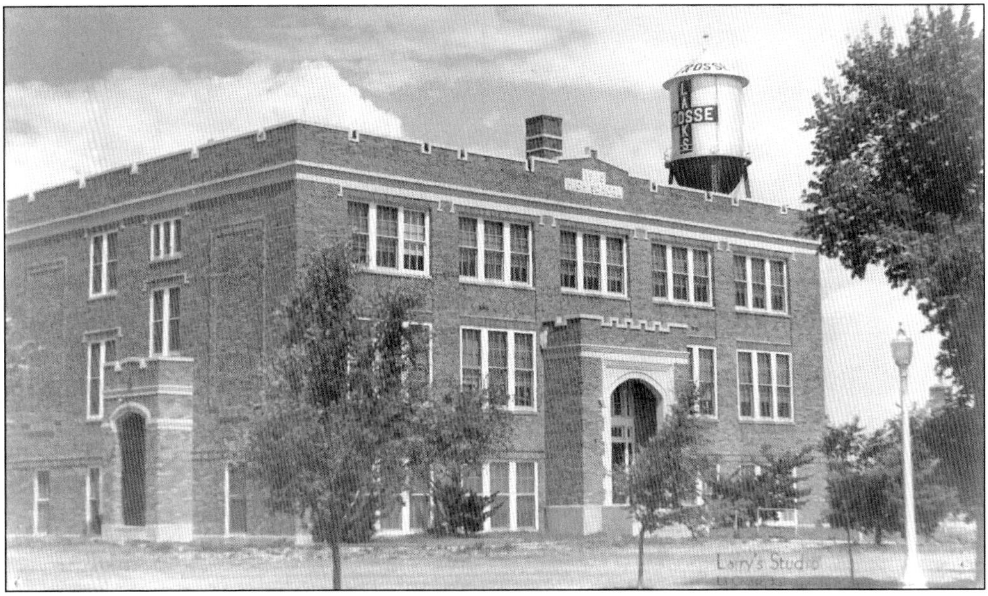

The rapid growth of La Crosse necessitated the construction of a new La Crosse High School building in 1916 to replace the combination grade and high school structure built in 1890. The design of the new school reflected a trend that emphasized function over design, all but eliminating the use of Post Rock. This school was razed after a new building was constructed in 1957.

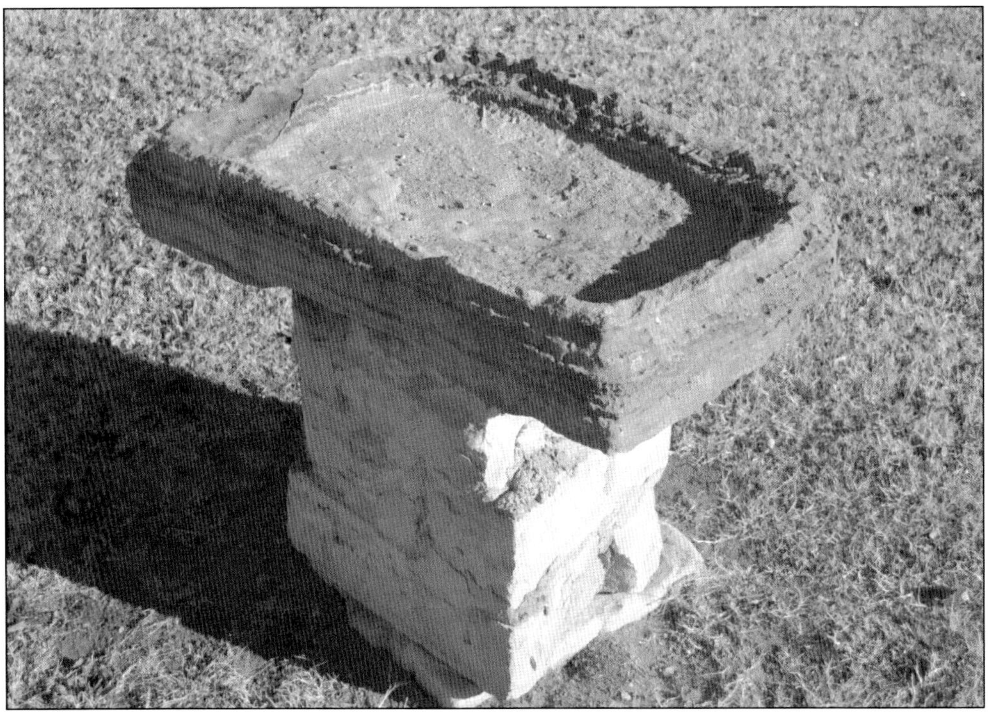

This birdbath located in the La Crosse City Park is an example of the versatility of Post Rock. The base is constructed in standard fashion, and the top was quarried, hollowed out, and sanded to allow it to hold water. The design is similar to that of cattle feeders and water troughs carved from large slabs of stone by the pioneers.

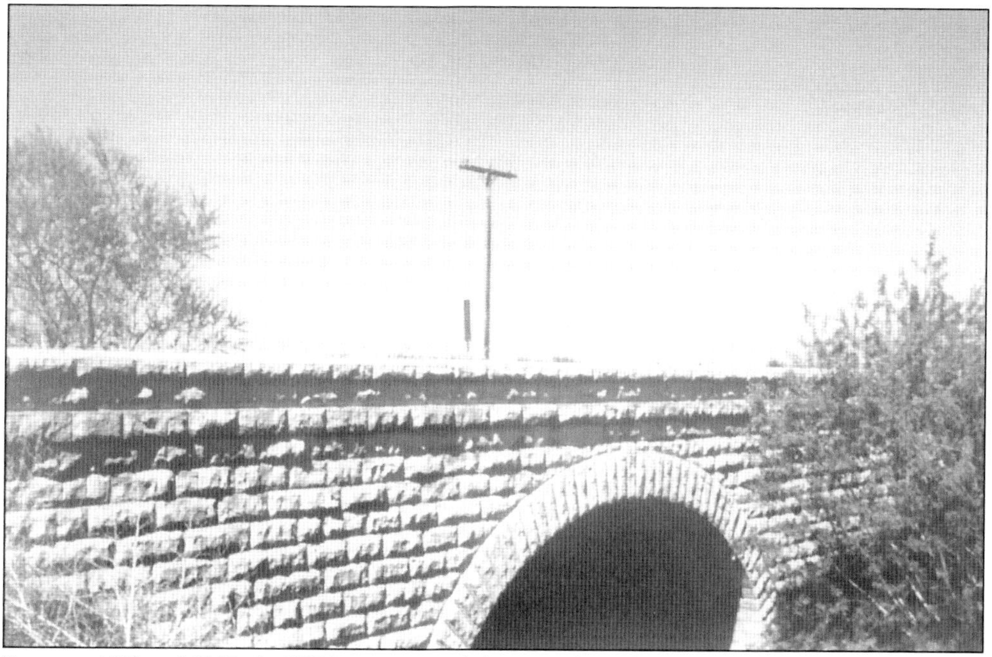

Between 1939 and 1940, the WPA constructed three single-arch limestone bridges in the southern part of Rush County over tributaries of Walnut Creek. The bridges ranged from 20 to 25 feet in length and 20 to 26 feet in width. Exposed stones were dressed in the pitch-face style with smooth-cut capstones and quarry-faced stones beneath the arch.

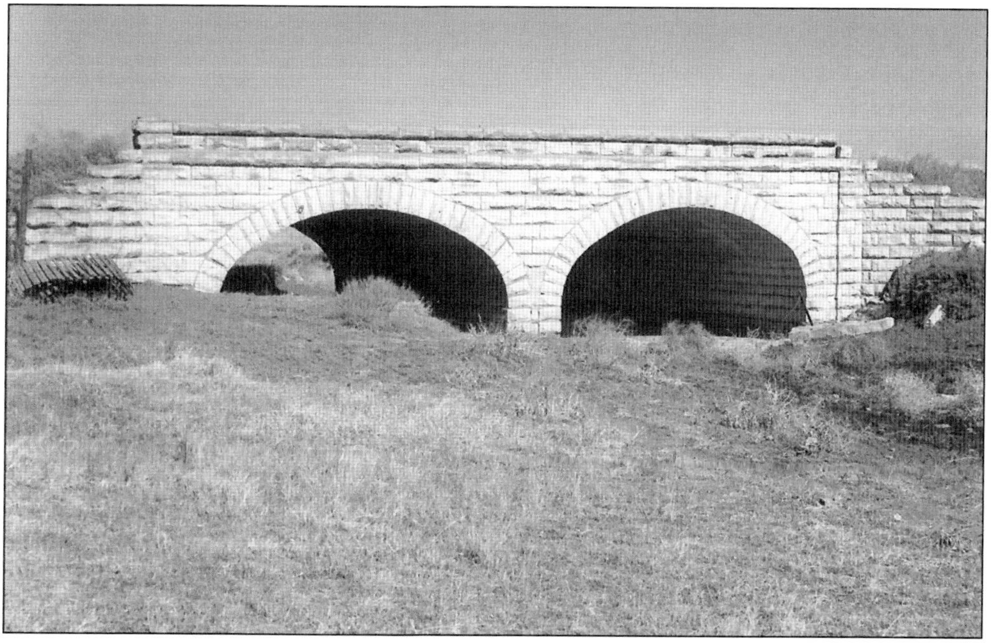

Between 1938 and 1942, the WPA constructed four double-span stone-arch bridges—two in the La Crosse area over small creek beds, and two in the Alexander/Nekoma area near Walnut Creek. Each of the bridges shared the same design, with earth-filled decks and low stone railings that extended from the sides of the bridges with smooth-cut capstones.

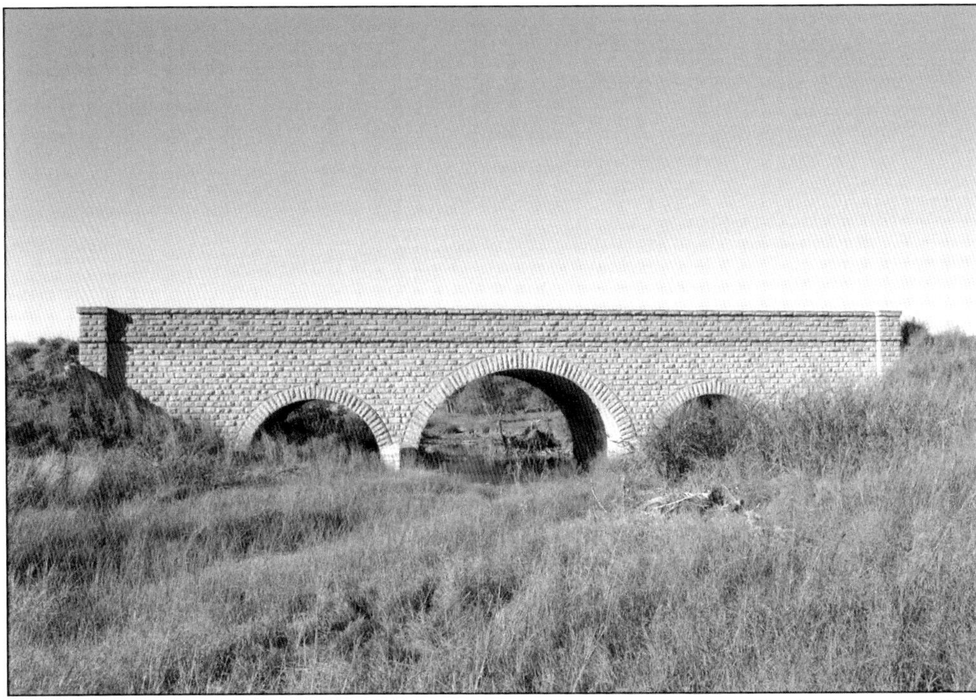

The WPA constructed this triple-arch limestone bridge in northeastern Rush County in 1936. The bridge was 99 feet long with a deck of just over 20 feet—narrow by today's standards. Built as a cooperative project between Rush, Ellis, and Russell Counties, the bridge was situated near the confluence of the three counties on the Rush/Russell County line, about one mile east of the southeastern corner of Ellis County. The bridge was listed in the National Register of Historic Places in 1986. After over 75 years, heavy traffic took its toll on the structure, and it was demolished.

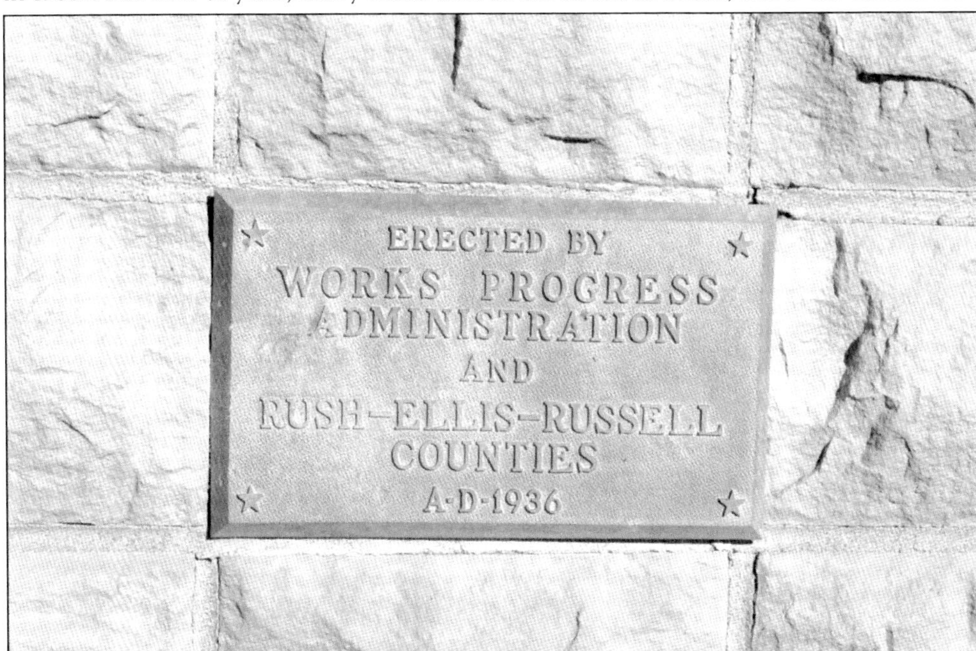

Six

Post Rock Abandoned

Post Rock all but vanished in new construction in the 1920s. Bricks were readily available and reasonably priced, and since bricks were mass-produced, builders no longer had to invest considerable time and labor in quarrying and dressing stones. Local brick mason Henry Welch, who built several early structures in La Crosse, produced his own bricks on site during construction jobs, casting and firing them with makeshift equipment. The labor required was far less than that needed for quarrying, transporting, and handling 300-pound stones.

With the advent of steel posts, the use of Post Rock in the construction of fences was dramatically reduced. Farmers reused existing posts while maintaining their fences, but if a post was broken, it was replaced with a steel post.

In the latter part of the 20th century, Post Rock came back into style. Farmers reconstructed stone fences along well-traveled roads, stone buildings were sandblasted and repaired, and—as a tribute to the region's heritage—posts or slabs of Post Rock limestone were engraved for use as signs in front of homes and businesses.

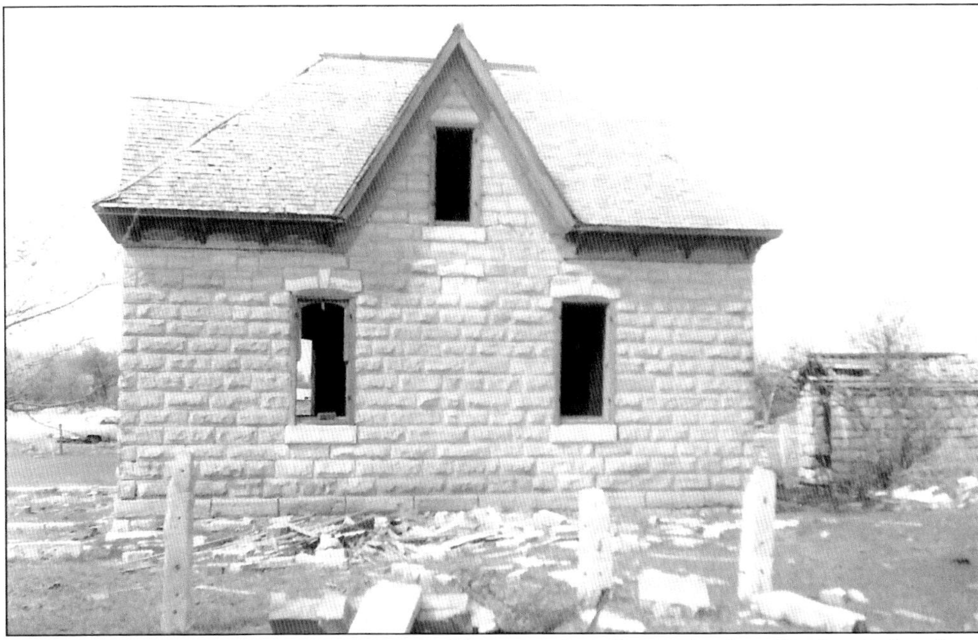

This one-and-a-half-story house and outbuilding stood on the south edge of Liebenthal and was one of the town's first homes. Although the windows have been removed, the structure appears to be intact in this c. 1960 photograph. Later residents placed a modular home on the property, leaving the stone to decay. This, the stone home, has been dismantled.

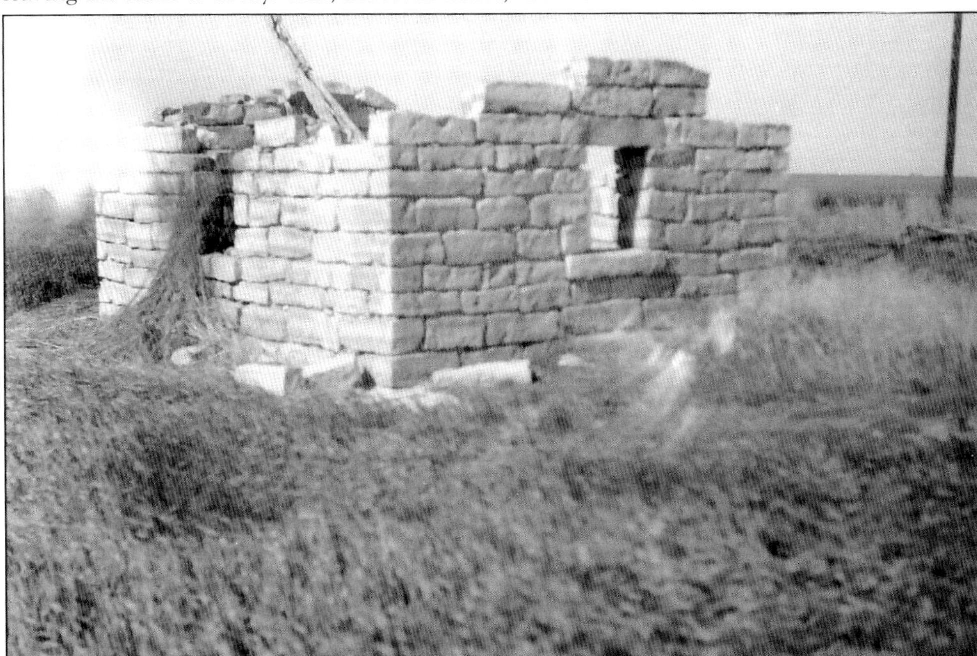

These are the ruins of a stone farmhouse near Bison in the 1960s; nearly all of the wooden sections are gone. This home was one of the first built in the county and is an excellent example of basic quarry construction with minimal use of mortar, which gives the appearance of stones that were loosely stacked.

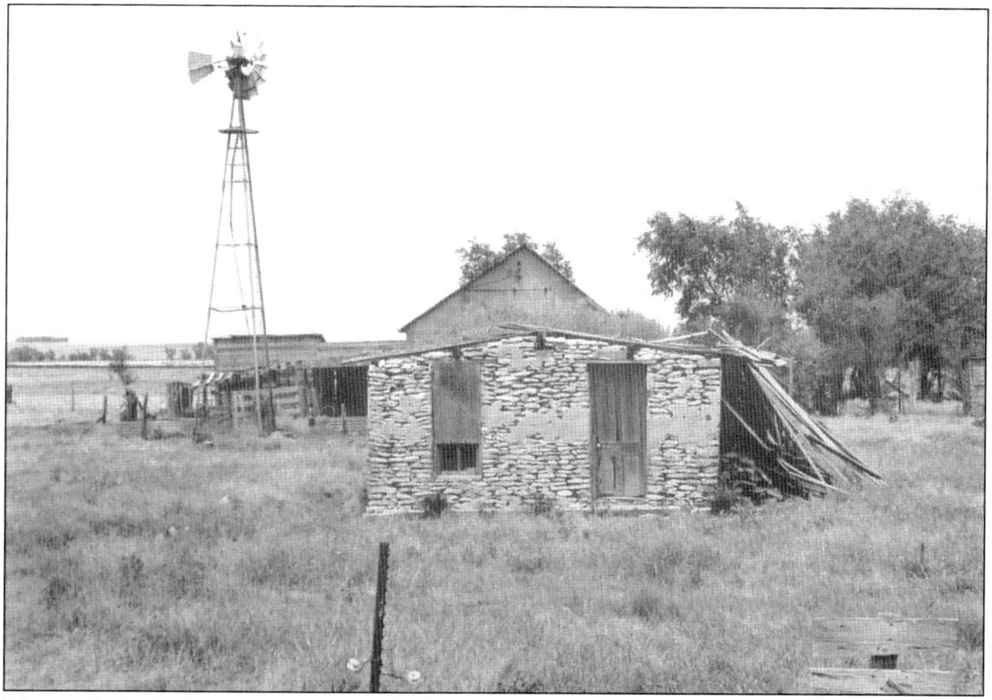

This early Rush County structure is built from dry-stacked stone. Dry-stacked walls are built without mortar to allow stones to shift slightly to avoid cracks or shifts from freezing. The exterior of the structure was covered in a stucco-type material to seal out moisture and help bind the stones. The barn and windmill were added later. (Photograph by the author.)

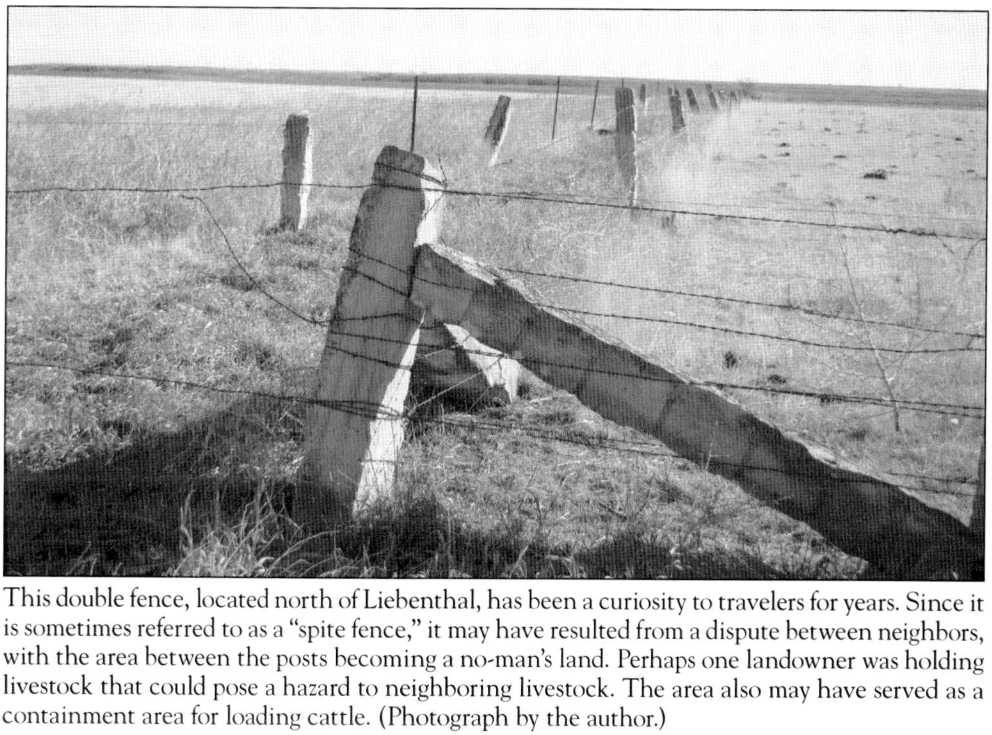

This double fence, located north of Liebenthal, has been a curiosity to travelers for years. Since it is sometimes referred to as a "spite fence," it may have resulted from a dispute between neighbors, with the area between the posts becoming a no-man's land. Perhaps one landowner was holding livestock that could pose a hazard to neighboring livestock. The area also may have served as a containment area for loading cattle. (Photograph by the author.)

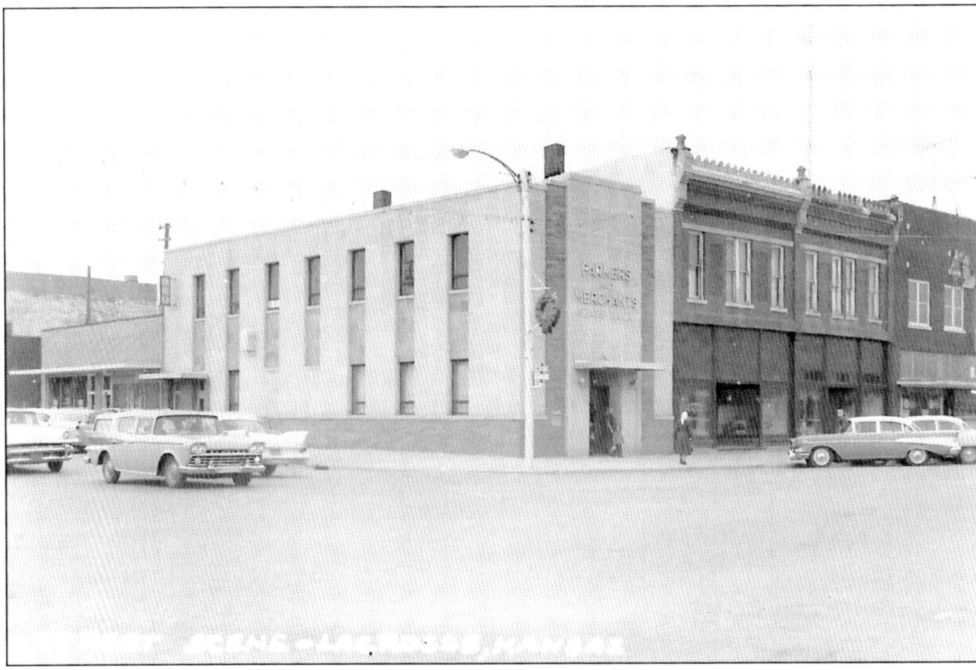

On April 1, 1954, major renovation began on the southern third of the Farmers & Merchants State Bank building. The columned, arched portico and corner entrance were removed, and the floor was lowered to street level. The ornamental cornices were removed, and the native-stone and brick exterior was covered in nonnative Silverdale and Colorado stone. In 1974, the lower level of the center section of the building was modernized, and both portions of the building were covered with a metal grate. In 1982, the building again underwent renovations, and the entire structure was covered with a new brick veneer. The image above shows the building in 1955; the picture below shows the totally transformed building in 1983. (Both, AC.)

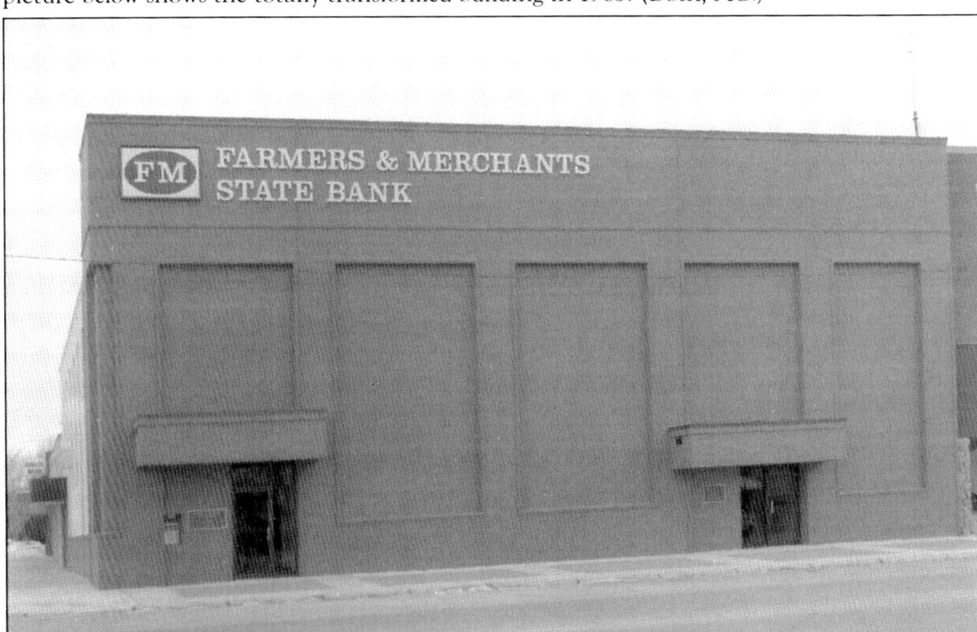

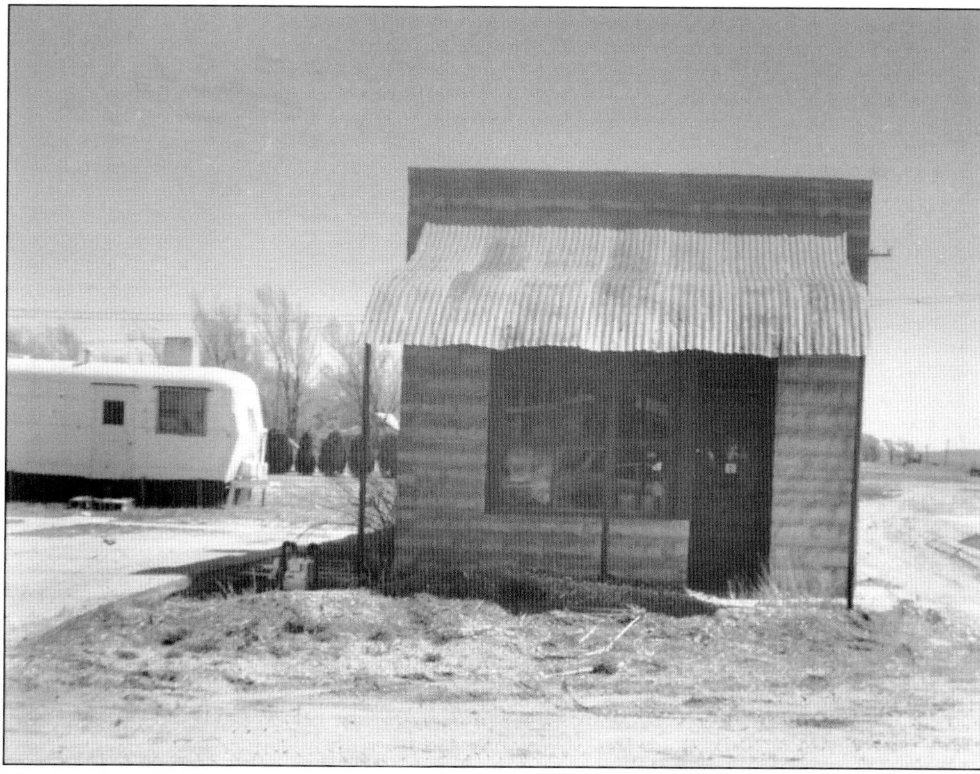

This small Post Rock store appears to sit abandoned on the south end of Main Street in Alexander. At one time, Main Street in Alexander had several stores; a lumberyard; a post office; a bank; grain elevators; and an eye, ear, nose, and throat hospital. By the end of the 20th century, only the elevator and post office remained. (AC.)

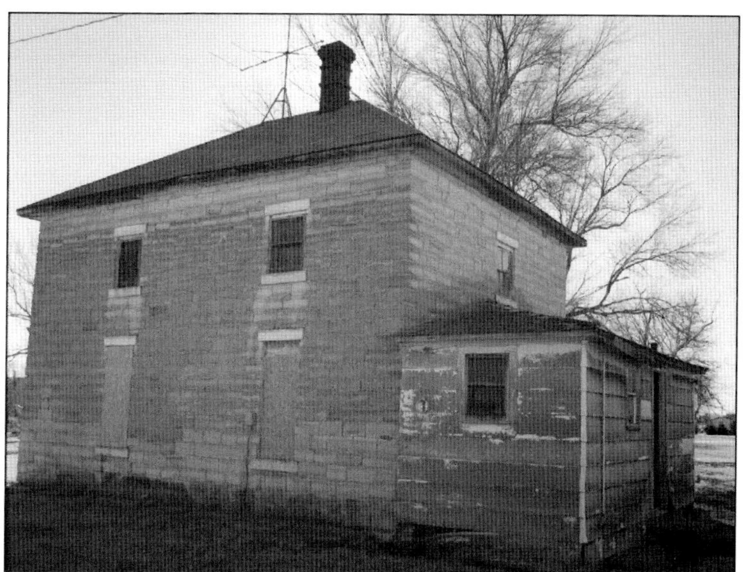

This house is believed to be the oldest standing home in Liebenthal. Jacob Herrman Sr., one of the original settlers who arrived in 1876, built it in 1886. The rectangular house—with four rooms on the main level, a hip roof, and a central chimney—was characteristic of the Volga German architecture in Herrman's homeland in Russia. (AC.)

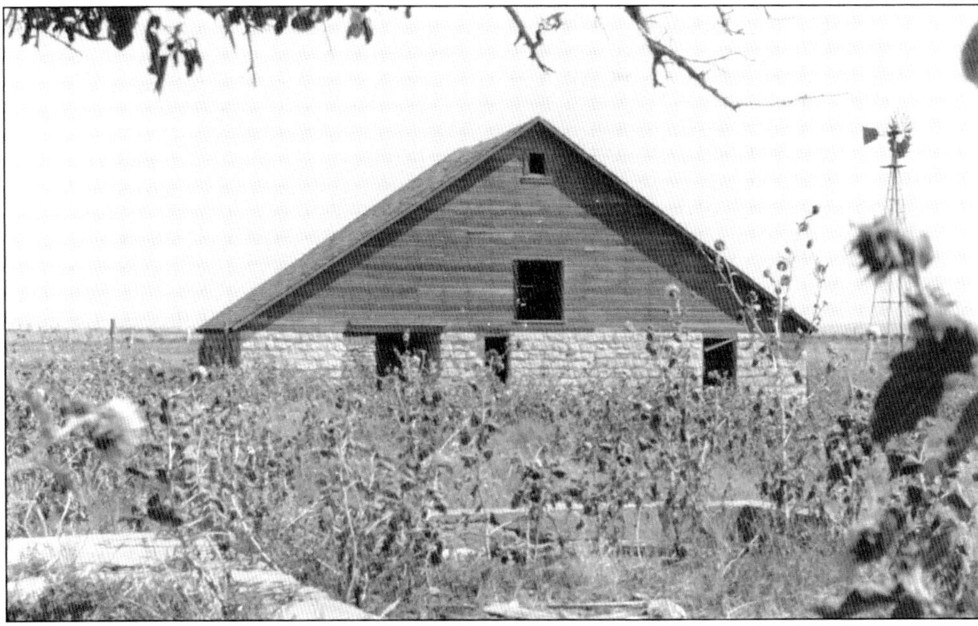

A number of barns were built in this style using Post Rock for the main level and conventional wood-frame construction for the upper floor and roof. The heavy stone walls created a strong enclosure to shelter livestock. After this barn, located north of Liebenthal, was abandoned in the late 20th century, the building burned; only a portion of the stone walls remains. (AC.)

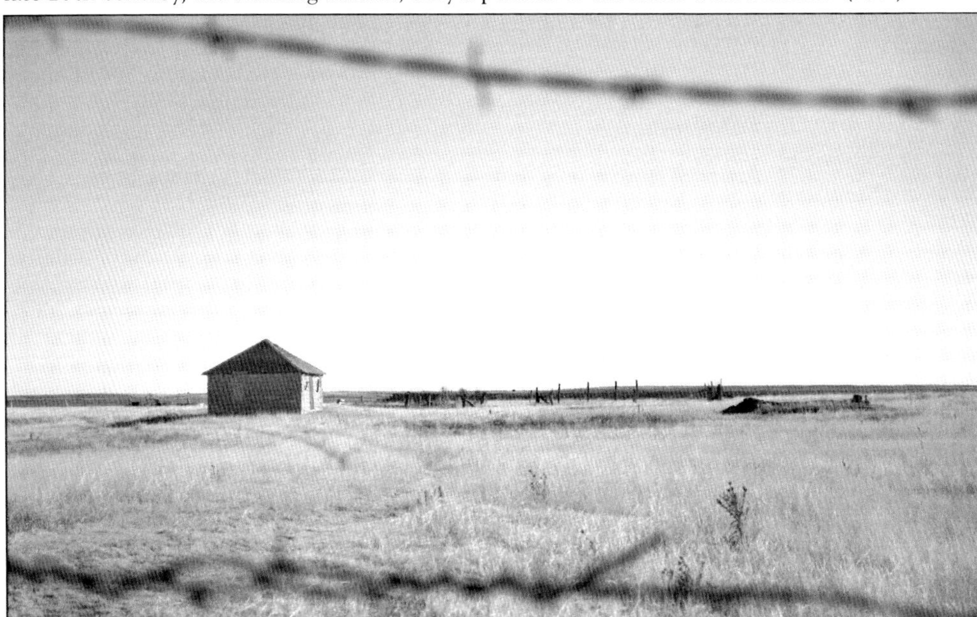

This isolated stone house stands a short distance from US Highway 183 north of Liebenthal. As with many abandoned farmsteads, unusable frame buildings were removed, leaving the stone foundations. Limestone buildings are more difficult to tear down and were left standing. Sometimes livestock could roam around the building, or the land was farmed to the edge of the building. (AC.)

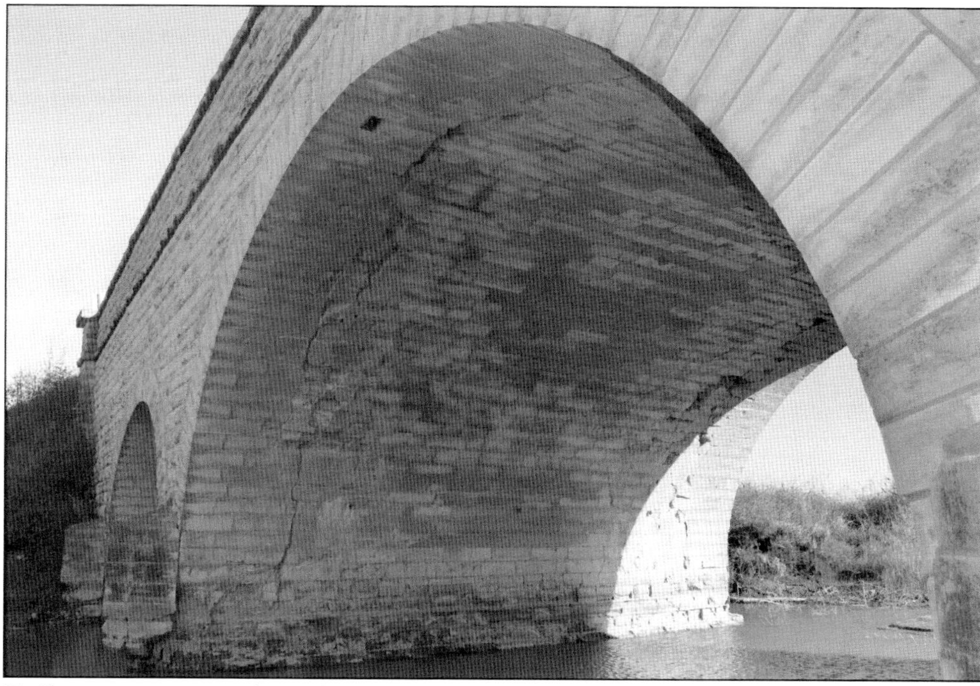

Traffic put excessive weight on the triple-arch bridge built in 1936 by the WPA on the Rush/Russell County line. Vibration from heavy-equipment traffic caused the limestone walls to separate from the stone arches that supported the earth-filled deck. Repair costs were deemed too high, and the bridge was condemned and destroyed in 2014. (Photograph by the author.)

Throughout the late 1800s and early 1900s, this Post Rock wall supported a pin-truss bridge that crossed Walnut Creek south of Rush Center. When the county built a new highway bridge, the old abutment was abandoned and overgrown with vegetation. The limestone was removed in April 2010 during grading for a new bridge. (Photograph by the author.)

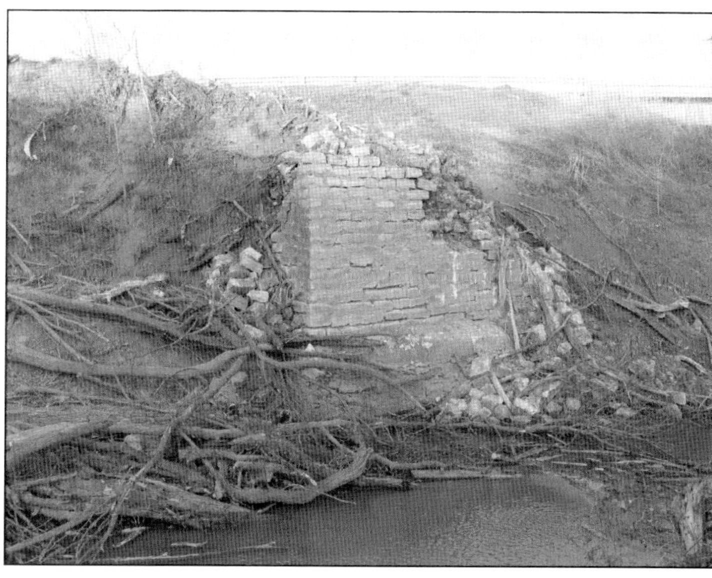

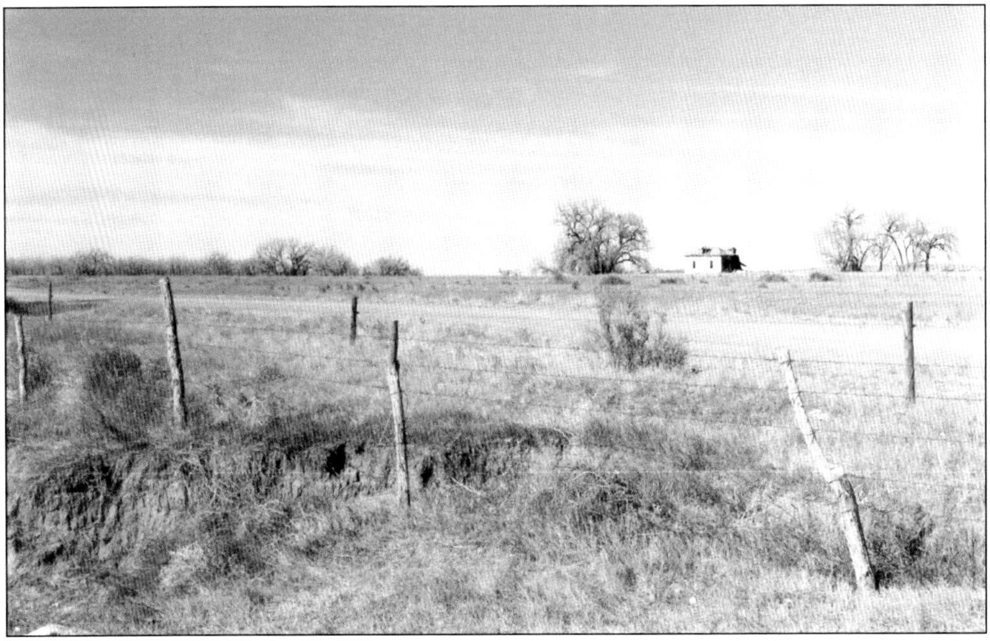

This homestead—located in western Kansas, to the west of Post Rock Country—was settled sometime before 1923. Lester Settle lived here as a child for about two years with his grandparents while his parents were building a stone house modeled after the home on the property (shown below). The last family to occupy the house was the Marcus family. The house had a double wall with mud used for mortar and between the two walls for insulation. The stone used for the house was quarried from the Post Rock bed and shipped by wagon in slabs—two at a time—to the site. (Both, courtesy Patricia Duffey.)

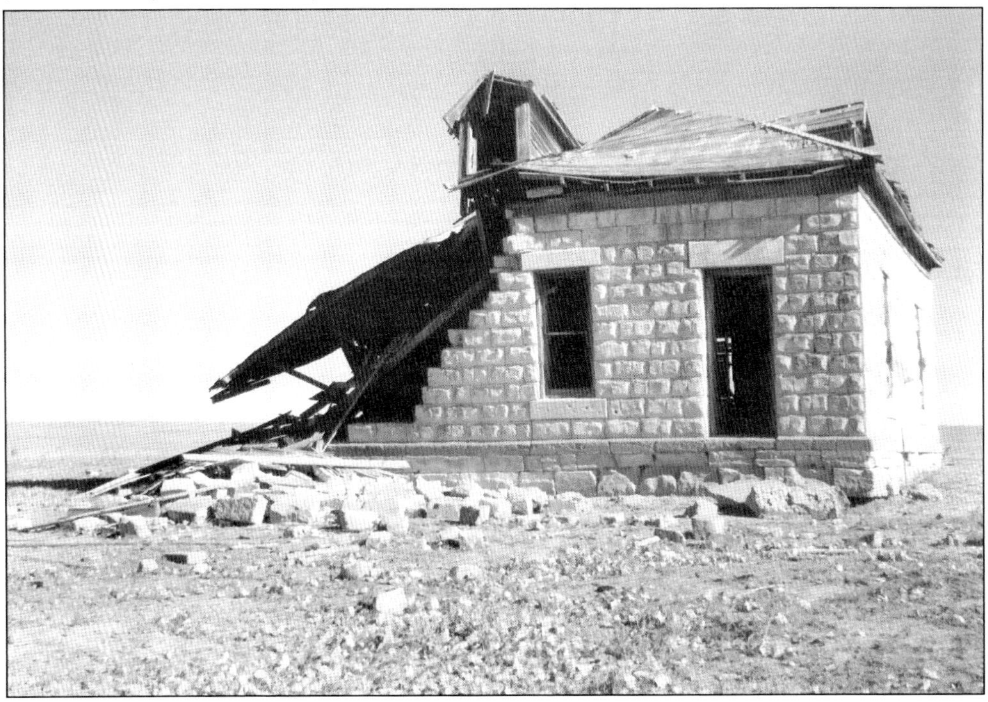

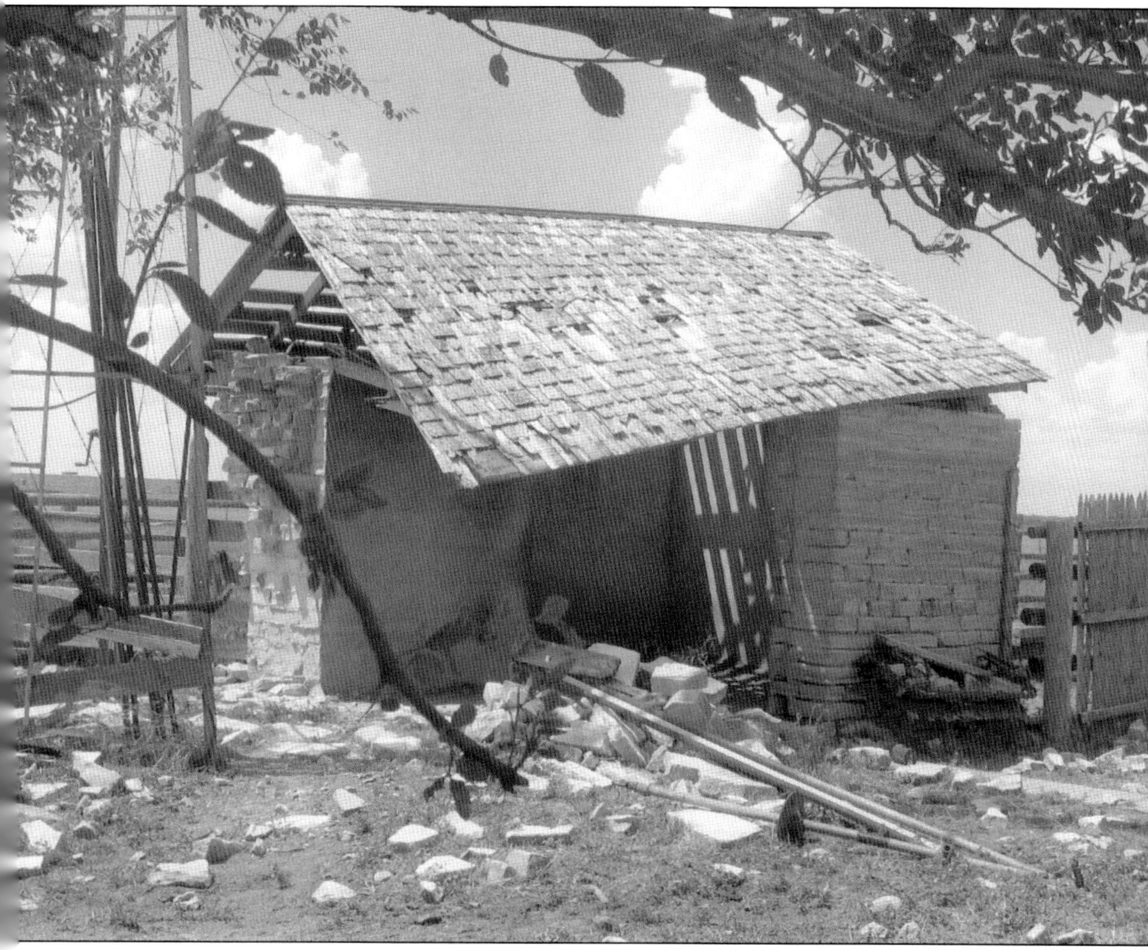

This picture shows the remains of a Post Rock limestone cooling house located south of La Crosse. Cooling houses were used in the 1800s and early 1900s for water and food storage; they could also serve as washhouses. Cooling houses were typically constructed next to a windmill, with a pipe from the well pump to an inlet at the top of a storage tank located inside the building. When the tank was filled, a release valve at the bottom of the tank could be opened, and gravity—combined with pressure created by the weight of the water—provided a pressurized water system. This building was constructed using multiple thicknesses of limestone in the walls to provide insulation and keep the interior cool. After the invention of refrigeration, cooling houses were no longer needed and were abandoned. (Photograph by the author.)

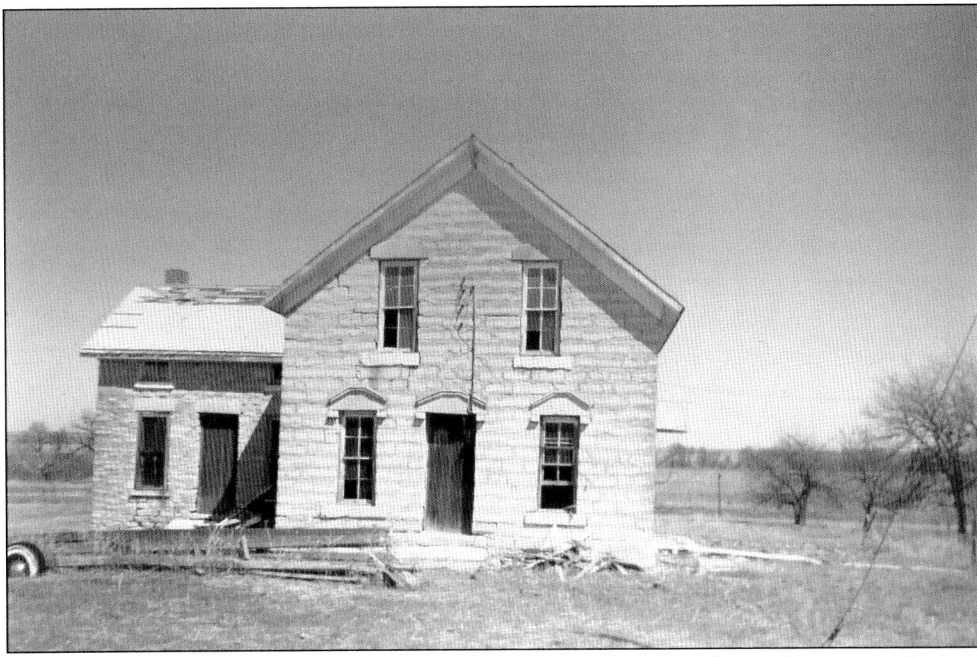

This abandoned homestead, photographed in 1979, stands east of Nekoma. The one-and-a-half-story home is constructed from native limestone. A later addition was constructed of an entirely different style of stone cut into a much smaller size. (AC.)

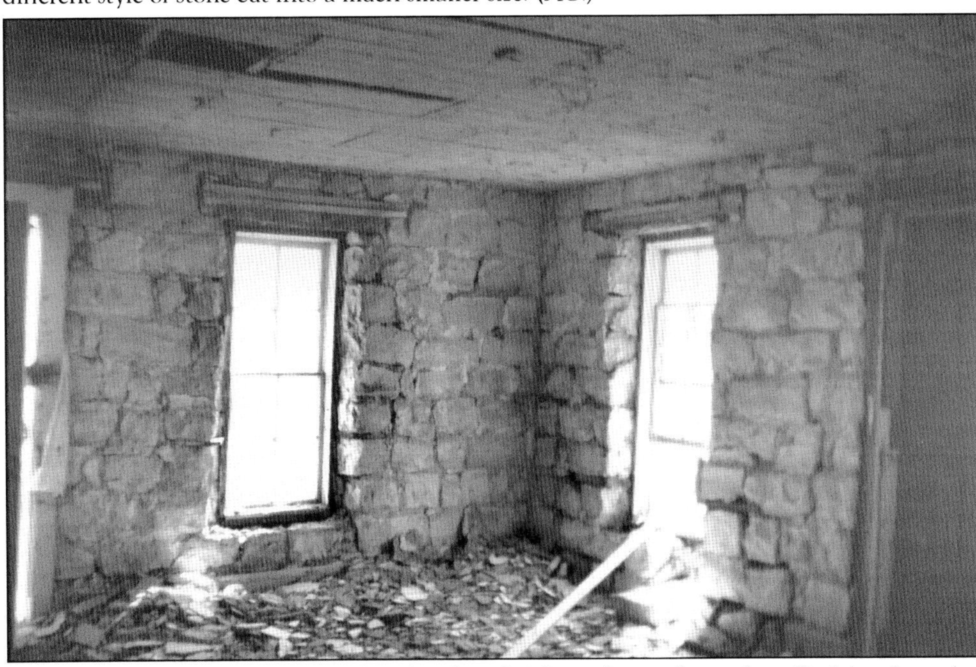

This photograph of the interior of the abandoned Nekoma house shows that all of the plaster has fallen from the first-floor interior of the limestone home. Much of the mortar from the interior layer of the double-walled house has also started to deteriorate. Note that the headers over windows and doors on the interior were constructed of wood, although exterior corbels were cut from large pieces of stone. (AC.)

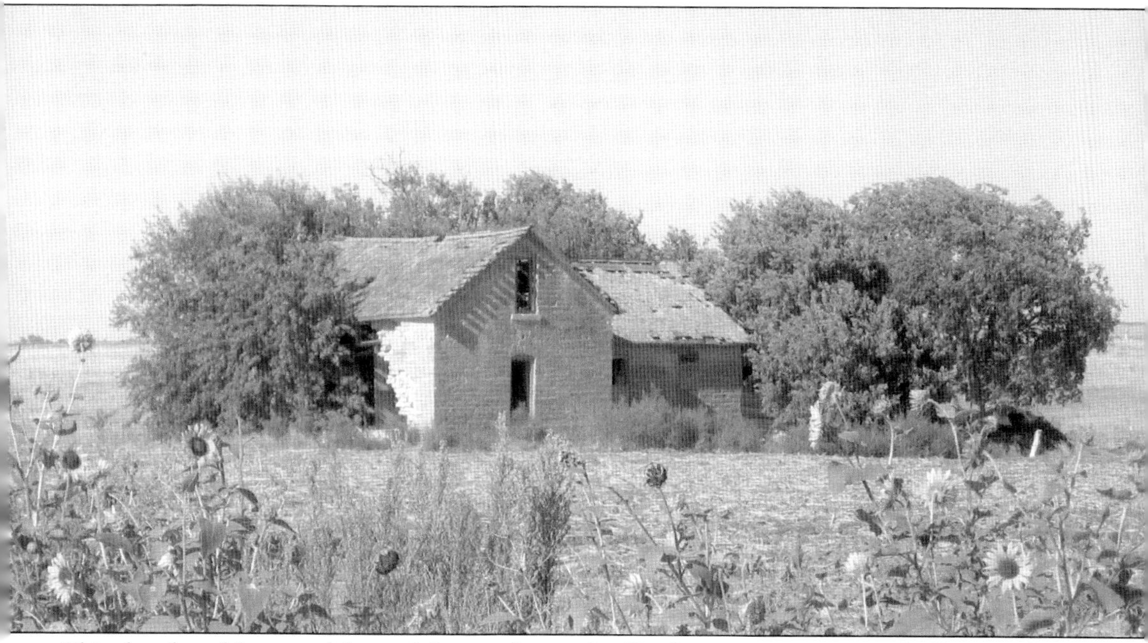

This abandoned farmstead, located three miles north of La Crosse, was constructed of Post Rock around 1900. After being abandoned for several decades, the home is almost obscured by trees and vegetation. With its collapsed wall, missing windows, and decayed roof, the building is a typical example of many abandoned farms (and their outbuildings and barns) throughout the region, most of which have long since been removed. As the number of family farms began to diminish after World War II, more and more structures were left to decay. During the latter part of the 20th century, the country saw a resurgence of interest in rural homes—minus the farmland. Unfortunately, most of the beautiful homes had reached a state of decay that made renovation not economically feasible. (Photograph by the author.)

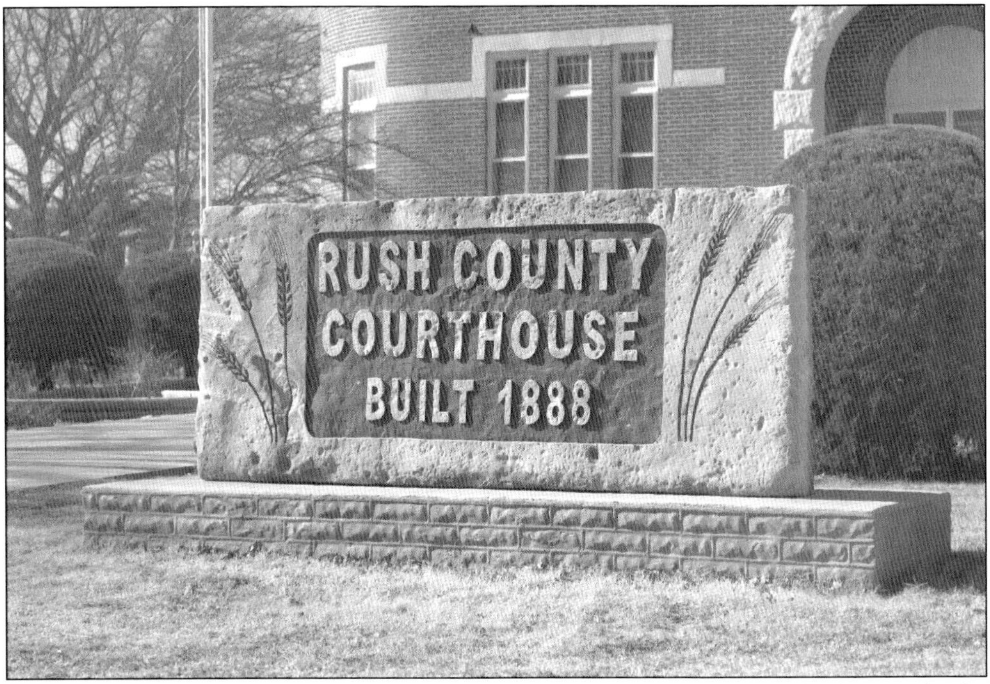

In recent years, Post Rock that would have been scrapped has been repurposed. This sign for the Rush County Courthouse is carved from a slab of Post Rock that once served as a step for the sheriff's office and jail. When the county constructed an addition to connect the sheriff's office to the courthouse, necessitating the step's removal, the stone was carefully engraved and placed in this upright position. (Photograph by the author.)

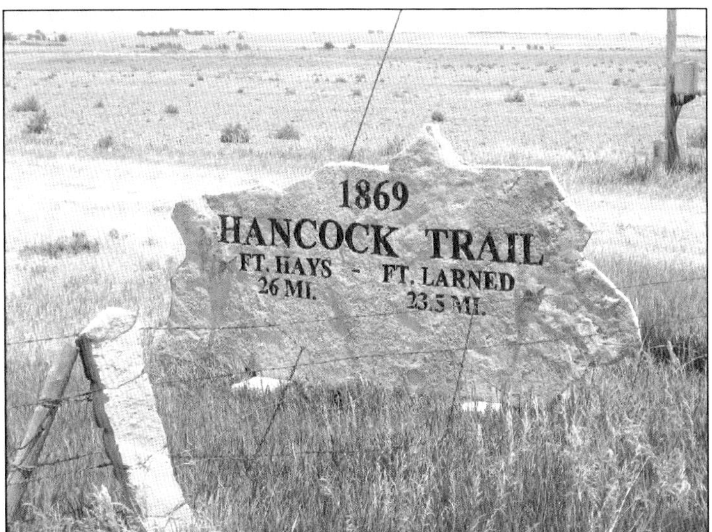

The Gen. Winfield Scott Hancock Trail served as a freight and mail road between Fort Hays and Fort Larned. This marker, located southeast of La Crosse, was carved from native limestone quarried nearby. Post Rock Country contains many public buildings with signs engraved in Post Rock, as well as fence posts engraved with family names and used as yard decorations. (Photograph by the author.)

Seven

A Museum for Post Rock

The idea for the Post Rock Museum began with longtime La Crosse barber Bill Appel. While visiting with clients, Appel frequently fielded questions about the peculiar limestone posts alongside the highways. In 1963, Appel organized a meeting with Harry Grass, president of the Farmers & Merchants State Bank; Roy Ehly, manager of the Southwestern Bell office; and other interested citizens. After some "barbershop talk" and $100 seed money from Appel, the group began building a museum about Post Rock. The group reactivated the Rush County Historical Society, which had been dormant since the celebration of the Kansas Centennial in 1961. The society was reactivated on May 1, 1963, with Ehly serving as president, Oliver Wilhelm as vice-president, Grass as secretary, and Stan Merrill as treasurer. With donations totaling $7,500, the group embarked on the task of locating a building to house the museum.

After considering a number of vacant native-stone homes and buildings around the county, they chose a vacant home situated on a parcel of land owned by Martin Hemken, an officer in Grass's bank and one the individuals involved in the historical society, and Hemken donated the late-19th-century home to the society. Stone-by-stone, the house was dismantled and moved from its original location south of Nekoma, Kansas, to Grass Park in La Crosse. Dozens of local individuals and organizations donated their time, talents, and materials to help create the museum. The museum was dedicated on May 17, 1964.

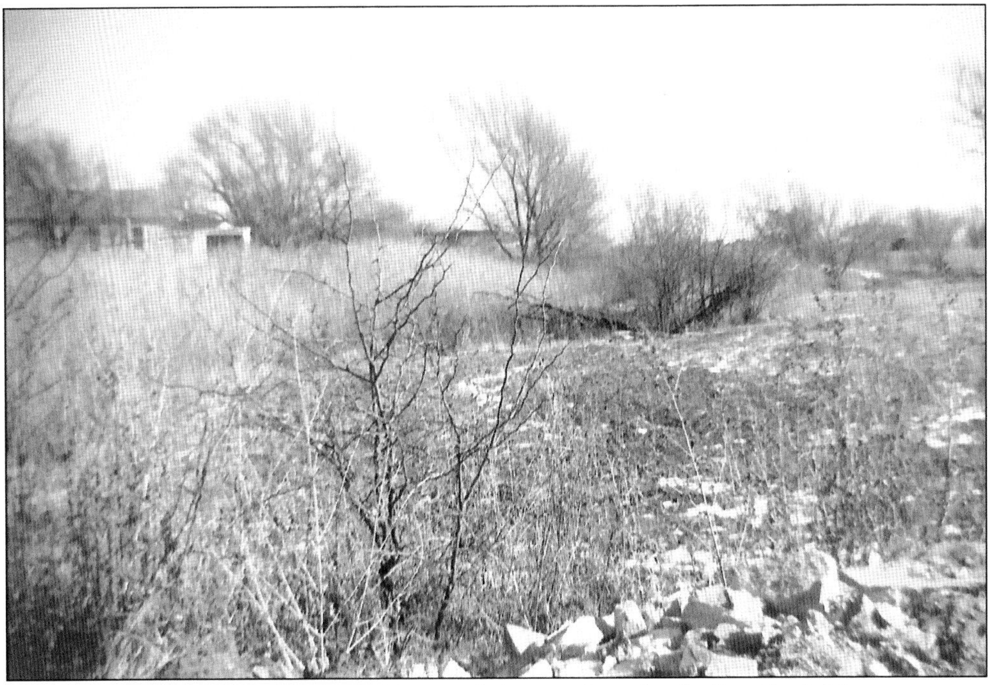

The location that the Rush County Historical Society chose for the Post Rock Museum was an undeveloped area known as Grass Park and located at the southern edge of La Crosse. The family of Harry Grass Sr. had donated the nearly four-square-block parcel of land to the city in 1954. A portion of the land next to the highway was used as a state-maintained picnic area; however, the rest of the land was undeveloped.

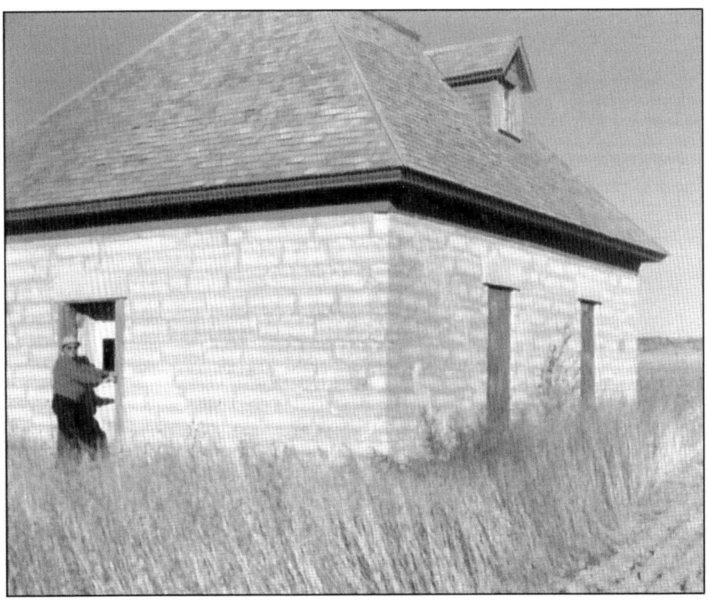

Representatives of the Rush County Historical Society scouted the county in 1962 in search of a stone building to house the museum. A number of types and sizes of abandoned buildings were reviewed before the group found the right structure. This is the building they selected—a single-level stone house located south of Nekoma. It was about 28 feet by 28 feet with a partial second story and two dormer windows.

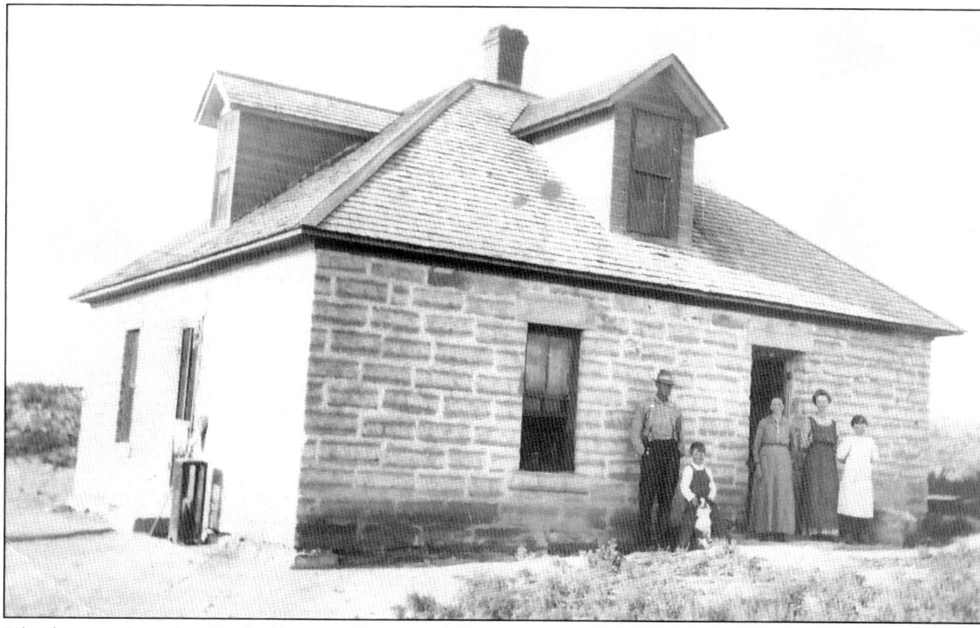

The house that the Rush County Historical Society selected was known as the "Murphy house" and was located southwest of Nekoma. Dan Haley constructed the house in 1883, and it was later occupied by the Sam Murphy family. Pictured here are, from left to right, Sam Murphy; his son, Kim Murphy; his mother, Rose Murphy; his wife, Ida Murphy; and his daughter, Rose Murphy.

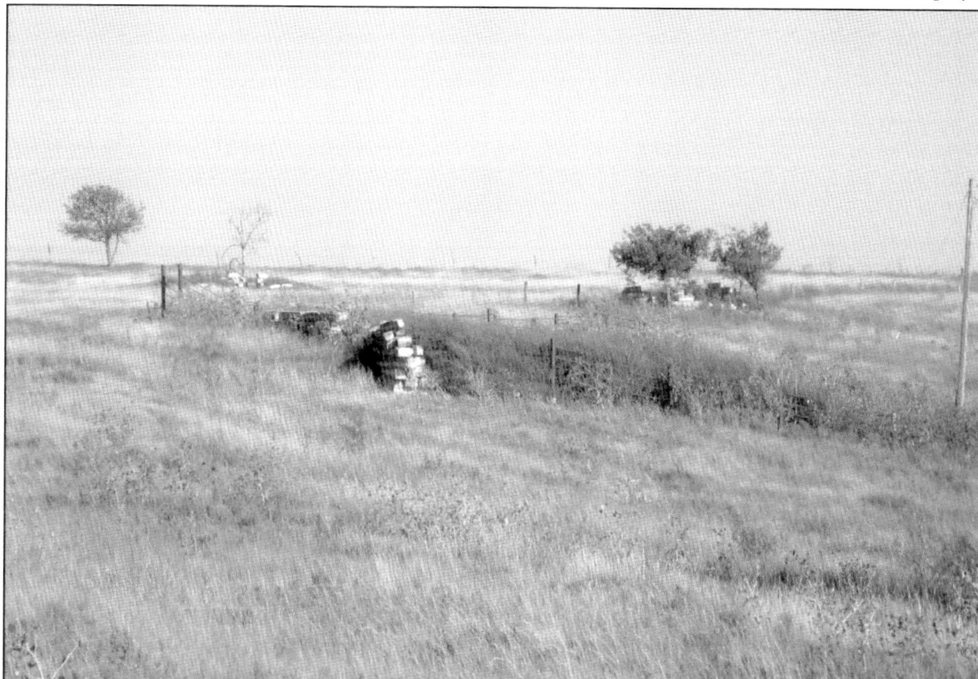

Historical records indicate that the stone for the Murphy house was quarried near where the home was built. In 2007, Brad Penka researched the original location of the Murphy house, and these remains of a Post Rock barn and other buildings were discovered nearby.

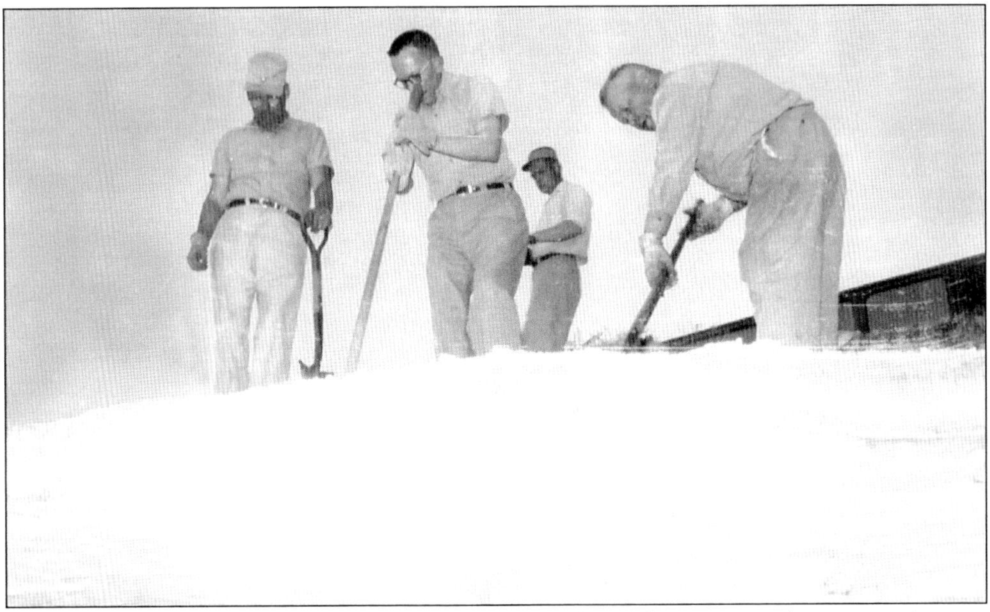

The Rush County Historical Society planned to include a full-size quarry diorama in the new museum. The society selected an existing quarry, owned by Emma Meinen and located four miles west and four miles south of Rush Center, to obtain the large slabs of rock. Pictured here are, from left to right, Allen McChristian, Harry Grass, Ben Payton, and A.W. Carbaugh—they were just beginning to remove the overburden (soil) to expose the Post Rock layer.

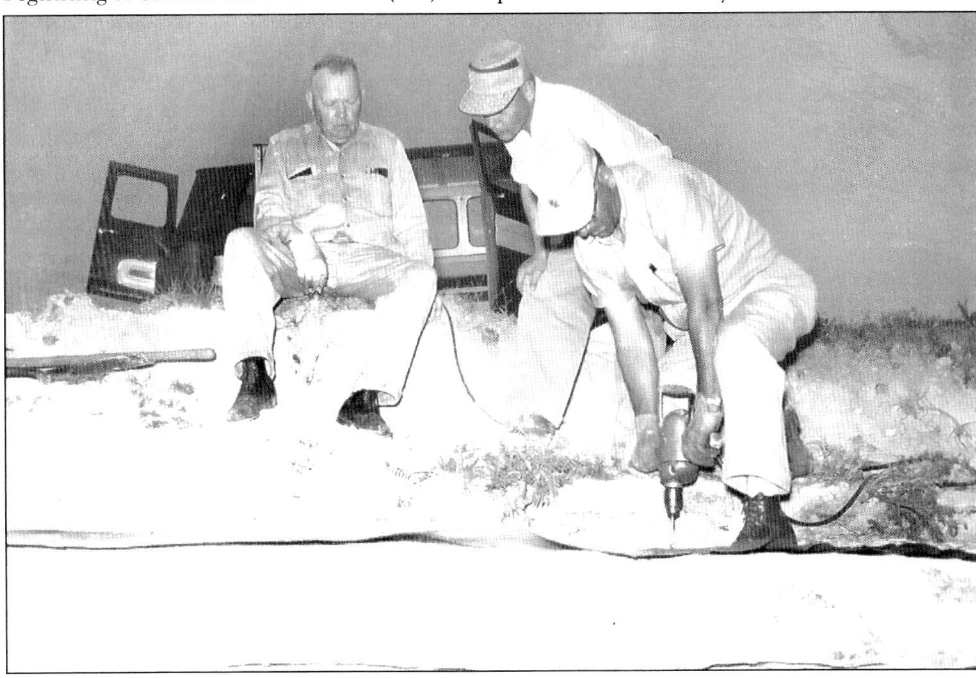

To create the diorama, volunteers had to quarry and remove large slabs of Post Rock from the bed in addition to salvaging surface sod and layers of rock beneath the Post Rock layer to create an authentic depiction. Preparing the stone for removal are A.W. Carbaugh (left), Ben Payton (center), and Allen McChristian.

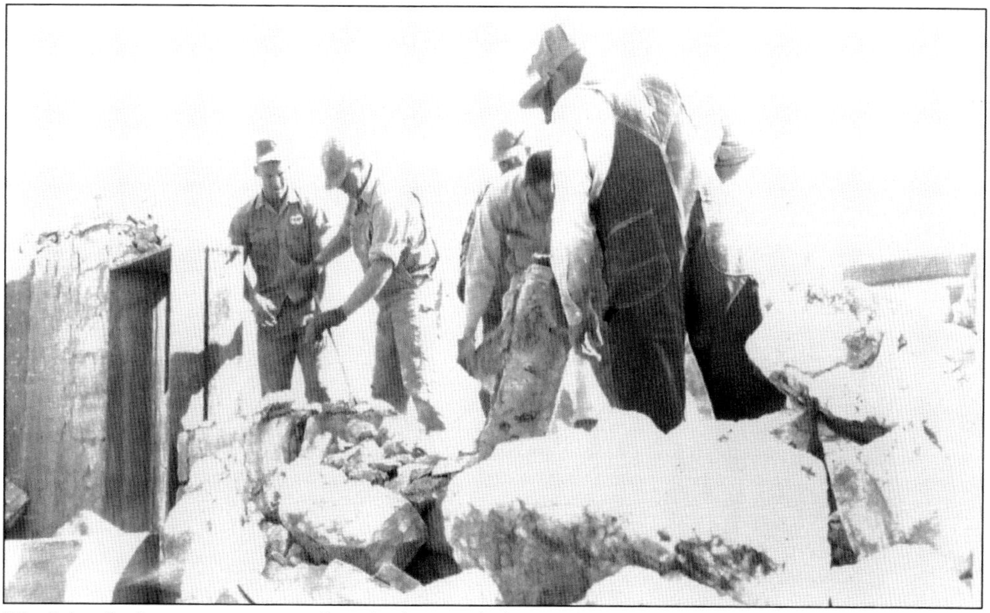

The Murphy house was painstakingly dismantled stone by stone. Each stone was numbered and carefully loaded so that the house could be reconstructed in the exact way it stood on the original site. Those involved in dismantling the house (some of whom are pictured) included Leon Karst, Garry Bott, Martin Hemken, Bill Schoendaller, Hobert Carson, Leo Pivonka, Harold Rife, Cecil Johnson, Harlye Seltmann, Bob Seltmann, Fred Keener, Clyde Bryant, and Orvin Jones.

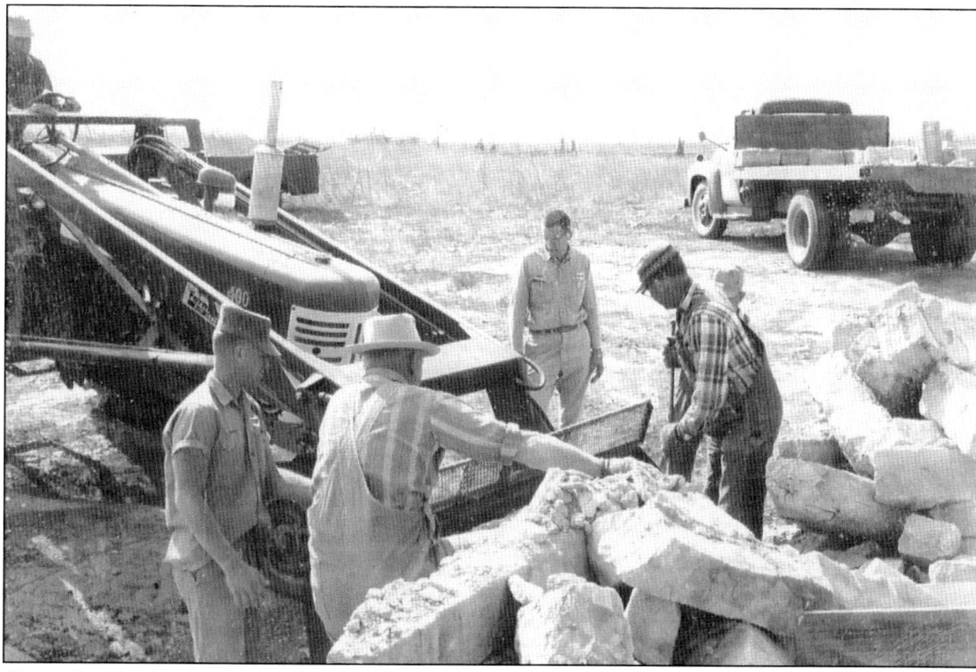

Once the stones were removed from the house and labeled, they were loaded by tractor and stacked on a flatbed truck for transport to La Crosse. Pictured here are, from left to right, Leon Karst (on tractor), Garry Bott, Martin Hemken, Bill Schoendaller, and Hobert Carson (the man behind Carson is unidentified).

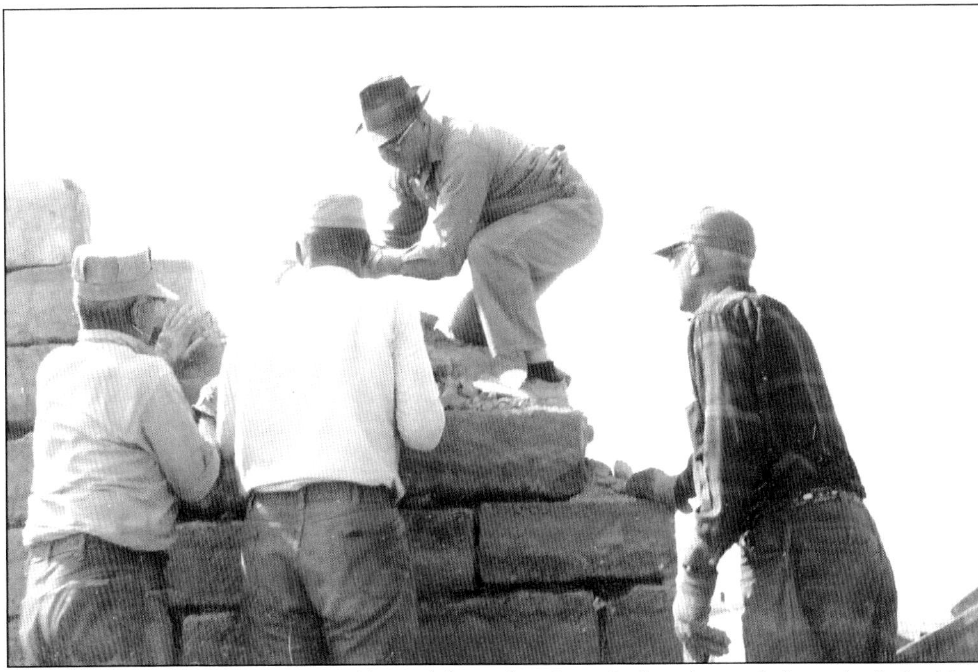

Once the Murphy house stones had been delivered to Grass Park and sorted, the task of rebuilding the house began. Local stonemason Henry Basgall was responsible for laying the stone. The numbered stones were placed in their original positions, and the gaps were filled with mortar to strengthen and seal the walls.

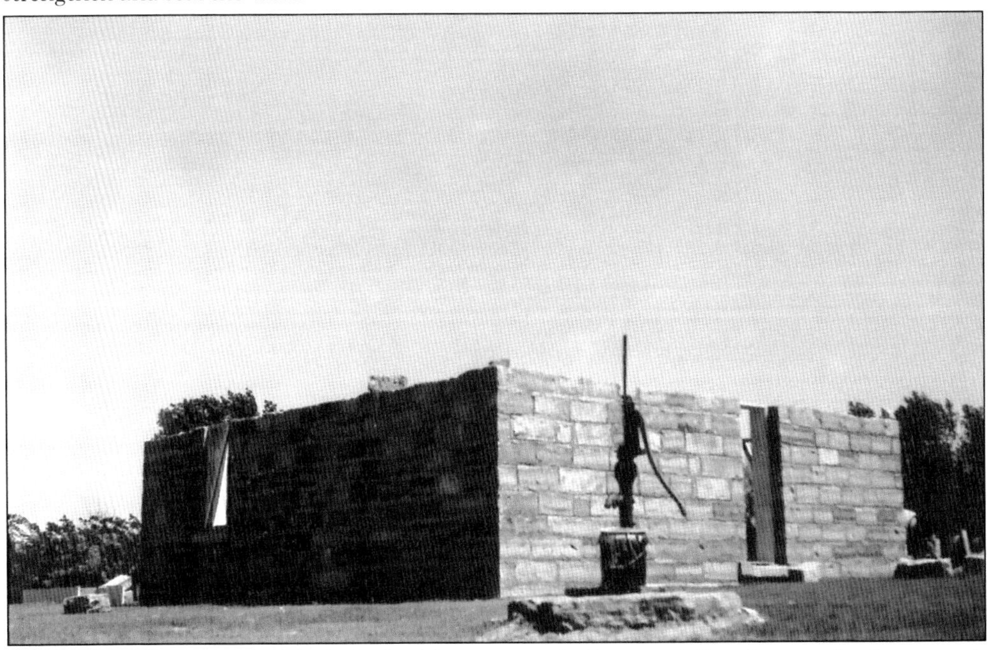

Once the walls were completed, the building was ready for a roof. Simultaneously, the grounds around the building were being prepared to re-create surroundings that would have been typical in a period farmyard. The limestone well cover under the pump in the foreground was donated by Henry Gillaspy.

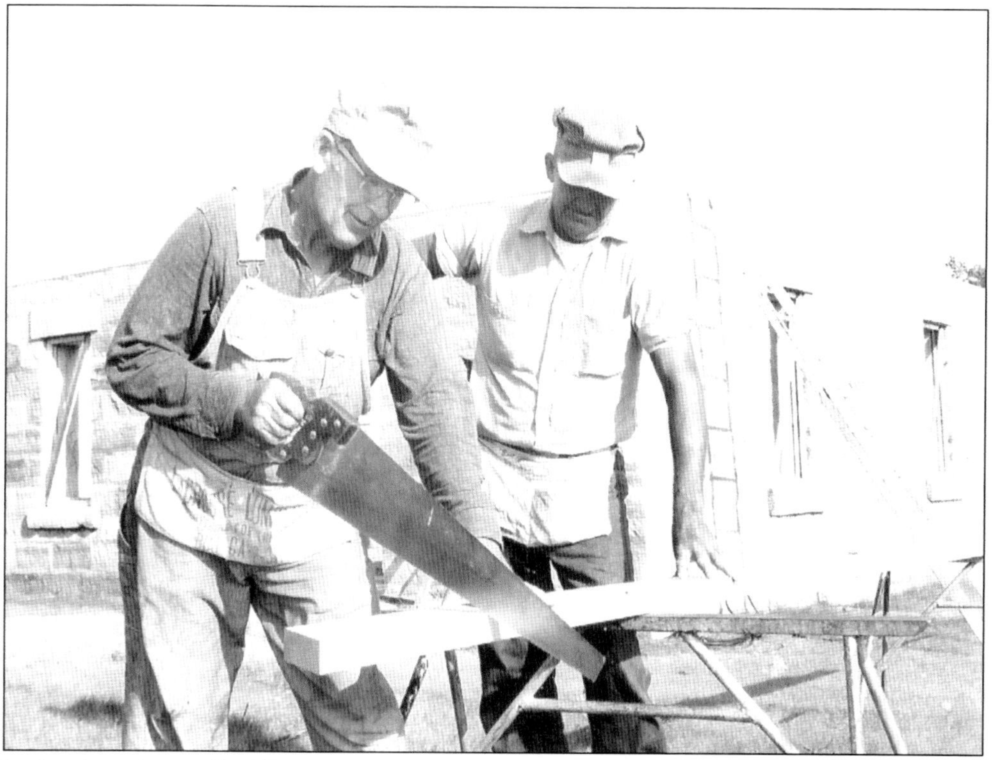

In the above image, Fred Brening (left) and Alex Schenkel are cutting rafters for the new museum. New lumber was used to recreate the roof in the exact style as in the original Murphy home; however, the builders chose not to replace the original attic dormers. Windows were placed in the original attic space to create an upstairs room that was probably used as sleeping quarters for children.

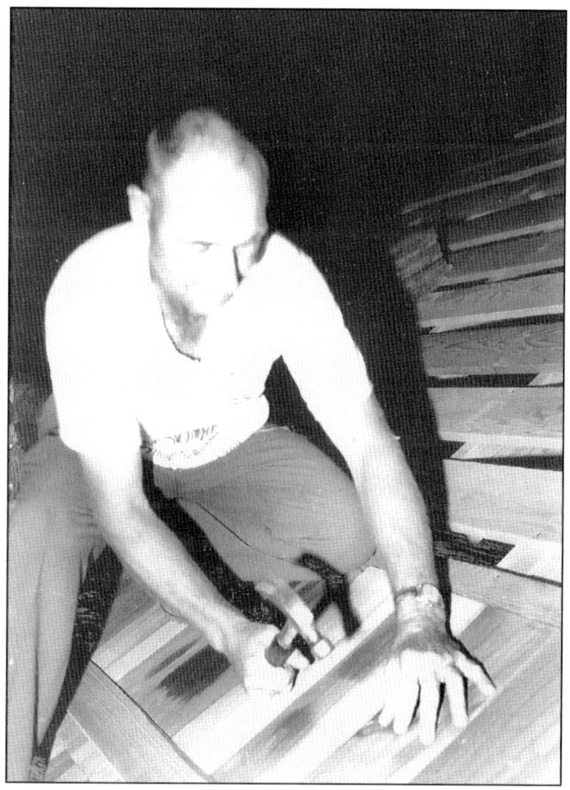

Workers installed wood shingles on the building to maintain the authentic appearance of the roof. Typical installation for wood shingles required that the roof decking be made of wood strips rather than solid sheeting to allow shingles to breathe. The picture at right shows Bill Maneth doing some of the shingling.

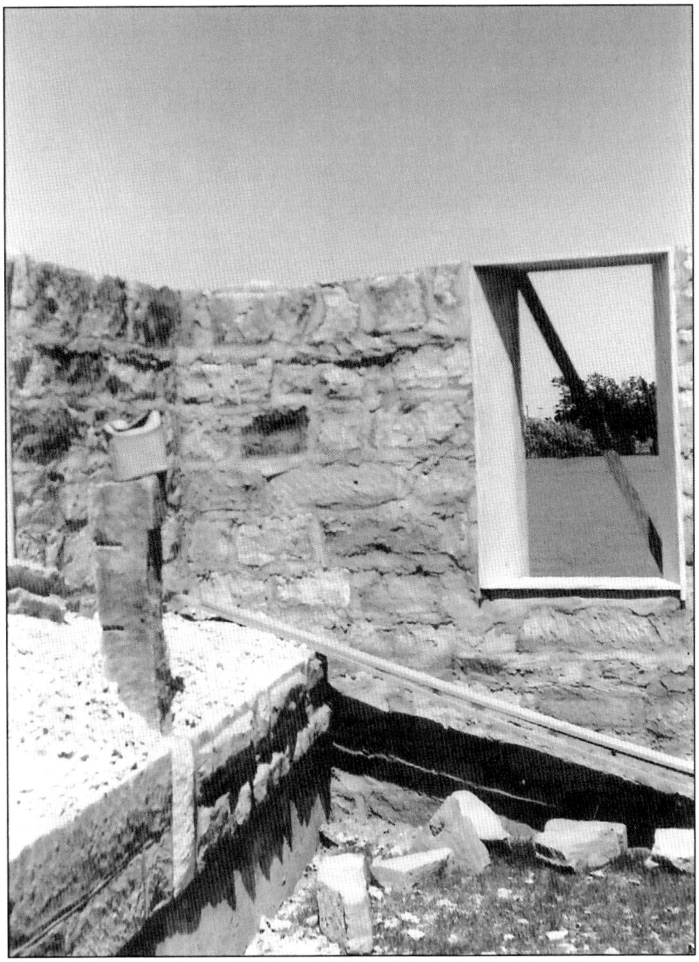

Because of the massive size of the quarry diorama, the stone slabs for the display had to moved and put into place before the walls were reconstructed. The June 1963 image at left shows the interior of the incomplete building before the roof and concrete floor were installed. Henry Basgall completed the masonry for the quarry display.

When the quarry was finished, it correctly depicted the base stone, the Post Rock layer, and the overburden. The image below shows the Post Rock bed with one layer removed and feather and wedges set in preparation for removal of the second. Stone drills and other tools were placed as they would have been used. The front depicts various methods of dressing and placing stone.

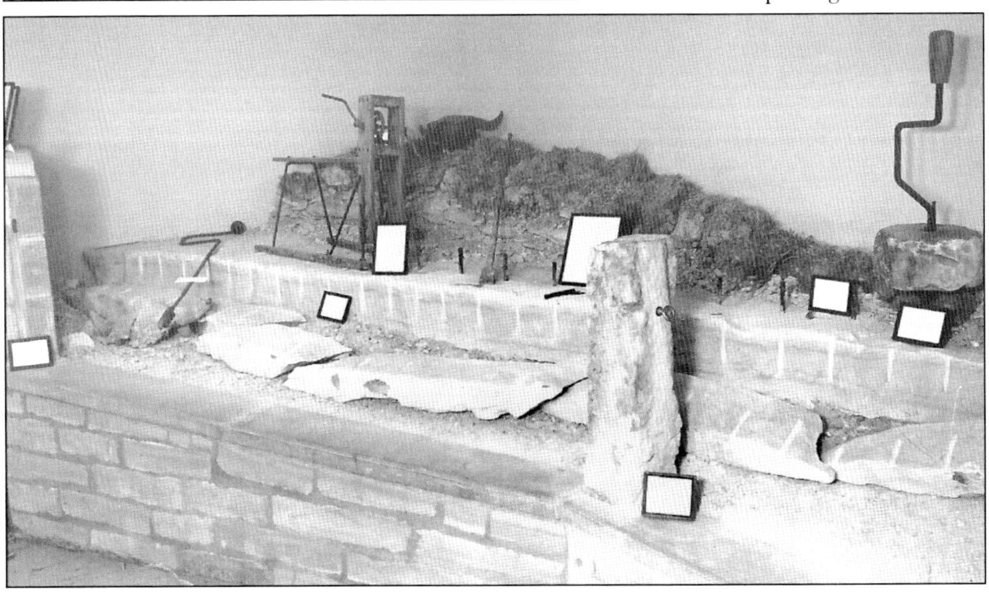

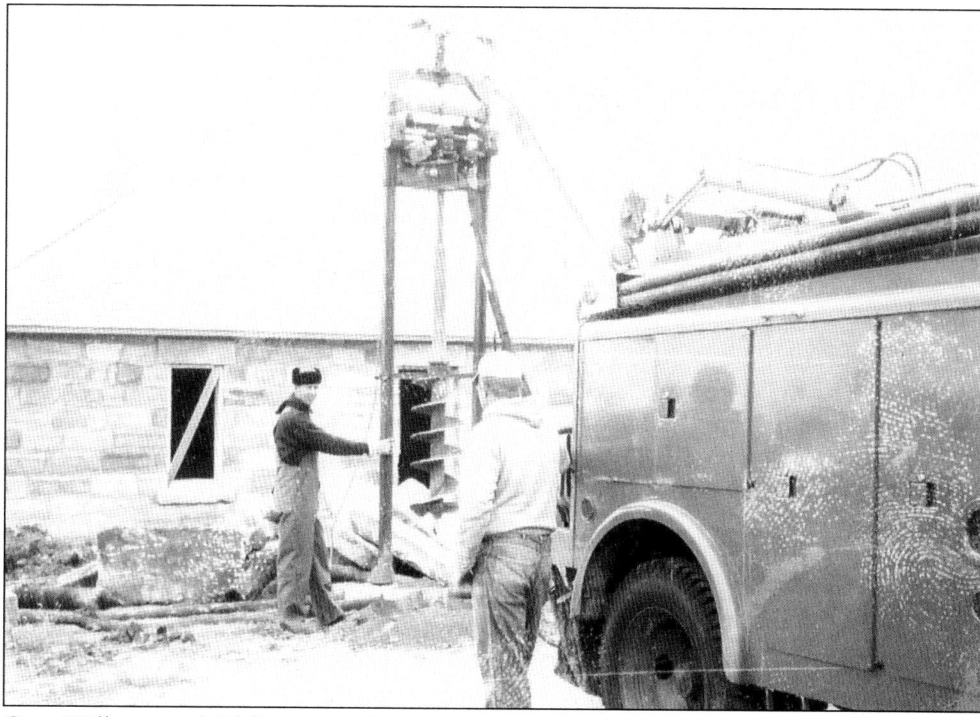

Gary Williams and Ed Drees are shown using a truck-mounted power auger to drill holes in preparation for setting posts for a fence to surround the museum. The Post Rock fence was designed to illustrate various materials used in fence construction over the years, including wood slats and barbed wire.

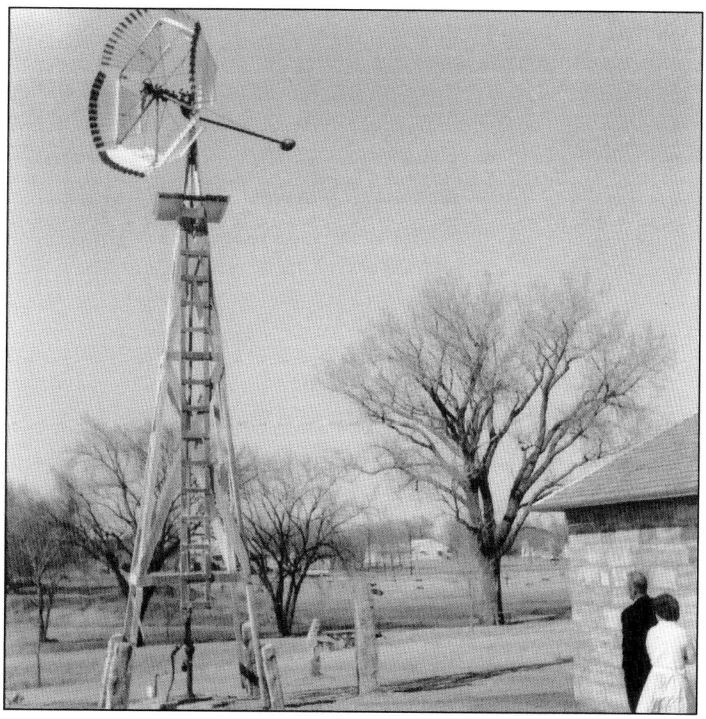

A windmill and hand-dug well were necessities on pioneer farmsteads. The 19th-century wooden windmill and tower adjacent to the museum originally stood on the Pete Rixon farm near McCracken. Emerson and Emmett Sloan and the Rush County Highway Department moved the windmill and set it in place.

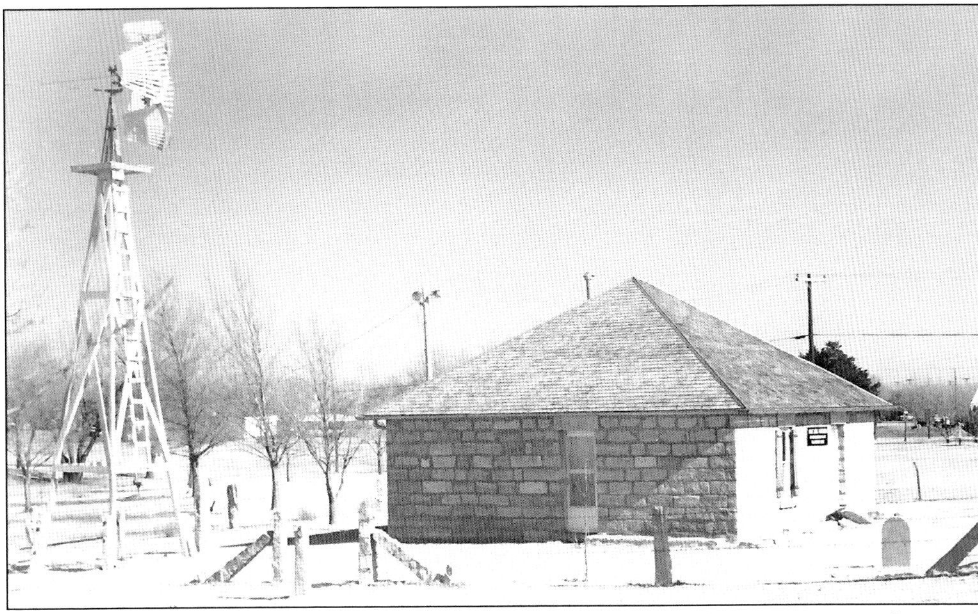

Once reconstruction of the Murphy house was completed, volunteers began to create a "farmyard" around the house. The 19th-century wooden windmill was anchored to the ground by Post Rock and situated over a hand pump mounted above a Post Rock well cover. This photograph shows the west side of the building in early 1964. It was 20 years before additional museums were added to the complex.

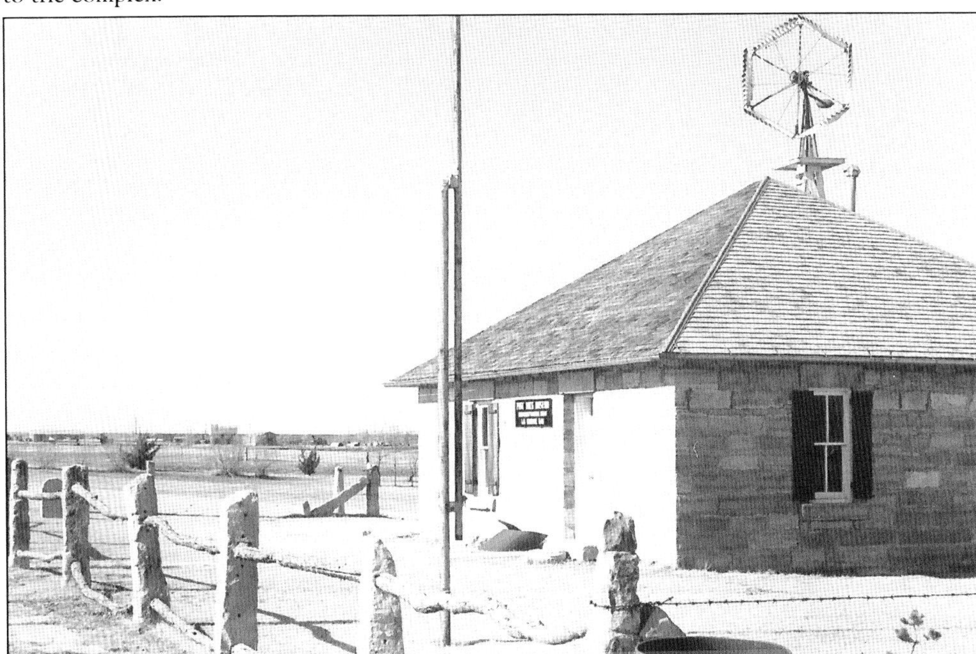

A Post Rock fence surrounds the museum and "farmyard." The La Crosse High School Future Farmers of America installed the fence, which is constructed of Post Rock and split rail. The La Crosse Knights of Columbus constructed the side and back fences using Post Rock and various styles of barbed wire.

Many people have used Post Rock for decorative or artistic purposes. Some stone buildings include intricate decorative carvings. An unidentified Rush County artist carved the face of Abraham Lincoln in relief into a slab of Post Rock. The piece (pictured at right) was donated to the Post Rock Museum in the 1960s.

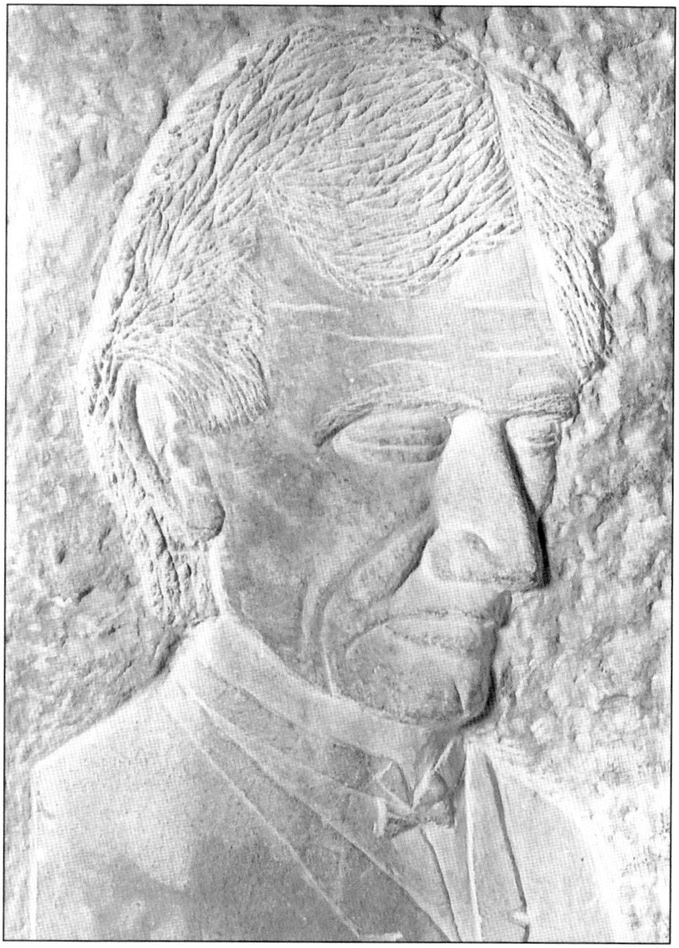

This replica sled, which is displayed in the Post Rock Museum, is modeled after one owned by James Serpan. Wood for the original sled was secured from along Walnut Creek west of Timken. The sled, drawn by oxen, was the family's only method of conveyance and was used in winter and summer to haul water, stone posts for fencing, and other supplies.

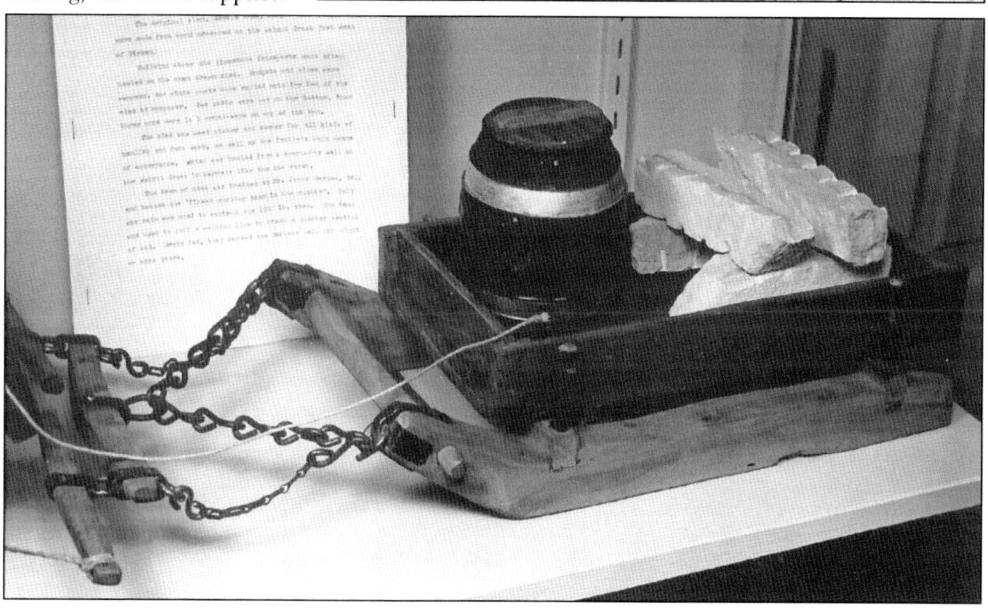

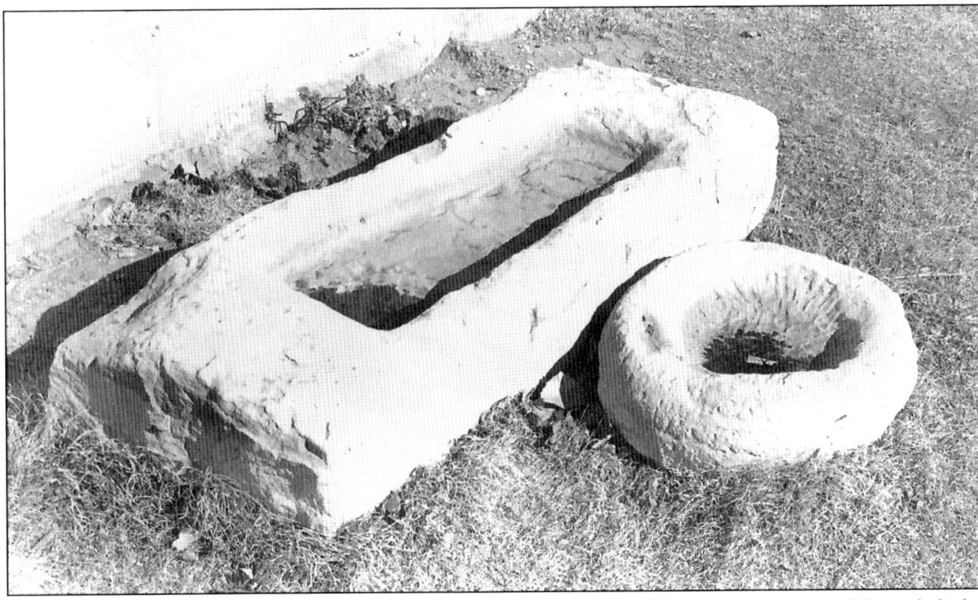

Post Rock was useful in a variety of ways. Hollowed-out slabs of the stone were used for salt licks, chicken-feeding troughs, and water troughs. The heavy substance was well-suited to the harsh environment, long-lasting, and inexpensive.

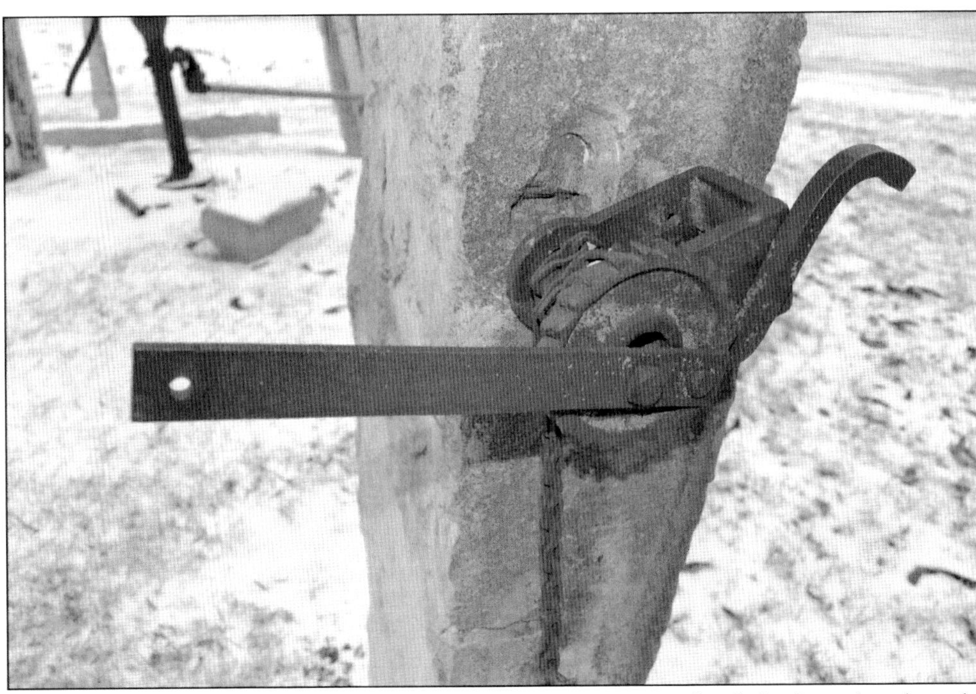

This wire stretcher, mounted to an extra-tall fence post, is part of a clothesline placed on the grounds of the museum in 1963. A second oversized post was set several feet away on the other side of the yard. Metal rings were anchored to this post with an iron bolt; wire or rope was then stretched between the two posts to create a clothesline.

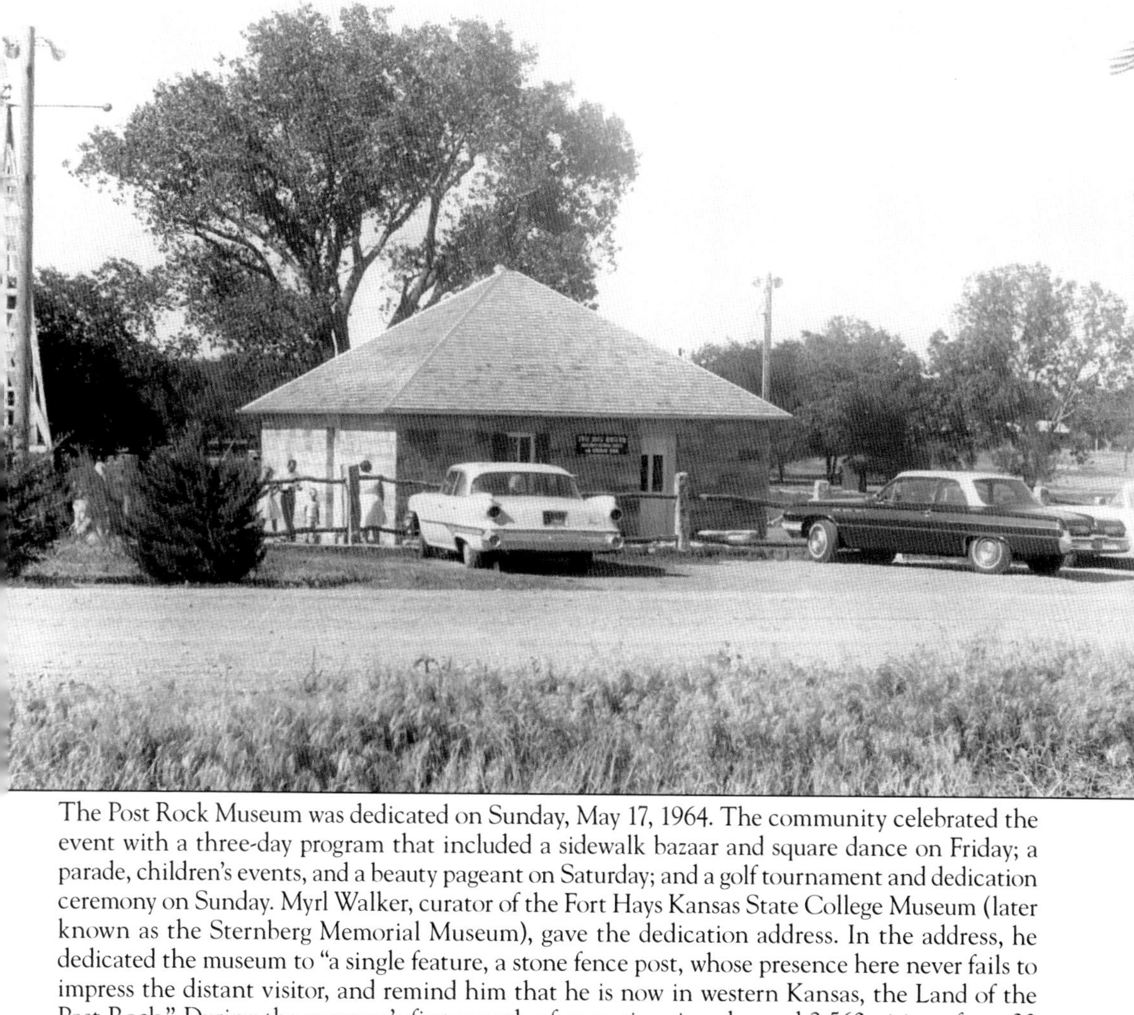

The Post Rock Museum was dedicated on Sunday, May 17, 1964. The community celebrated the event with a three-day program that included a sidewalk bazaar and square dance on Friday; a parade, children's events, and a beauty pageant on Saturday; and a golf tournament and dedication ceremony on Sunday. Myrl Walker, curator of the Fort Hays Kansas State College Museum (later known as the Sternberg Memorial Museum), gave the dedication address. In the address, he dedicated the museum to "a single feature, a stone fence post, whose presence here never fails to impress the distant visitor, and remind him that he is now in western Kansas, the Land of the Post Rock." During the museum's first month of operation, it welcomed 2,560 visitors from 30 states and 3 foreign countries.

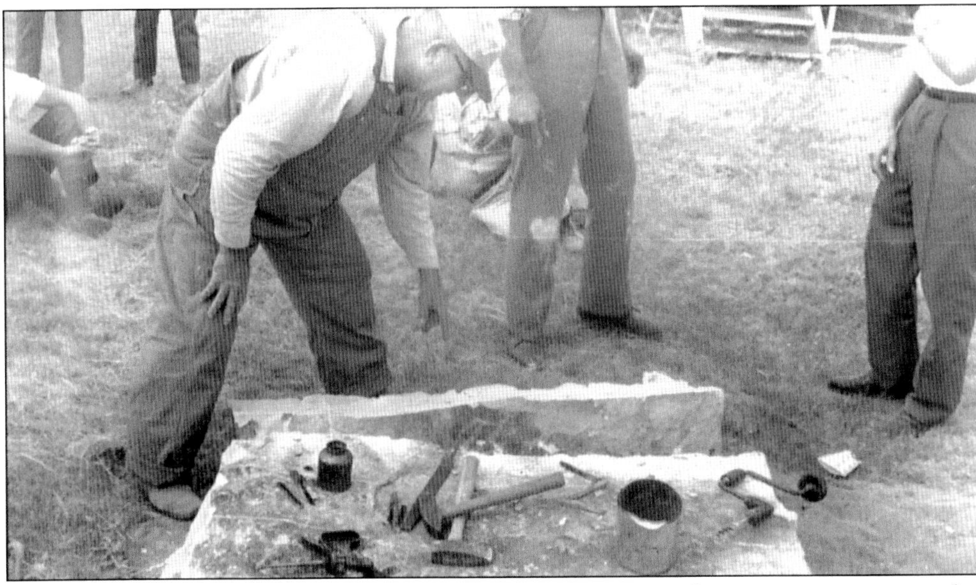

In 1969, the Rush County Fair held a stone post–cutting contest. Contestants were required to cut a stone by boring holes with an auger and bit along a line, inserting metal feathers into each hole, putting a wedge between the feathers, and tapping the wedges until the stone split. The contestant who did this in the shortest time was Rush County resident Henry Basgall, who was declared the winner with his time of four minutes and thirty-three seconds.

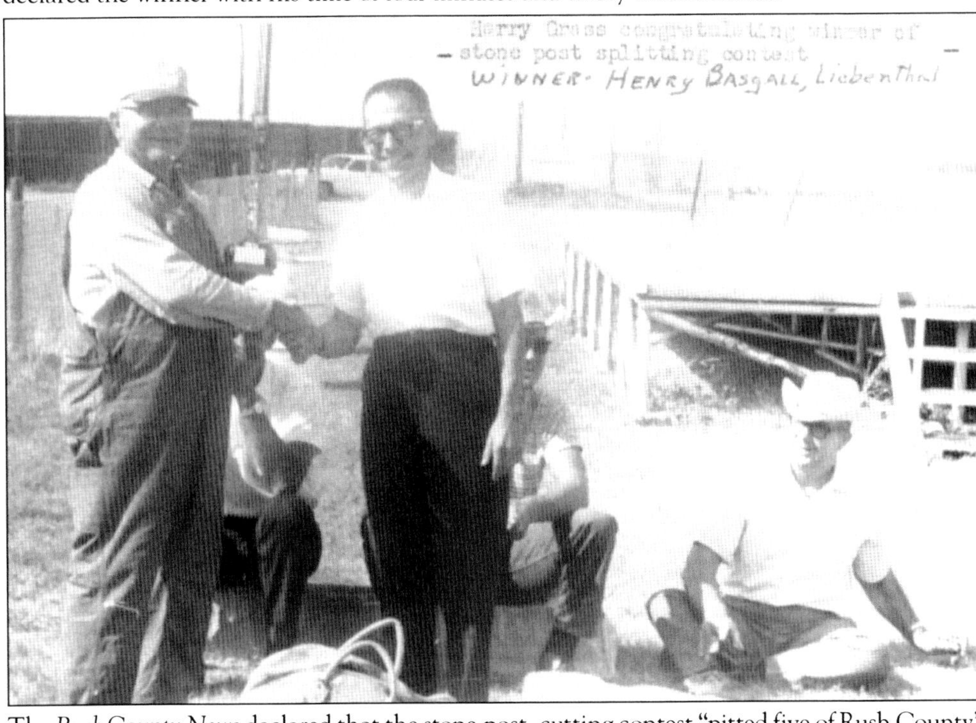

The *Rush County News* declared that the stone-post–cutting contest "pitted five of Rush County's best stone cutters against each other." Here, Harry Grass (right, standing) congratulates the winner of the contest, Henry Basgall (left). Other contestants included E.M. Herrman, Jerome Randa, Bill Legleiter, and Bill Moeder.

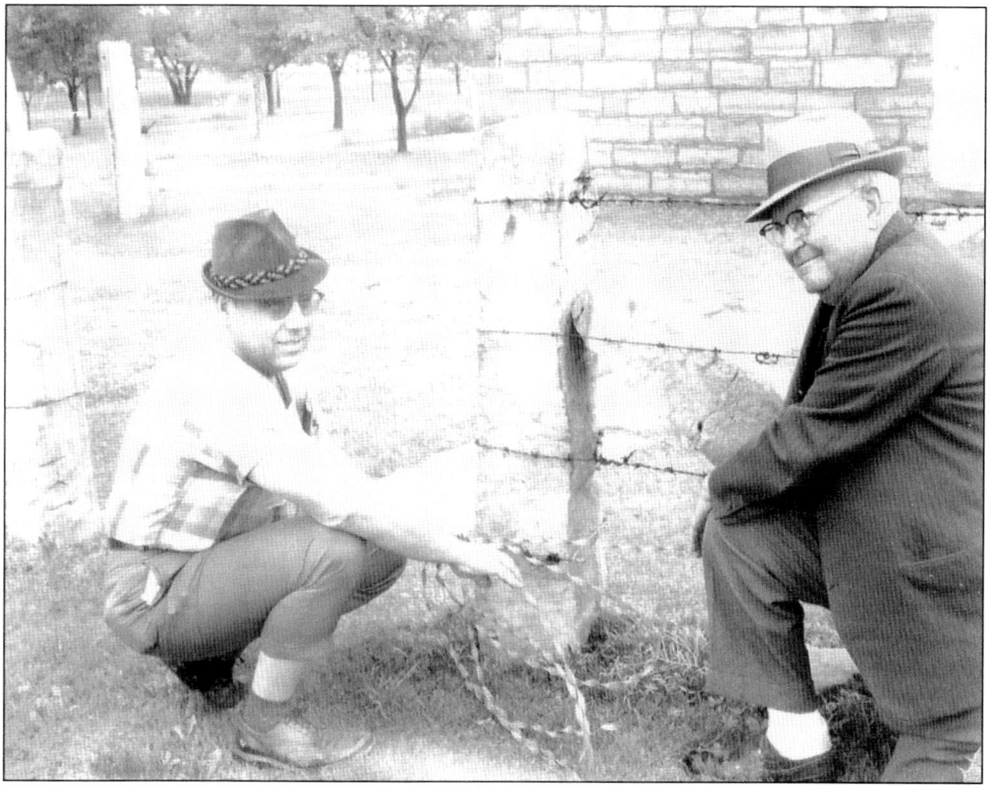

After Joseph Glidden patented his first barbed wire design in 1874, it forever changed the way pioneers fenced their land. Barbed wire was an inexpensive and easy-to-use option for protecting crops from animals roaming the free range in central Kansas. Here, Roy Ehly (left) and Bryce Logan attach a strand of Allis Sawtooth ribbon wire, patented in 1885, to a stone post. (KBWM.)

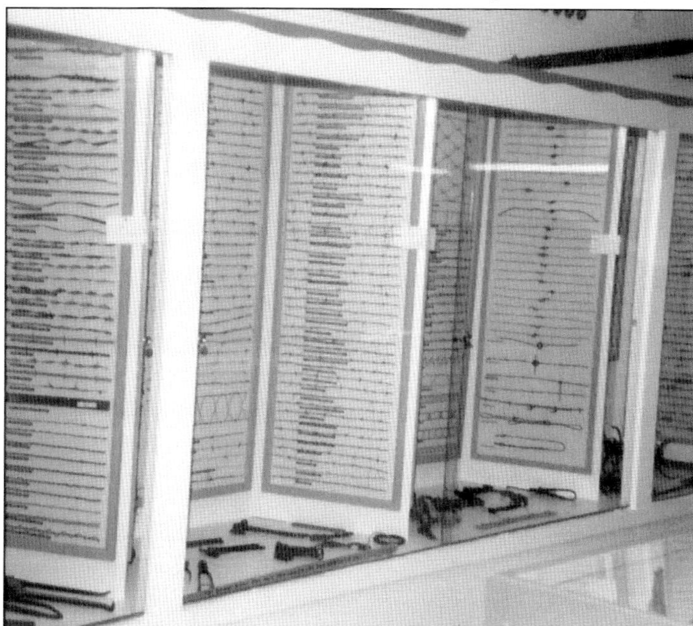

One of the displays in the Post Rock Museum is a plaque with several strands of barbed wire attached to it. Museum workers began to notice that visitors took a strong interest in the display, and several actually had their own wire collections. The picture at right shows a collection of barbed wire assembled in the 1960s by Leo Schugart of Hoisington, Kansas. (KBWM.)

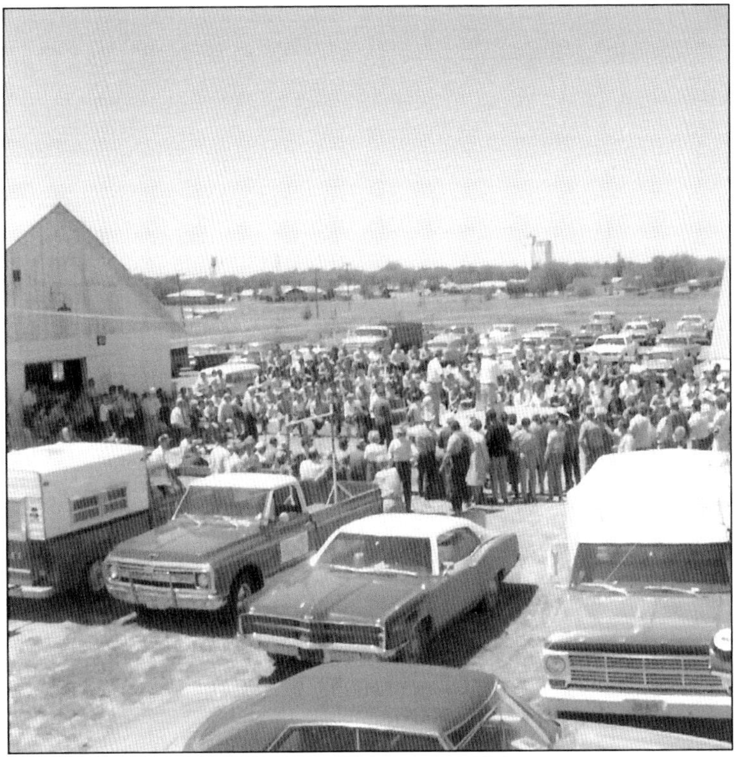

In 1966, following the creation of the Post Rock Museum, Roy Ehly, Ivan Krug, and Bill Robbins incorporated the Kansas Barbed Wire Collectors Association as a way to unite collectors of the unique fencing material. The Barbed Wire Swap and Sell, the first show of its kind, was held at the Rush County Fairgrounds on the first weekend of May in 1967. The gathering attracted over 2,000 people from across the United States. (KBWM.)

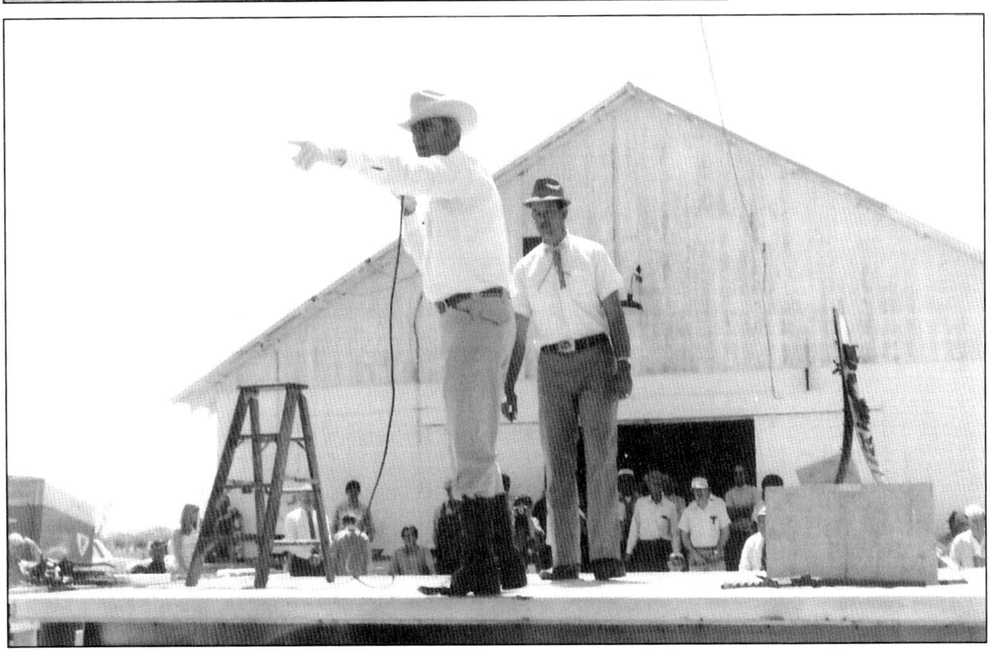

When it was introduced, barbed wire sold for pennies per pound. As interest in collecting grew, so did the value of rare wires. At the annual Barbed Wire Swap and Sell auction, 18-inch segments of barbed wire can sell for over $300 each. In addition to barbed wire, the auction includes other fence-related items. As of 2013, auctioneer Russ Lohrey (holding microphone) had conducted 46 of the 47 auctions; the man behind Lohrey is Don Stites.

A highlight of the Barbed Wire Swap and Sell is the World Champion Barbed Wire Splicing Contest. Eventually, fence lines would break and require repair. Contestant must splice a third piece of wire to two others attached to posts by twisting the pieces together in the same manner employed by early settlers. Here, Ivan Krug (foreground) and Ray Weiser (kneeling at right) help with the ladies' "powder puff" competition. (KBWM.)

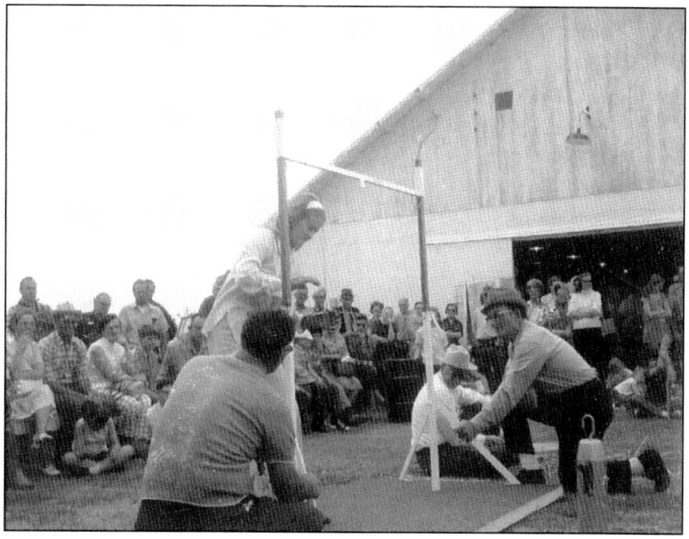

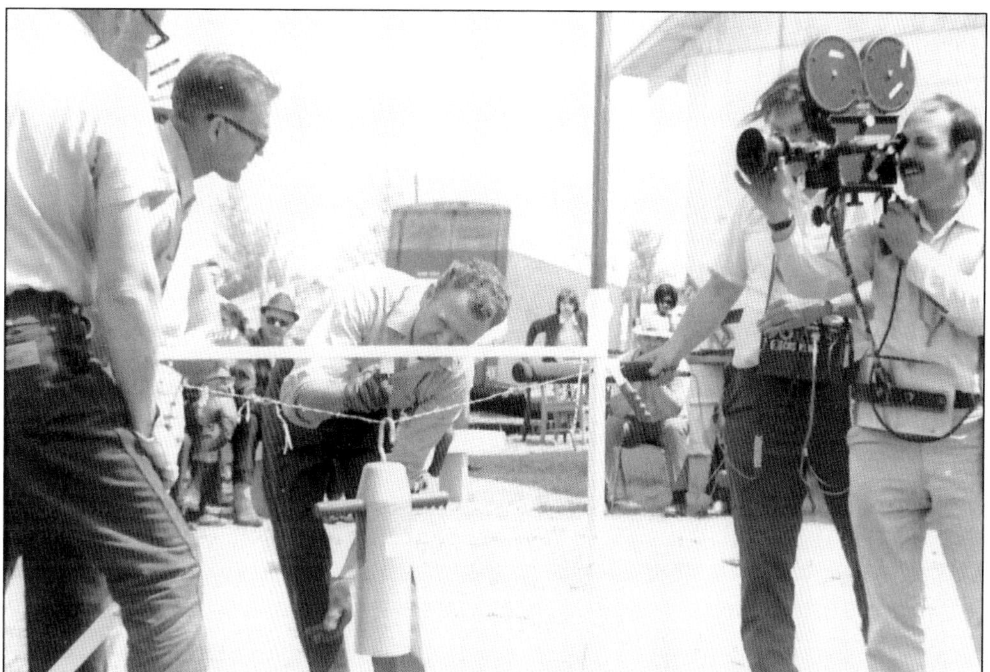

Contestants in the World Champion Barbed Wire Splicing Contest are judged by speed and the strength of the splice. No tools are permitted, but contestants may wear gloves. The splice must be able to support a 75-pound weight. Scores are tallied using a formula that adds the splicer's time to the amount of sag. (KBWM.)

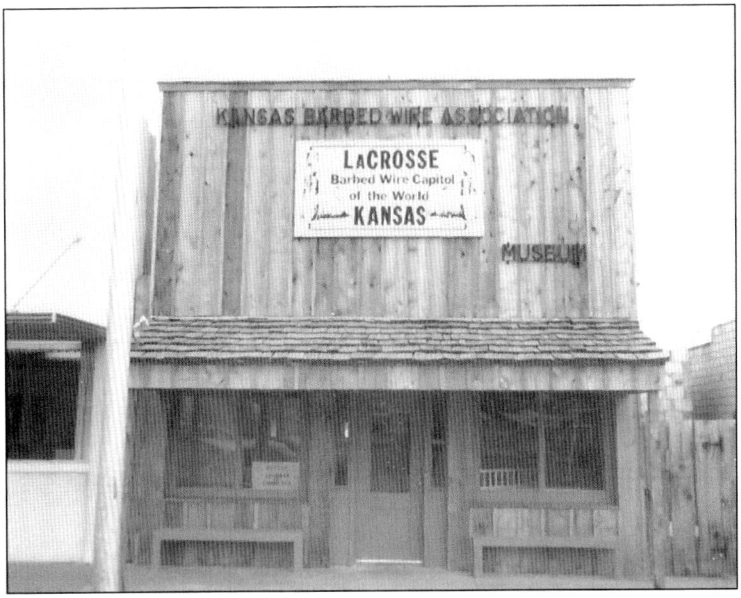

In May 1971, the Kansas Barbed Wire Association dedicated the first barbed-wire museum in a small storefront in downtown La Crosse. The Barbed Wire Museum proved an excellent complement to the Post Rock Museum. The popularity of the hobby and the museum helped La Crosse to earn the nickname "Barbed Wire Capital of the World." (KBWM.)

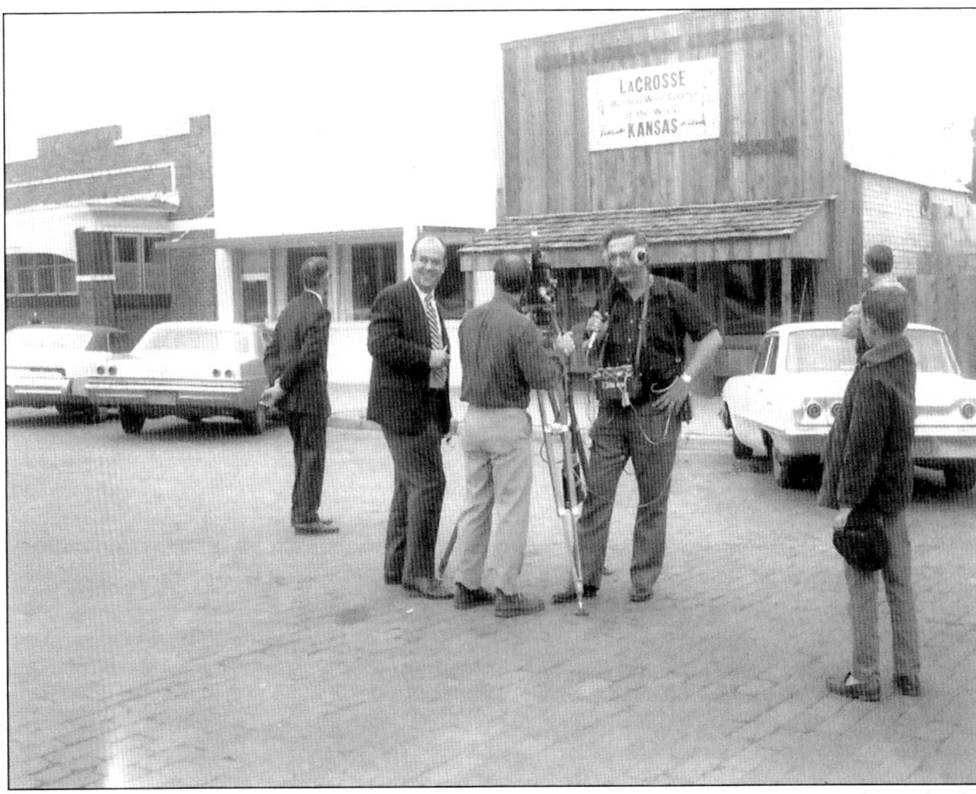

In May 1970, the still-incomplete Barbed Wire Museum drew national attention when Charles Kuralt (second from left) filmed a segment for his *On the Road* television program. One year before, Ivan Krug, secretary of the Kansas Barbed Wire Association, appeared on the *Tonight Show Starring Johnny Carson* to discuss the area's heritage and demonstrate barbed wire splicing. (KBWM.)

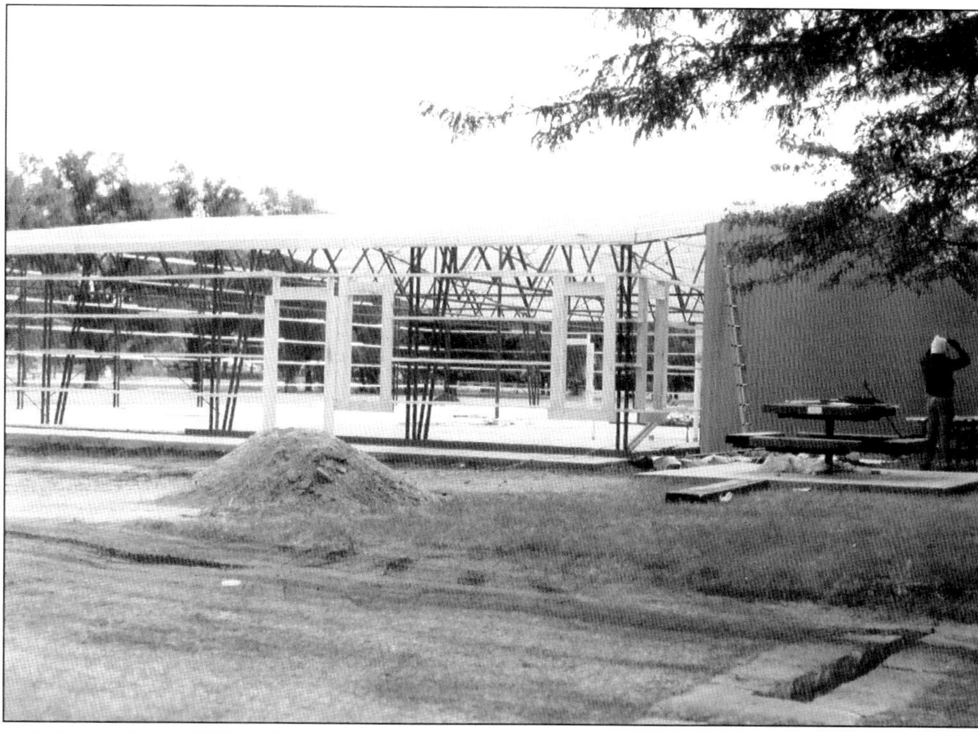

In 1990, the Barbed Wire Museum received two large collections of barbed wire and fence-building and -repair tools. With limited space in the small storefront, the community began to raise funds for a new 5,400-square-foot building in Grass Park adjacent to the Post Rock Museum. Placing the new facility adjacent to the Post Rock Museum helped to physically demonstrate how barbed wire and Post Rock are interconnected. (KBWM.)

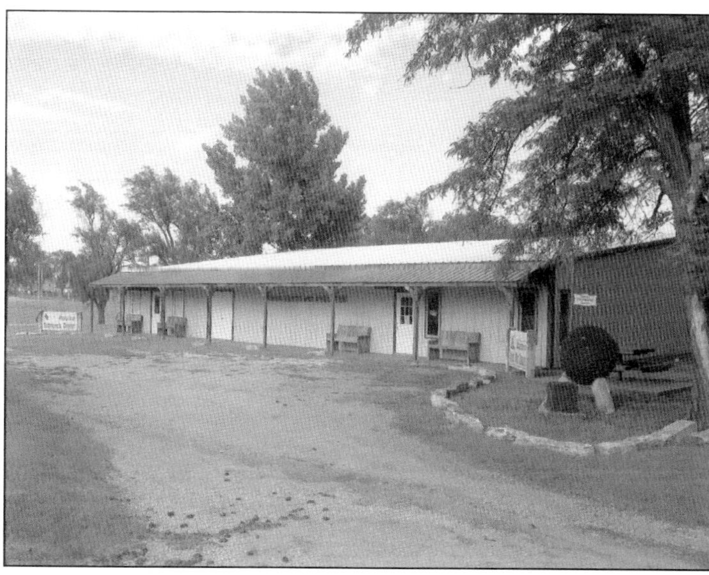

In May 1991, the new Kansas Barbed Wire Museum was dedicated with a mission to preserve the history and tell the story of how this type of fencing changed the face of early Kansas. After its initial construction, the museum was expanded with a 1,000-square-foot addition to house the headquarters of the Antique Barbed Wire Society. (KBWM.)

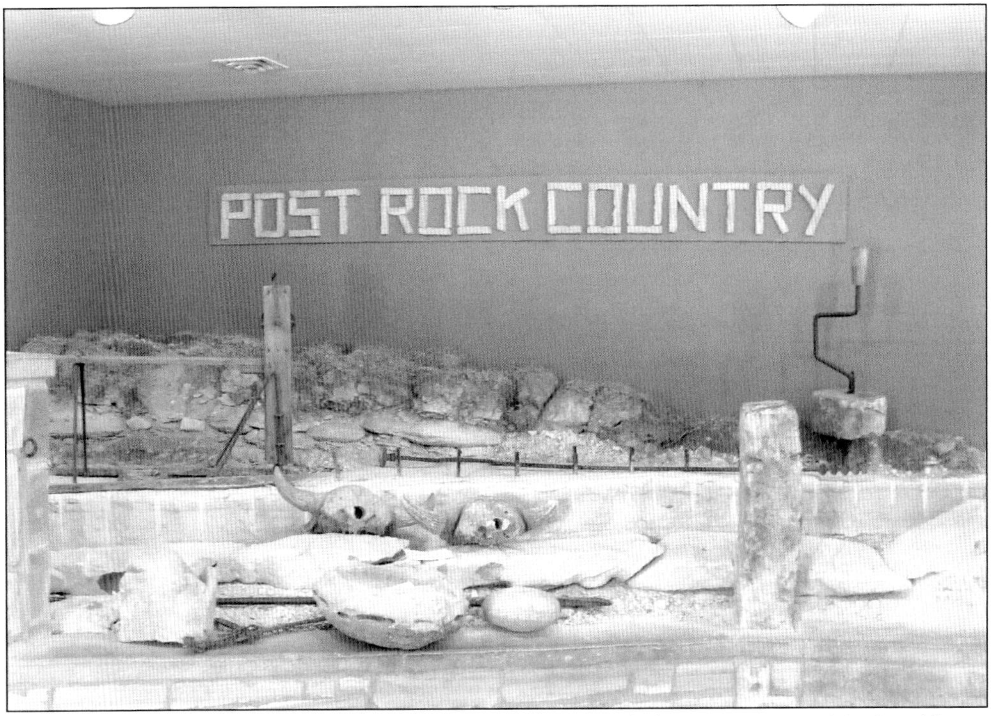

Post Rock Museum has been updated and improved since its dedication in May 1964. In addition to the original collections, many new paleontological specimens and artifacts of human history have been added. A Post Rock addition, used for storage and restroom facilities, was built in the 1980s. The original life-size quarry diorama, installed in 1963, continues to be a main attraction that depicts the 60-million-year history of Post Rock with great accuracy. As the museum moves beyond its first 50 years, with all of its improvements, it still retains its original character and respect for the founders who intended to preserve the history and tell the story of Post Rock Country. (Both photographs by the author.)

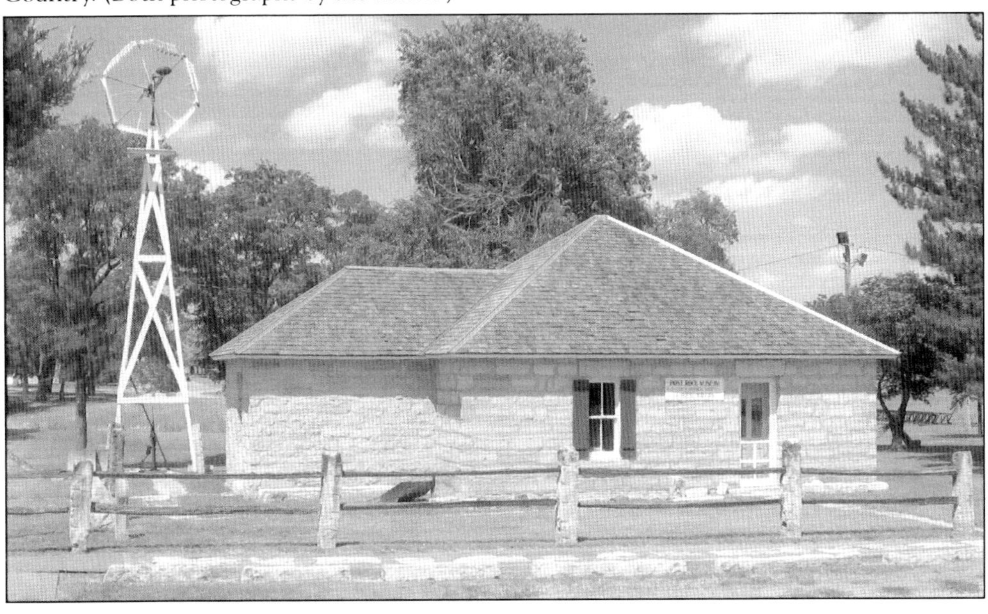

About the Rush County Historical Society

The Rush County Historical Society was organized in 1960 to promote the county's observance of the Kansas Centennial. After being disbanded following the celebration in 1961, it was reorganized in 1963 to establish the Post Rock Museum. In May 1975, the society acquired an 1887 Santa Fe Railroad depot from Timken and moved it to Grass Park for use as the Rush County Historical Museum. The depot building houses over 1,000 photographs and artifacts relevant to the citizens of Rush County. In May 2003, the society moved a wood-frame bank building from Nekoma to house a museum of banking. In May 2007, volunteers restored the interior of the bank to its 1916 appearance and opened the Nekoma Bank Museum. In 2013, the society proceeded with plans to secure a one-room school to join the four existing museums. The organization continues to partner with the Kansas Barbed Wire Museum to manage the museum complex. Today, the museums continue to work toward the preservation of the history of Rush County and Kansas through the diverse five-part educational program presented through five interrelated museum facilities.

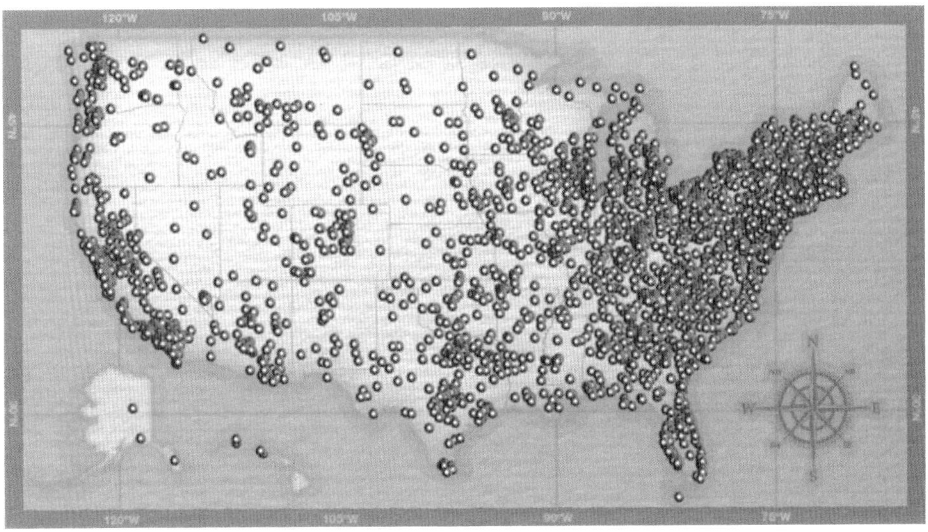

Consistent with our mission to preserve history on a local level, this book was printed in South Carolina on American-made paper and manufactured entirely in the United States. Products carrying the accredited Forest Stewardship Council (FSC) label are printed on 100 percent FSC-certified paper.

MADE IN THE USA